The Matter of Vision

Thank you, Kate

The Matter of Vision

Affective
Neurobiology
& Cinema

British Library Cataloguing in Publication Data

The Matter of Vision
Affective Neurobiology & Cinema

A catalogue entry for this book is available from the British Library

ISBN: 9780 86196 712 4 (Paperback)

Cover design: Simon Esterson

Published by
John Libbey Publishing Ltd, 3 Leicester Road, New Barnet, Herts EN5 5EW,
United Kingdom
e-mail: john.libbey@orange.fr; web site: www.johnlibbey.com

Distributed worldwide by **Indiana University Press**,
Herman B Wells Library – 350, 1320 E. 10th St., Bloomington, IN 47405, USA.
www.iupress.indiana.edu

Printed and bound in China by 1010 Printing International Ltd.

Contents

Foreword:
War of the Word

There is a covert war raging in our culture, a secret hidden even from its most committed warriors, and for whom this conflict is so deep in their psyches that it is unconscious. If their allegiance is challenged they react with ferocity, utter conviction and total disparagement towards the enemy. These are ideal soldiers in any war, largely unaware of their dedication to the cause, virtually automatons unable to question it.

Such a war exists and furthermore is at the heart of our culture. No one is unaffected by it, every single person strides its battlefields every day of their lives. No one dies in this war, it is after all a cultural war, but its effects go so deep and so far back in time as to dwarf human history. You are a victim of this war and you have been so all your life, but you will very probably be unaware of it. Most wars have their -isms, such as National-ism or Imperial-ism, and this war has its own-ism too, Logocentrism, the war of the Word against Vision.

Logocentrism, in the sense it has here, places a greatly exaggerated value on the Word, creating a status for it far above its real capacities, glorifying it whilst at the same time viciously denigrating potential opponents, in particular its oldest adversary, Vision. Logocentrism places the Word at the centre of culture and attributes magical powers to it. It is almost unheard of for a voice to be raised in opposition to its universal rule, so pervasive is its influence. This project at last raises the standard for its most noble and ancient opponent, Vision. The day is near when Vision will be restored to its pre-eminence. I see therefore I am.

* * *

This book started from a couple of ideas, hunches might be a better word. The first is that Vision is much more powerful than we realise. The second is that the vast majority of information we take in from a film is absorbed unconsciously.

1

I came to both ideas in the course of making films. The notion of the power of Vision came partly from the sense of how much information there is in a film, and the feeling that most people are not aware of most of it. We rather take films rather for granted and that increasingly seemed to me an odd and striking injustice. The sentiment is usually accompanied by a casual disregard for the monumental achievements of Cinema in the face of a really rather intractable medium, all too often while simultaneously bowing down before what I would contend are the scant resources of the Word, in the assumption that it is by far the superior medium. I became convinced that was a myth, and that in fact Cinema wielded such power without apparent effort that it was both ironically invisible and hugely underrated, even among those one might think would know its riches. People I came across who made their living from Cinema, as well as critics and theorists, including most film-makers, seemed to share this largely unconscious assumption that Cinema might be fun, might on occasion achieve distinction, but compared to the masterly Word it was a mere trifle.

I could see no one, anywhere, giving the credit to Vision and Cinema that was their due. That was a strange position to be in. After all, it was only a hunch, and against it was ranged not just the expected adversaries but also the considered views of most potential natural allies. Apart from the odd drunken conversation with directors of vaguely similar persuasions in dark corners of film festivals, snatches of suppressed thoughts rather than fully-expressed ideas, there was nothing. Not even the most fervent Cineastes seemed to take their partisanship further than the idea that a number of directors had achieved works of art despite the pressures of crass commercialism, particularly in Hollywood. Even the radical claim that the best of Hollywood was vastly superior to the best of European Art Cinema, pleasingly offensive though it was to many sensitive minds, stopped short of claiming superiority for Cinema to the traditional arts. Film Theorists, even where they shared a love of Cinema, by no means the majority, were so wrapped up in the Word as to be barely aware of Vision, except where it was almost certainly a bad thing, the guilty Look. This was not a healthy position to be in. It suggested either the whole world was wrong, or I was – like Humphrey Bogart in Casablanca for the waters – misinformed. Naturally, I resented the implication, even from myself, and it seemed wise to keep the idea under wraps in a climate of wholehearted repression. However, going against the grain was too attractive an idea to surrender.

I had one further instinct that seemed to be on my side of this great and cavernous divide. When we meet people for the first time we tend to make up our minds about them rather quickly, in a matter of seconds, perhaps even fractions of seconds. It occurred to me that there must be a huge amount of processing going on of various kinds to reach such a judgement in so short a time. The downside is that we sometimes get it wrong and are forced to revise our opinions as we learn more about a person, but in the main first impressions stick. Those impressions, it seemed to me, must have an awful lot of information being assessed to arrive at them – and in such a short time. That process is very largely, I reasoned, a visual one. We are used to the idea these days that 'body-language' tells us a lot about a person, and that we interpret that material both quickly and decisively. It also seemed to me that this process was largely unconscious, as both the speed and volume of information involved could only possibly appear fragmentarily in consciousness. Such thinking would lead me towards Science to discover what evidence existed, and that is the story of this book.

Another realisation that set off this study was that in a culture where the ideology of the Word dominates we have no experience of articulating visually, and that extends to those for whom we might assume it to be second-nature. Working with third-year students at a film-school in London developing their graduation film-projects, I asked one group to sketch out a scene portraying jealousy. They were initially stumped but then immediately fell back on devising dialogue. These were very good final-year students on a highly-competitive course attracting up to a thousand applicants for around forty places. Yet their first reaction to visualising a scene was to resort to dialogue. That experience was anything but unique, in fact to find the opposite was highly unusual. These were bright students, keen to make their graduation films as cinematic as possible, yet their whole cultural formation had not equipped them to articulate visually. We had students from around the world, Japan and Norway, Turkey and Columbia, Spain and Germany, so this was not merely a local problem of the land of Shakespeare. When they were banned from dialogue, with a little prodding here and there, they would soon get into shifting their brains into the mode for thinking visually. It was not an insuperable problem, it didn't require radically new skills, just the exercise of a mode that existed in their heads but had hardly been consciously exercised their whole lives, a whole continent, a galaxy awaiting exploration.

It was fascinating to watch their brains tick over, searching for the mode that was required in the absence of dialogue to visually express jealousy. Very soon they began to imagine how a man and a woman might stand, facing each other, perhaps facing slightly away from each other. The jealous person might hold themselves differently, their shoulders could be tense, hunched up. Perhaps the others would avoid eye contact if they felt guilty, or look challengingly if they felt the jealousy was unfounded. You could see a whole world of possibilities whirring around in their heads and coming out in suggestions between each other, negotiating the visual, the emotions, forming the drama visually, seeing it in the characters' physical stances and behaviour.

It was like clicking a switch. With a simple shift of thinking, instead of resorting to Language it is quite possible to think visually in terms of emotion and its expression. Only a small shift, but showing how we are conditioned to turn to language, yet have the channels of thinking visually easily available, as it were next door. There is a price to Logocentrism, a whole world of thinking differently that it seems to exclude, and exclude forcibly.

Film-making has a lot to do with presenting information in such a way that the audience takes it in – in the right order and at the right time. If the film-maker misses out an important link in the chain, the audience will start to get lost straight away. The result tends to be that the film-maker sets out to cover all the bases, so that the audience has all the information it needs to follow the story. Experience soon tells you that a lot of that information is missed or not recalled, some by some people, some by others. However, I began to think that in fact audiences take in a lot more information than they realise. In other words, a lot of the information that goes in does so unconsciously, just as it does when we meet a new person for the first time.

As a sort of experiment to test those ideas I once took the rather risky strategy of teaching a single film to a class of fine-art and graphics students for a whole term as their introduction to Cinema. I was a little nervous at taking the chance, because if I was proved wrong the students would soon get bored and I would have done them – and Cinema – no favours. When I told the students we would be spending a whole term studying a John Wayne Western from the 1950s, the sense of anticipation was negligible. The film was *The Searchers*. The title-card, a painting of a brick wall, accompanied by what today sounds like a corny cowboy song did not augur well for my bold experiment. As we began to look closely at every element of the film and spot the details, the atmosphere changed. The students were surprised that, through a broadly Socratic method in which they were repeatedly questioned about what they were seeing, they were discovering that there was far more to this film than they had assumed and that they had seen far more than they realised. Each session began with a student presentation and a few weeks in the fine-art student who had been among the most sceptical and a leader of opinion among the group made his presentation, in which he declared that John Ford was a genius. I was delighted and relieved. The experiment had paid off. I learned a lot myself, in fact I was probably the greatest beneficiary as, despite making and analysing films full-time, I had not realised the depth that a film I thought I knew well contained.

Some years later I did something similar on *Psycho*, and again the same sense came across that there was so much information, and what has been called 'exformation'[1], the material discarded in the process of creating something, in this case perhaps with regard to the finessing of the screenplay, elaborating back-story for the characters. The overall sense was what Freud called, in relation to the unconscious, the iceberg-effect. Ninety-percent or more of the 'hidden-history' around the characters and the story is either invisible or only hinted at, but in this case the fact that it existed in some way and at some time in the process gave a feeling of immense solidity to the film. It is fairly well-known that Hitchcock would spend a lot of time and money on preparation of the screenplay for his films, spending $225,000 on *Marnie*, for example, a substantial investment in 1963, and my modest work on *Psycho* began to reveal to me the depths of story that investment of time and money had facilitated.

That feeling of solidity was even more marked when I happened to see a presentation of *Vertigo* as part of a gallery installation. I chanced upon the scene where the recreated Judy emerges from the bathroom in the hotel room, surrounded by a green glow. The feeling I had watching it on a small screen in a warehouse-gallery setting was that the scene was carved from rock. Somehow there was nothing arbitrary about it, it felt as though no element in the scene could have been any other way. It somehow communicated a feeling that it was perfectly constructed, an immovable depth to it that defied the fragility of film-making as a craft.

In the course of making films I had learned that the most unlikely instincts, and without exception, turn out to be the most valuable. In this case it gave further support to the feeling that films contain more information than we are aware of, but also that when they are built with great skill they can realise the potential of the medium in such a way that they give a glimpse of the immanent depths of which it is capable.

That feeling was extended in relation to Classic Hollywood Cinema where, in certain films, I felt that you knew 'where you were' much more clearly, knew what

---

1   An idea from the Danish science-writer Tor Norretranders in his *User Illusion*, Penguin, New York, 1998.

was going on, what the film was about, what was at stake. A prime example was *Mildred Pierce*, a Hollywood film-noir of 1945. The odd thing was not so much the comfort of knowing what the story was about, but a feeling that you knew the emotions that Mildred, played by Joan Crawford, was going through. It struck me forcibly that the heart of the Classic Hollywood period was what Sam Fuller said in Godard's *Pierrot Le Fou*, that Cinema is, in a word, Emotion. What a film like *Mildred Pierce* succeeded in doing was somehow to make emotion visible. It was not a question of dialogue but of being able somehow to see what emotions were at stake and absorb that information in the course of the story.

Looking at Hollywood films from earlier in the sound period, they generally lacked that lightness of touch, that sureness in guiding the audience, but things seemed to change, not in a formal sense, but perhaps in the confidence and experience with which film-makers applied the formal paradigm that was already in place by around 1930. That ability to 'know where you are' is no mean achievement, as I had learned from numerous errors making films myself. We tend to take it for granted that a story will be reasonably clear in Cinema today, but the work by generations of film-makers, by which I mean to include screenwriters, directors of photography, editors and hands-on producers as well as directors, was a gradual improvement of firstly technique and then its use, to tame the recalcitrant medium of moving-pictures in the cause of narrative clarity. I had a sense that around 1939, often described as a landmark year for Hollywood releases, the skills had been honed to the degree that a film like *Mildred Pierce* feels distinctly modern, where films from the early 30s usually feel stagey and static, only partly due to the limitations of sound-recording technology in the early years of sound.

This is all informal and subjective, but experience gained in film-making has time and again suggested to me that informal knowledge, often unspoken and 'tacit', of the kind wordlessly or incoherently passed between an editor and a director in the cutting-room, is considerably more valuable than the more formal kinds of knowledge that we associate with the Academy. However splendid and irreplaceable instinct may be as a place to start, it was however only a starting-point. The story of this project is my setting out from there to see where I might find evidence one way or the other to test those instincts. Film Theory[2] had an almost lordly disregard for the visual, so unconsciously in league was it with the Word. I was

2   By Film Theory I mean to suggest the ideas, mainly from France, that hit England in the early 70s in the film journal *Screen* (in which I was peripherally involved as an enthusiast), via *Cahiers du Cinema*, in turn taken from a whole generation of mainly French thinkers broadly in the tradition of 'Continental Philosophy', involving semiotics, psycho-analysis and theories of ideology.

6

quite lost as where to start with the ideas that I was then familiar with from those brave and exciting days of the mid 1970s, when the new approaches from France poured in to the staid English scene. They had nothing to say about Vision, as though it did not exist, and indeed for them effectively it did not. It seems to me now a perverse impasse that we gave over Cinema to what were in effect its natural enemies, but as a result I found myself in a dead end.

The only place I found the kind of evidence that made sense to me was far from the arts and humanities, in Biology and Neuroscience. That was both unexpected and a major challenge, not least as the matter of the interpretation of experimental results immediately crosses over into the territory of philosophy. I am neither a scientist nor a philosopher and therefore the only sensible approach to the ideas put forward below was to try to keep close to my background in film-making. My limited knowledge of both science and philosophy makes the propositions in this book necessarily tentative, although they have crossed over deep into those territories. My reading of the literature in those sallies forth suggested a range of connections between contemporary neurobiology and Cinema, and it is a sense of the significance of those connections that prompted a Theory of Film based upon them. The ambition of previous generations has often been to bring the discipline of science to bear upon Cinema, but it can be argued that it is perhaps only at this point in the development of neuroscience that one may arguably see beyond generalities to sense a number of profound connections between the way the brain works and the way we respond to Cinema. Those connections potentially form a foundation so much deeper than Language as to reduce any of the traditional parallels between that relatively recent evolutionary arrival and Cinema largely redundant.

This project proposes the notion of using Language to serve Vision rather than its current approach of disregarding and relegating it to a minor role. That would be a new role for Language, but both an eminently possible and valuable one. Language derives many words from Vision and, as with my students learning to think visually, it is as simple a shift as the use of words to attempt to adequately describe the multiple dimensions and richness of a visual scene instead of using words as a shorthand symbol – the comparison between a carefully-drawn portrait and a stick-man.

The antique nomenclature of the 'Major' and 'Minor' hemispheres of the brain, the first broadly associated with Language skills, the second with Visual skills, is an example of how Language has been used to relegate Vision to a position of inferiority. Neuroscience has almost dispensed with those terms as research has revealed the truth to be rather different, but the prejudice lingers. 'Verbal' and 'Non-verbal' skills in IQ tests is another example, as though Visual skills have no autonomy.

In one sense the real challenge of this project is to begin to uproot the very deeply-held feeling that Language is superior. I suggest that is a myth and on the contrary that it is Vision that is almost infinitely superior both quantitatively and qualitatively. Quantitively in that it processes much more information, and qualitatively in that not just the depth and breadth of information it handles, but *the wisdom that information contains*, is vastly in excess of anything of which the Word is even capable. It is perhaps above all the wisdom of Vision that is extraordinary. We see so much more than we are aware of and so much more than finds its way into Language. I see therefore I am.

The Matter of Vision

The Matter of Vision has three meanings for both terms – Matter in the scientific sense, as in the world is made of matter, Matter meaning Issue, and Matter indicating a Materialist explanation for phenomena – that is the belief that everything is capable of explanation in time through Science. Likewise, Vision has an adjectival connotation, as in a man of Vision, it also is technical, the capacity of the eye for Vision, and a reference to Cinema as a Visual art.

1

The Matter of Vision

Modern society[3] has been the prisoner of three stern gaolers, Language, Consciousness and Reason. Each member of the troika has succeeded in imposing an image of its hegemony upon the mind of modern culture. The result has been the incarceration and repression of their opposite number, the target of this relentless campaign; Vision, the Automatic[4] and Emotion.

The task of those images is to boost the prestige of their masters at the expense of their opposite numbers, and in that they have been remarkably successful. Jealously painting-out the real role of their opponents, they have consistently sought to reduce their status.

Language, Consciousness and Reason (LCR) are seen here in terms of their status as cultural[5] artefacts, that is not things themselves, but the 'ideology' attached to each of them that reifies them above their real status. The question is not of their real relationship to their opposite numbers but the ideological ones that have developed around them.

This project suggests that Language, Consciousness and Reason, in contrast to their image in the public mind, are not quite the peaks of being human that have been promulgated, but more limited in their achievements and reach than their 'ideologies' would claim. Those ideologies also have an aggressive attitude towards their opposite numbers and have set out to demote and 'denigrate'[6] Vision, the Automatic, and Emotion (VAE).

The aim of this project is to restore Vision to its real status as the noblest and wisest facility of man, and to turn the tables on the vulgar upstart Language.

---

3   From the time of the Industrial Revolution.

4   The Automatic is the term I suggest as a replacement for the negative term, the unconscious, p. 10. See Commentaries for further discussion.

5   'Cultural' is used here in a Darwinian sense discussed later.

6   See 'Downcast Eyes: The Denigration of Vision in Twentieth Century French Culture', Martin Jay, University of California Press, 1999.

Likewise, to promote the massive role of the Automatic compared to that of Consciousness, and to aid the return of Emotion to the prestige and position proposed for it as early as 1739 by David Hume in the face of the inflations of Reason.

* * *

In the late 1950s it was calculated that the eyes absorb a million times the information of which consciousness is aware.[7] In 1965 a physiologist put it that "only one millionth of what our eyes see, our ears hear, and our other senses inform us about appears in our consciousness".[8] Of the range of *external* stimuli Consciousness handles a millionth, but for *internal* activity the figures for the brain as a whole suggests it handles between ten and thirty billion times the information of Consciousness.[9] That would suggest the possibility that the rest of the information is handled outside Consciousness, yet Language provides us with only a negative term for that activity – the 'unconscious'. The proposal here is to dedicate an independent term to that area – the Automatic.

Although Consciousness has a limited capacity for information-processing, as in the fabled seven objects that can be held in Consciousness at any one time, it has evolved for the tasks it carries out, and information-processing capacity is not coterminous with value. In other words, Consciousness is more than Information. The brain works to reduce information that is not necessary, a reducing valve,[10] and Consciousness in particular does not necessarily require large numbers of neurons to carry out it important functions. However, given that caveat, the issue remains that both the very substantial work of the Automatic and its significance is arguably consistently undervalued, even by neuroscientists.[11] It is not that Consciousness is not valuable but that arguably in relation to the Automatic it is an epiphenomenon, an effect rather than a cause, a by-product of brain-function, whereas the image often proposed is of an all-powerful phenomenon, and that of the Automatic a shadowy and uncertain one.

It is suggested here that the Automatic does nearly all the work and directs the

---

7   By Kupfmuller, an Information Theorist – quoted in Norretranders op. cit., p. 143.

8   Dietrich Trinker, also quoted in Norretranders.

9   Quoted in Norretranders, op. cit., Ch.6 'The Bandwith of Consciousness', p. 124, and Part III 'Consciousness', p. 211.

10   The term used by Simon Raggett see: www.quantum-mind.co.uk

11   Dehaene, 2014, details extensively the work of the unconscious but asserts that Consciousness is like an executive choosing from vast amounts of material prepared for its decision by the unconscious, whereas my sense is that Consciousness is the passive partner, presented with the choices for attention by the Automatic and reporting back on them to the Automatic in a constant feedback loop.

limited capacities of Consciousness to attend to the few stimuli it is capable of handling at any one time, effectively tasking it with reporting back on the significance of, and any changes to, those stimuli as part of a feedback loop energised by the Automatic.

The image this project disputes is that LCR are the Major partners and VAE are the Minor partners. This nomenclature echoes an old distinction that used to be made between left and right hemispheres of the brain, with the Left, language-oriented hemisphere, termed Major, and the Right, vision-oriented hemisphere – termed Minor. That terminology reflected an old prejudice that Language is more important than Vision, a prejudice that is the prime target of this project.

Again in raw numbers, Language processes an average of around ten bits per second of information. Vision processes around ten million bits per second, again a differential of a million times.[12] Yet the ideology around Language, here referred to as Logocentrism, unequivocally suggests that Language is superior to Vision – with Vision characterised as superficial and lacking in depth compared to the profundities of which language is capable. The proposition here is that quite the opposite is true, Vision is deeper and broader, more sophisticated and mature than Language could ever hope to be. Wisdom resides in Vision, not in Language, which is a narrow medium of translation. Thought, for example, takes place not in Language but in Vision, and only in Vision. Thought is translated into and manipulated in Language, but only actually takes place in Vision.

Neuroscience has also revolutionised our understanding of the relation between Reason and Emotion. From twenty years' work with brain-damaged patients, Antonio Damasio[13] concluded that Emotion is possible without Reason, but that Reason is only possible with Emotion. In other words, Reason is contingent upon Emotion and it is Emotion that is autonomous. That conception turns upside-down the conventional valorisation of Reason and concomitant pejorative image of Emotion. In relation to Cinema, Hitchcock said that Cinema is stronger than Reason, and Godard went further to declare that Cinema *is* Emotion. The conception here is that Emotion is the alarm-system that the body/brain uses to alert itself to a threat to survival.

The other side of that pairing is Reason, seen here as more of a noble ambition than a universal truth. Man's ineluctable subjectivity inevitably condemns him to rationalisation rather than grand Reason. And it in that rationalisation that we

---

12   From Norretranders, op. cit., Ch 6 in general, pp. 143–144 in particular

13   Damasio, *Descartes' Error*, Quill, New York, 1998.

11

witness the operations of the subjective in the body of Reason. Recent neuroscience has turned the negative aspects of subjectivity into strengths. Subjective experience should be seen not as out-of-bounds, but as right at the heart of understanding consciousness, for example, by treating it not as evidence, but as raw data.[14] A similar approach has yielded valuable insights both with Dreams and with the study of Emotion, and it is in that last area that I would suggest that by including Emotion within a reformed paradigm of scientific method, a revolution of Newtonian proportions has quietly occurred, reinvigorating empiricism and substantially extending its reach. The proposition here is to view Emotion as the raw-material of the brain, the fuel that drives it, and also gives it ignition in its constant movement. It is a commonplace that to live is to feel, but that has a deeper and profound truth in the very mode of the operations of the brain and the body/brain system as a whole.

This project would restore liberty to Vision, the Automatic and Emotion and in so doing repair a serious imbalance in our culture. Lacking a proper hearing for Vision, the Automatic and Emotion we are not losing one half of the picture but in fact sustaining a greater loss. The Major factors have been painted as Minor and the Minor factors as Major. The aim should not, however, be simply to turn the tables, replacing one structure of dominance with another, but to restore the balance in a context that understands how evolution developed such apparent opposites into an integrated whole where both sides play an invaluable role. The reverberations from properly correcting the imbalance would be a revolution in how man thinks of himself in the world.

LCR v VAE

Vision

The starting-point of this enquiry was a sense that Cinema is more powerful than it is given credit for, and that power comes from its nature as a visual medium. The conception of Vision that accompanies that view sees it as the source of virtually all our knowledge about the World. Unlike Language, we do not in general have to practice Vision.[15] With Language there is a search for every word, sometimes conscious, often unconscious or Automatic. With Vision we do it

---

14   A point well-made by Dehaene, *Consciousness and the Brain*, Viking, New York, 2014, pp. 12, 41–43.

15   While we do not perhaps have to practice Vision as we do Language, as a technical facility, that is distinct from whether we learn *from* Vision – which evolutionary logic suggests is primary – which things are food, which might suggest danger, which are poisonous etc. Its capacities evolved for survival, but exaptation has made that enormous capacity for information available for Cinema, as it were. See Gould, S.J.; Vrba, E.S. (1982). "Exaptation – a missing term in the science of form", *Paleobiology* 8 (1): 4–15.

without thinking (even where we get it wrong first time around). There is immediately an irony in that situation in that we tend to take the power of Vision for granted. That might be thought of as the Tragedy of Vision.

Language is said to be around 40,000 years old, with recent estimates putting it as 100,000 years old, and speculation that it might be considerably older, even up to a million years old or more. Man is said to be around 2.4 million years old, depending on how you set the boundary between Man and his predecessors, but the first anatomically modern human fossils date back only 195,000 years, however primates with semantic communication seem possibly to predate 'man' which could set the origins of language further back.

Vision is eons older, evolutionarily, than Language. The notion that Cinema, a visual medium, could even be imagined to be 'structured like a Language',[16] a relatively addition to the evolutionary scene, makes little sense (when added to the disparity in processing capacity). The reduction of Cinema to Language would be ahistorical in the extreme and Idealist in philosophical terms. From the perspective of evolution, Language can be argued on the contrary to be contingent upon Vision. For example, between two-thirds and three-quarters of words are said to represent Vision (or Sound, but with a much lesser number devoted to Sound). Language is a development that is based upon Vision.

One element of my interest in Vision was to look at the development of the eye. What could that tell us about Vision? The evolution of the eye can be traced fairly accurately and linked to certain geological changes on Earth. At the time in question the planet was covered with mist and geological changes raised the ambient temperature a few degrees, sufficient to disperse the mists. Before that, vision was useful but of only local significance. Afterwards, vision was at a premium, as the ability to see a potential predator, or indeed potential prey, obviously possessed biological value. Following these events, the eye accelerated in development over a relatively short period in biological terms, a period known as the 'Cambrian explosion', between 542 and 543 *million* years ago.[17] By the end of that million year period, the sophistication of the eye was not much different from ours today.

The eye developed as the most efficient method of alerting creatures to a survival-threat. The reason for its efficiency is its capabilities in registering movement – as in the movement of a predator. Movement is the best sign as an

16 See 'Cinema and Language' below, p. 24.

17 Andrew Parker - *In the Blink of an Eye*, Simon & Schuster, London, (2003).

early-warning of the approach of a threat to survival. Our eyes respond with alacrity to movement in peripheral vision, and that is an inheritance of evolution. It is, of course, also significant for Cinema, for moving-pictures.

The Wisdom of Vision

Vision may be vastly older and vastly more powerful than Language, but what I would like to draw attention to here again is the quality of Vision. There is a common view in my culture that it is Language that is the subtle medium, capable of the depths of expression of Shakespeare, while the visual sense, and in particular Cinema, is crude, obvious, and superficial. I would guess that part of that attitude comes from the fact that Language has to be practiced to gain its effects. We are more conscious of making an effort to manipulate it on a daily, hourly, constant basis. With Vision, as I have said, it is automatic, often unconscious and we are much less aware of any effort involved.

This conception has Vision as an intelligent medium. In other words it is not merely a passive vessel through which information passes, but an active mediator that has a role in identifying what is important to be looked at and passes back information it assembles about those things to the body/brain system in a constant feedback loop. Horace Barlow, twenty years after his 1953 experiment in frog vision sensed something similar: "a large part of the sensory machinery involved in a frog's feeding responses may actually reside in the retina ... each single neuron can perform a much more complex and subtle task than had previously been thought ... the activities of neurons, quite simply, are thought processes".[18]

The notion I want to develop here is that we do not realise the quality of information we receive from Vision. I suggest that everything we know we learn from Vision. It is not merely a question of the amount of information that we receive, although that is an indication of how much we are picking up, but of the depth, the intelligence, the sheer *wisdom* that Vision brings. What I mean to suggest by wisdom is that the nature of the knowledge gained from Vision goes far deeper than common currency would suggest. Wisdom suggests insight, perhaps combined with mature reflection. The wonder of Vision is that it is intelligent in the sense of making discriminations, judgements – just as in the first moments we lay eyes upon a new person – and those judgements would seem

---

18   Quoted in Norretranders op. cit., p. 193.

to involve millions, perhaps billions of discriminations. That means the brain[19] making choices, according to biological criteria, what might be called instinctive, tacit, or natural wisdom – dare I say the best kind – rather than the rational Darwin's List type,[20] the formal kind of the Academy. It is worth stressing that the criteria of this wisdom are biological rather than sociological or philosophical. That means the discriminations are about survival (for reproduction). Evolution makes those choices solely on their being advantageous for survival. For the most part those discriminations are Automatic and do not appear in consciousness. This wisdom, this intelligence is unconscious.

My suggestion would be that many of the qualities we think come from Language in fact come from Vision.

As a prime example, I would contend that Thought takes place in Vision. Not only that but Thought *only* takes place in Vision.[21] Thought does not take place in Language. Language translates what Vision provides into its own medium, but it is not a source of meaning, merely a medium of translation. Language is contingent upon Vision.

My thought is that virtually all the information we gain about other people comes from our Vision, and again mainly unconsciously. When we are told about somebody we compare that information to what we see of them, and it is that latter information that is decisive. The reason is that 'seeing is believing', we gain a much richer field of information in Vision, more complex, with more dimensions than anything Language can provide. What wisdom we have comes entirely from Vision. Intelligence is about the application of imagination to making distinctions and judgements. Imag-ination could almost be a synonym for Vision. Christian Keysers[22] has shown us that the easy assumption of philosophers over the ages that we cannot know what is in another's head is not quite true. On the contrary we cannot avoid knowing, not in the literal sense of seeing thoughts but in empathising with what they are going through emotionally and mirroring that unconsciously in our emotions through what he has called Shared Circuits.

Those processes also obtain in Cinema as we watch people on the screen. We gain

---

19 According to Bennett and Hacker's 480 page survey, *The Philosophical Foundations of Neuroscience,* Wiley-Blackwell, London, 2003, it is not sensible to talk of the brain separate from man, but their whole comprehensive survey is based on a fragment from Wittgenstein to that effect, which I admire on principle as eccentric, but not in practice as creating more problems than it solves, and to no effect, an echo of a current view of their sponsor.

20 See p. 106 for Darwin's List.

21 Those born blind cannot think in Vision, but as it has been suggested that the brain provides optional overlapping systems where sight is not available, it may be possible that for the blind thought occurs through those systems.

22 Christian Keysers, *The Empathic Brain,* Social Brain Press, 2011.

less intimate information than being in somebody's company, but what films show us is people in action, with a far broader range of actions than we would normally experience with an individual, the process of drama, the intensified emotions of actors seen on a bright screen in a darkened room.

The articulation of Vision

One problem Vision has is that of articulation. Language could be much more active in articulating Vision, but the ideology of Logocentrism tends to deny and demote Vision, minimising and denigrating it. The result is that, although Language is heavily dependent upon Vision for its references in its own medium, it has not often been used to taking on the positive task of articulating the qualities of Vision. In the letters of Cezanne we see the attempt of an artist to put into words his daily struggle with expressing himself in painting and in Rilke's letters on Cezanne we see something related, a poet trying to find ways to express the poetry of the Visual in a great painter. It is possible for language to articulate Vision, to serve Vision, and it is suggested here that would bring some balance to the role Language plays, against the tide of Logocentrism. Language serving Vision would be both appropriate and constructive, a role of which it is capable, but in which it is much less experienced than is good for Vision.

I see therefore I am.

The Automatic

I would see it as another instance of Logocentrism that the area beyond Consciousness receives only the negative of the term as its title – unconscious. The terms suggest that Consciousness is the privileged one and its opposite number relatively unimportant and therefore deserves merely the negative term.

The information-processing numbers explored in the 1950s suggested Consciousness has a capacity of only around one-millionth of the area outside it – which we know as the unconscious. In proposing the term The Automatic, I want to draw attention to the notion that this area beyond Consciousness gets on with its many tasks outside our awareness, in silence as it were, and automatically – that is without conscious direction from us.[23] The area appears to be substantial

---

23 The area beyond consciousness includes the autonomic, reflex, homeostasis, and their status would need to be clarified as part of a greater understanding of the terrain of the 'Automatic'.

and neuroscientists often refer to the relevant processes as automatic, so that the term is already in current if informal use.

The comparison William James is said to have made between the conscious and Automatic as a pin in the Albert Hall gives an image of the difference of scale between the two, in which case Man is arguably an unconscious creature.

One of the main ideas behind this project was that we take in most of what we absorb from a film unconsciously/Automatically. Film-study could make a contribution to the understanding of the brain through helping to devise experiments that use films to assess what information audiences do in fact absorb Automatically. The difficulty is how to untangle information absorbed Consciously and that taken in Automatically.[24] While there has been much work over the last twenty years on identifying the threshold between conscious and unconscious absorption, which has tended to suggest the extent of unconscious operations in the brain, there is a difference between crossing the threshold and, as it were, evaluating the building you are entering, between a first step and the universe beyond. Threshold analysis has certainly demonstrated the significance of emotion and the subjective, and that is congruent with the approach taken here towards Cinema. An advantage of working with films is that they can be viewed repeatedly, that is their output is a constant, and their content catalogued exhaustively to compare with audience recall in a variety of ways to find what works most effectively. Experiments with films have demonstrated differential brain activation, with a Hitchcock-directed TV film (*Bang! You're Dead*, 1961), for example, scoring around 50% higher than *The Good, The Bad & The Ugly*. 'Hitchcock was able to orchestrate the responses of so many different brain regions, turning them on and off at the same time across all viewers'.[25] Even that rather basic experiment, using fMRI scanning (2008), provided evidence of the relation between mise-en-scene and attention, and between objective measurement of brain activity and the subjective experience of the audience.[26]

Emotion

Emotion is central to this project. In terms of the question of what Emotion is,

24 See Dehaene op. cit. for an account of such experiments since the 1990s. The 'threshold' method his laboratory uses would perhaps require some development to deal with the issues of Cinema discussed in this book.

25 Hasson et al., *Neurocinematics: The Neuroscience of Film*, Projections, Vol 2, Issue 1, Summer 2008, pp. 1–26.

26 The issue of developing experimental methods to analyse unconscious activity from films is one to which I hope to return.

I take the line of LeDoux (*The Emotional Brain*) that the key thing is what Emotion does rather than being too concerned with definitions of what it is, which tend to end up either diffuse or circular. Emotion is seen here in physical terms as the response of the body/brain system to a perceived survival-threat (or opportunity) in the external environment.[27] It functions as an alarm-system that warns of a potential threat, and takes the form of internal activity, blood flow, synapses connecting, galvanic skin response, sweating, etc and only at the extremes does it make an appearance in Consciousness. Most Emotion is unconscious or Automatic (for which there is considerable evidence, see LeDoux). Everything that happens in the brain is seen as prompted by Survival, and Emotion is, as it were, the raw material that the body/brain system produces as a response to potential danger.

The evolutionary sense of a threat may seem too broad and general to apply to everyday life, but if we take the notion first suggested in *The Descent of Man* that sees human culture as the successor to genetic evolution, in other words cultural evolution as the adaptation of genetic evolution that developed in human society, then the definition of a threat becomes much wider. By a process of adaptation, or 'exaptation', what originally served the purpose of an alarm against predators can become a mechanism to help choose a handbag or breakfast cereal. In the choice of a handbag there can be many competing images that battle for victory in the buyer's mind. Is it really me? Is it too young/old, posh/flashy for me? Can I afford it? Will it go with other things? "The only thing that separates us from the Animals is the ability to accessorize" as Dolly Parton put it.[28] The Emotions that are part of the process of taking a decision will be partly conscious, but also unconscious. It can be argued that no one ever took a decision rationally – even with an exhaustive list of pros and cons – as in the famous example of Darwin trying to decide about marriage (and concluding it was better than a dog). Emotion makes the decision for us as Reason has its limits.

That point is also related to Damasio's crucial conclusion noted earlier – that Reason is contingent upon Emotion. Emotion without Reason is possible, but not Reason without Emotion.[29] That view overturns centuries of philosophy but also suggests the power of Emotion. Kant reacted against Hume on the epistemology of induction, but it was Hume who declared that 'Reason is and ought only to be the slave of the passions, and can never pretend to any other office

---

27 While the primary mention in the book is of Survival, it is implicit that survival for reproduction is the order of play.

28 In *9 to 5* (1980), Screenplay: Patricia Resnick & Colin Higgins.

29 Damasio, *Descartes' Error, Emotion, Reason and the Human Brain,* op. cit.

than to serve and obey them'. Hume's wisdom on emotion appears prescient both for his time and in opposition, as it were, to the view Kant would later take.

What might be called The Logic of Nature is seen in Emotion, as Emotion is survival. That is to say that Emotion arises as a survival response, and survival is basic to evolution alongside reproduction. We survive in order to reproduce, that is the logic of evolution and therefore the Logic of Nature.

Cinema is Emotion, according to Sam Fuller in Godard's *Pierrot Le Fou*, where he was asked to define exactly what is Cinema: "Film is like a battleground. Love. Hate. Action. Violence. Death. In one word ... Emotion". Cinema is drama, and dramatising uses the strongest emotional situations.

There are two immediate connections between science and Cinema in regards to Emotion. The first is that the eye responds to movement. It is natural for our eyes to follow movement. It is built-in as a biological response. Movement may equal danger so we are particularly alert to it. The second connection is Emotional movement. A film is an arc of the hero/ine's emotional status. Each scene is centred on a change in that status, for example success or happiness. The arc of the hero/ine's emotional status is the string the audience follows. A film is, in ideal formal terms, all emotional movement. It is not 'about' emotional move-ment, but is emotional movement. Cinema is Emotion.

Life is change. Without change, without movement, there is no life. Life, in the biological sense, is a process of change. The Logic of Nature is change, in the large; evolution. Emotion is a process, a process of change. Movement is central to Life. Cinema brings photography to life. Cinema moves and Cinema moves us. Cinema is Emotion.

Emotion has had a bad name with scientists. After all, it is the opposite of Reason, the foundation of science. The growth in interest in Emotion in neuroscience has met with far from unanimous approval, but I would argue that it as an invaluable advance because it brings the 'subjective' within the orbit of scientific method – of experiment and testing, as Dehaene has done in relation to Consciousness. A similar thing could be said of Dream Science, which has taken what were considered to be irredeemably personal experiences, dreams, and subjected them to scientific methods and procedures with striking outcomes – not the least the notion of overturning Freud's speculative claim that the unconscious hides guilty secrets. Dream Science has suggested the truth to be the direct opposite – the unconscious reveals rather than conceals – it is all about revealing and has nothing to do with concealment.

With the study of Emotion in neuroscience, subjectivity is within the gates of scientific method. I argue that is something of a revolution, extending the reach of science into areas previously excluded. If we accept Damasio's argument that Reason is contingent upon Emotion the autonomy of Reason falls. However, Emotion complementing Reason is a more balanced picture, an expanded view of Reason encompassing subjectivity in a scientifically-disciplined manner. The task remains to chart the dimensions of unconscious Emotion in order to understand more about that complementarity.

Affective Neurobiology (ANB)

This term is not strictly speaking an existing discipline, nor is it a proposal for one. It denotes an approach to the various Matters of Vision, particularly Cinema, that brings together neuroscience and evolutionary biology but with an emphasis upon Emotion, or Affect. The distinction between affective and cognitive is said to originate with Aquinas in the 13th Century. While the affective is concerned with Emotion, the cognitive is often seen as being concerned with thought, and implicitly with the notion that thought occurs in language. The proposition here, as indicated above, is that thought occurs in Vision. Further than that, thought is not seen as occurring in Language at all, but only in Vision. What we think is a process of thought occurring through Language is our second-hand experience of Vision that has been translated into Language. I have made the argument above how much older Vision is than Language, and therefore the notion that Cinema is structured like a Language seems unlikely in evolutionary terms. In fact, the different approaches to tasks shown by the two sides of the brain overlap to a degree with the opposition here between Language and Vision. Language is a tool that tries to focus in, on the right word for example. Vision tends to be a sweep across a visual scene, stopping along the way, but making sense of the scene as a whole. That 'holistic' quality is identified with the approach of the other, right hemisphere.

Neurobiology is established as a discipline, or rather the yoking together of two complementary disciplines. The biology part is strictly evolutionary biology, and most neuroscience takes evolution as the background against which brain functions are assessed. For example in the left-brain/right-brain debate it is striking how most experiments share the epistemological framework of evolution, often with an emphasis on survival as the driver. There is a saying that nothing in biology makes sense outside evolution, and I would extend that to suggest that nothing in neuroscience makes sense outside evolution.

ANB as an approach to Cinema marks a break with traditions based in Language and a move to a proper science-based analysis. Christian Metz posed the question, how scientific can the study of Cinema be?[30] He asked that question 50 years ago, and as though neurobiology did not exist. That generation failed to answer the question directly by looking to science, instead turning in effect to Language (Semiotics is seen here as a subset of Linguistics). With the state of neuroscience today I would argue that the study of Cinema *can* be properly scientific. Neuroscience is perhaps only on the foothills of knowledge about the brain, but the potential can be glimpsed for a substantially better understanding of Vision and Cinema than would ever be even theoretically possible with analysis based in Language. The varieties of 'Theory' that have held the stage since Metz's question are not theories science would recognise, and have none of the predictive power required of a theory in science. Science would not regard such claims to the status of theory as legitimate.

The key to theories in science is their ability to be tested. Testing consists, in the classic method, of formulating ideas in such a way that experiments can be designed to assess the viability of the theory under laboratory conditions, a notion quite foreign to Continental Philosophy in all its guises. Theories have to be capable of being disproved. This is hardly news in science since Newton, but does not currently apply to any brand of 'Theory' in the Arts and Humanities, which all share Kant's claim for the autonomy of Reason. The aim of this project is to propose the formulation of ideas in just that way – so they can be tested and are capable of support or disproof. The study of Emotion, Consciousness and Dream Science have shown that what was formerly thought to be subjective and not amenable to objective analysis can be approached scientifically. For example, there appear to be some parallels between the way the brain works in REM dreaming and while watching a film. The external referent part of the brain shuts down in both cases. Dream diaries have been used successfully to chart the forms that dreams take and to begin to challenge some of the myths around dreaming. Researchers have found, for example, that the bizarreness of dreams tends to be greatly exaggerated and that the great majority of dreams have a functional structure that is rather more coherent and rational than previously claimed.[31] Dreams are seen as having a biological function like everything else, and as a result

---

30 Metz: 'Le cinéma: langue ou langage?', 1964, Volume 4, No 4, pp. 52–90.

31 'dreams are most often reasonable simulations of waking life that contain occasional unusual features in terms of settings, characters, or activities (Dorus et al., 1971; Foulkes, 1985; Hall & Van de Castle, 1966; Snyder, 1970)' in Domhoff, G. W. (2005). *Refocusing the neurocognitive approach to dreams: A critique of the Hobson versus Solms debate. Dreaming*, 15, 3–20.

are brought down to earth, which is one of the great achievements of science – the ongoing process of replacing myth with experimentally-tested fact.

Dream diaries could perhaps form one example of how viewers' responses to films could provide the material with which to start a scientific approach to Cinema. The close study of individual films, as in my little experiment with *The Searchers*, begins to yield up their complex content. It would be possible to analyse the development of the script, its range of references, the 'exformation' that was discarded in its writing, all as part of a reclamation of the 'unconscious' of a film, an archive of the information it contains. The task is then to devise experiments that begin to untangle the conscious from the Automatic. That is no easy task but I have a sense that the way forward is through the same issues of Survival, Evolution and Emotion. I noticed in teaching that we only take in what has emotional significance for us. Without that, information doesn't stick. In that sense knowledge seems always to be concrete. Abstract ideas tend to float away, but if there is something that attaches us to an idea, an identification of some sort, then we are much more likely to remember it. As with the study of Emotion, the combination of being able to track brain activity through imaging, like fMRI, and the constant relating of issues back to evolution, to Survival, perhaps offers a route to begin to define what information goes in Automatically and what Consciously. Such a process could also increase our understanding of how the brain works, shifting the ground of the study of Cinema to a collaboration with science. From the current introverted nature of academic study such a future seems far away, but it also seems to me to offer far greater rigour and a real contribution to society, with the considerable side-benefit of bridging the gap between the Two Cultures, bringing Art & Science back together, after a separation often seen as going back to the Eighteenth Century.

The approach in this project is a materialist one in which it is argued that everything has a solely physical explanation.[32] It is a materialism of a scientific rather than Marxist character. Marxism borrowed materialism from science in a similar sleight of hand to the variants of Theory in the late twentieth-century, but Marx turned Hegel upside down, which is not quite the same as rejecting it completely. The inheritance of German Idealism is an antithetical tradition to the empiricism of Newton, Locke and Hume. I would suggest that the proper inclusion of Hume's 'passions', Emotion, in the paradigm of scientific method,

---

32   See the later discussion, in On Method, about the boundaries between the physical and the metaphysical.

offers a revitalised and extended, a New Empiricism, an Expansive Materialism with explanatory powers exceeding any other framework.

Science is often accused of reductionism. There is an irony in that it is reductionism as a method that has facilitated the achievements of science. Scientific method involves identifying key variables in order to make predictions about cause and effect. The accusation is that in doing a similar thing to analyse art, science applies a coarse mesh that fails to capture the subtleties of artistic expression. My contention here is that neurobiology with an affective emphasis marks an epistemological advance from the limitations of classical scientific method that is so marked that the potential for a science of art, a science of culture (using an evolutionary definition of culture) is transformed.

Reverse-Engineering Cinema

The overall approach to Cinema that is proposed reverses the common route of moving from Nature to Culture, that is from Biology to (evolved) human Culture. Instead, it is suggested to 'reverse engineer' from the concrete cultural artefact that is Cinema, its archive, its history, its every moment formal and informal, to the biological base. For example, if we ask the question why does the eye follow movement in Cinema, the answer lies in tracing that fact back to its roots in the evolutionary history of the eye, going back many millions of years. The explanatory power of an evolutionary explanation is contained in that example – the reason the eye follows movement is biological in the evolutionary sense, and with a history of almost unimaginable antiquity.

The epistemological challenge of the reverse direction is that it would be practically impossible to imagine Cinema from the starting point of Nature. The detailed route that evolution took that arrived at the birth of the medium, let alone the Classic Hollywood Cinema in all its moments, is inevitably so complex as to almost defy human imagination. However, the reverse route is more capable of being traced as we start from the existence of Cinema and can unpick its history in terms of the logic of evolution. There is something in that approach of Bayesian inference, reasoning backwards to infer the hidden causes behind observations.[33] Beginning with the concrete facts of Cinema and working backwards is practical, where the reverse – imagining Cinema from the evolution of the Eye, for example – would be a virtually impossible task.

33 Description taken from Dehaene p. 94 op. cit.

Kuleshov & Gazzaniga

An example of the *Affective Neurobiology* approach to Cinema can be seen in links between two moments, the Kuleshov[34] experiments of 1917, which featured a famous actor with a neutral expression intercut with emotive shots – a crying baby, an attractive woman, a hot bowl of soup, and a famous experiment by the neuroscientist Gazzaniga around fifty years later. What interests me about Kuleshov is not the discovery of editing per se, for which it is best-known, but the idea that the audience filled-in the neutral expression of the actor according to what was in the succeeding shot – for soup he was said to look hungry, for a crying baby sympathetic etc.

Gazzaniga[35] worked with a split-brain patient who was presented with three objects – a chicken foot, a spade and a shed. The patient had no problem – the spade was for shovelling the chicken-poo out of the chicken shed.[36] I would suggest a rather similar process is going on in both cases, which is that the brain constantly seeks to rationalise the slim resources of Consciousness by linking stimuli in a meaningful way. Another way of seeing that impulse is towards narrative, a narrativising process. There are several other examples in the way the brain functions that show a related activity. That suggests there is a biological basis to narrative and suggests one reason why narrative Cinema has been the dominant mode of the medium.

The view of this project is that not only do we have very little idea of what we learn from Cinema, but little idea of how the brain responds to it. Neuroscience rooted in the historical sense of Evolution combined with an emphasis upon Emotion offers the possibility of overcoming those deficits and in the process adding to our stock of scientific knowledge of the brain. Compared to the analyses offered by Film Theory that would seem to be a rather more worthwhile project.

---

34 These experiments have become almost apocryphal in film-study, and represent an early interest in linking science to Cinema in the optimistic period after the Russian Revolution. They are often regarded as establishing editing as a unique element of the new medium, see http://en.wikipedia.org/wiki/Kuleshov_Effect

35 For the Gazzaniga experiment see p. 281 in Norretranders op cit.

36 It is worth distinguishing here between the 'natural' skills of Vision technically, as it were, and the 'cultural' evolutionary learning involved in their use, such as being able to distinguish between a mushroom that tastes wonderful and one that will kill you.

Cinema and Language

The notion that Cinema can best be analysed by reducing it to the condition of Language has a history going back to the earliest days of the medium, culminating in Christian Metz's declaration that Cinema 'is structured like a language'.[37] There was an echo in that statement of Lacan's assertion that the unconscious is structured like a language.[38] From the view taken here, both assertions are quite simply wrong, and reinforce the ideology of Logocentrism that denigrates and demotes Vision.

The Long Shadow of Immanuel Kant

Those two assertions are also symptoms of a philosophical approach that has proved 'unreasonably ineffective'.[39] In that regard there is an argument to be made that would be both unfashionable (at least in the humanities) and not uncontroversial. In the sciences, on the other hand, it would pass by largely without comment. There was a certain parting of the ways in philosophy that can be traced back to the eighteenth century, but with fundamental implications for contemporary debate both about philosophy and the vexed question of the relation between Art & Science, the Two Cultures debate so-named in the 1950s.

It all begins with Kant. Widely regarded as the greatest philosopher of the modern era, there is however an argument that he was also responsible for much of our present troubles. The two philosophers to whom Kant principally responded were Hume and Leibniz. He was exercised against Hume's idea that we apprehend the world solely through our senses. His desire was to assert that ideas form part of that perception of the world and in the Categorical Imperative it would appear that he claimed a certain autonomy to reason to that end, claiming a truth for philosophy that was independent of but equal to the truths of science in the tradition established by Newton and carried on in philosophy in his era by Hume (who died before Kant's response was published, although their lives overlapped). Kant felt he had achieved a Copernican Revolution in philosophy, distinguishing the world in our minds and an external world impossible for us to know directly.

---

37 Christian Metz, *Film Language*, University of Chicago press, Chicago, 1990.

38 Jacques Lacan, the leading figure in psycho-analysis in France at the rise of Film Theory. The French neuroscientist Stanislas Dehaene quotes his colleague Lionel Naccache to the effect that "the unconscious is not structured like a language but as a decaying exponential" – indicating the decay of unconscious memory that does not enter consciousness. See p 104 'Consciousness and the Brain. S Dehaene, Viking, New York, 2014, also see Commentaries on 'Consciousness and the Unconscious'.

39 See Steven Weinberg, *Dreams of a Final Theory*, Vintage, New York, 1993, commenting on philosophy.

There are interesting parallels between that view and current neuroscience discussions. Neuroscientists agree that we have only a representation of the world in our brains, partly due to the limitations of Consciousness and partly because, despite the idea that the brain is the most complex object known to man, it would not be possible to know the world completely in its every moment. Kant concluded for his part that it was the case that reason apprehended the world independently of the world outside the mind and that world could not, in principle, be known.

It is this autonomy to reason, an ideological perspective in Kant, that creates the problem. If reason is autonomous then philosophy by extension has a truth independent of the criteria of science. Those truths are not rooted in 'experience', that is in the material world, and are thus – in philosophical terms – Idealist. Kant arguably thus founded the tradition of German Idealism, which could be seen as passing in various guises through Hegel, inverted by Marx to his brand of materialism, which in turn fed into the thinkers behind the beginnings of Film Theory in the 1960s. In these synoptic strokes the line of argument goes that Marx, through an inversion rather than wholehearted disconnection from Hegel, erected Castles not in the Air (as Schopenhauer put it), but in the sand of Economics. It could be said that in eschewing the real materialism of Evolution after Darwin, Marx's brand of Hegelianism succeeded in creating another Idealism keen to take on the garb of materialism.

The continuities of German Idealism, however, took up slightly unlikely residence in Film Theory, via the thinkers behind it, in denying the materialism of science and substituting for it the false materialism inherited from Marx, in 'scientific socialism'. Returning to Kant, his assertion of an autonomy for reason found an interesting contradiction in Damasio's conclusion[40] based on work with brain-damaged patients rather than the abstractions of philosophy. His formula makes Reason contingent upon Emotion or, to put it another way, Reason has no autonomy. It is Emotion that has autonomy.

If we are able to accept that point, then Kant's wishes fall. Reason is not and cannot ever be autonomous. The historical echo is now with David Hume, in his famous assertion that Reason is and always should be under the control of the Passions. If you recall, it was partly Hume that Kant set out to deny.

The problem that leads back, in this sketch, to Kant, is that in the presentation to Reason of a licence to autonomy, Hegel's Castles in the Air[41] are echoed in the

---

40   see Antonio Damasio, *Descartes' Error*, op. cit.

whole of French thought that lies behind Film Theory. That tradition is anti-visual[42] while leaving a trail of idealisms often claiming to be materialist, but in reality nothing of the sort. Rejecting science out of hand, turning its back on the real materialism of evolution, let alone neurobiology, it is without the faintest thought of submission to the proper discipline of science. In science ideas must be testable, able to formulated in such a manner that experiments can be designed that will put the truth of those ideas to the rigours of laboratory conditions . No post-modernist relativism must ever be allowed to deny one jot of the achievements of real science. The notion that ideas must be testable is a universe away from the inheritance of German Idealism. A Lacan produces not Castles but labyrinths in the air, an unintended legacy of Kant that has permitted the creation of 'a tumbling ground for whimsies', as William James observed of Freud's conception of the unconscious.

Real Materialism

This project represents the rejection of the whole of that philosophical tradition originating with Kant and German Idealism, in favour of a materialist analysis based in science and upon scientific method. The notion of scientific method identified here is one enlarged by the addition of Emotion into the paradigm, a change regarded in itself as revolutionary. That diplomatic addition to the paradigm is seen as marking a step-change in the potential of science to analyse the Arts and Humanities. In contrast, the whole philosophical tradition behind Film Theory is viewed as irredeemably in thrall to the word. That is the major reason it is unable to say anything of consequence about Vision. It is, in effect, blind to Vision.

This project returns to Hume's closeting of Reason as necessarily always under the control of Emotion. The shadow of German Idealism falls sharply across the French thinkers of the 20th Century who form the background to Film Theory. Their 'materialism' is substantially rhetorical, a kind of wishful-thinking that is another form of Idealism, often fuelled by a wish to be associated with political radicalism. In fact, their abandonment of the Port Royal tradition of clarity in discourse, 'If it is not clear it is not French', seems historically to be part of a broader identification with German Idealism that parted company with materialism based in science even in the time of Kant.

---

41 Schopenhauer's view of Hegel's philosophy.

42 See Martin Jay, *Downcast Eyes – The Denigration of Vision in Twentieth Century French Thought*, op. cit.

New Empiricism

There is a clear line to be drawn here between what is regarded as a proper materialism, in which ideas have to be capable of submission to experimental testing, and the rhetoric of Film Theory and its intellectual parents. The latter often apes the garb of materialism, but in reality it is the King's New Clothes, nothing remotely to do with the essential discipline of science.

The call here is for a return to the fundamentals of real materialism, with the principle of testability as the gold standard. This is not however, it should be said, a return to the traditional logic of scientific method and empiricism of old, but one whose potential I would suggest has been radically changed by the inclusion of Emotion[43] within the walls of what might be thought of as a New Scientific Method. That change would seem to me to have the potential to be a revolution In submitting the formerly excluded area of what had been thought of as subjective, the opposite of and enemy to Reason – the foundation of science – to scientific analysis and methods, it has been shown that areas such as Consciousness, Dreams and Emotion are capable of objective analysis. This might be called a New Empiricism, a change that I would argue qualitatively extends the reach of scientific method, with profound implications.

There are certain parallels with the difference in perspective identified by the large body of research on 'hemispherical lateralisation' between the two hemispheres (the left brain/right brain debate). Current opinion is that both sides of the brain deal with the full range of problem-solving, but the left side brings a narrow, focussed and goal-oriented approach, whereas the right side brings a broader, more holistic and innovative approach. The inclusion of Emotion within the citadel of scientific method is as though science has been able in some way to embrace the complementary biological value of a 'right-side' approach, in an appreciation of the value of elaboration of a fuller picture than had been possible hitherto when focussing strictly on a 'left-side' rationality. The scepticism that remains among many scientists to consideration of Emotion indicates that would be over optimistic, if arguably worthwhile as an aim. There remains significant resistance to the inclusion of Emotion and other subjectivisms within the ranks of scientists, so it would be misleading to represent what is effectively a shift in epistemology as universally accepted. Even researchers in the area are reluctant

43 See section on Emotion (p. 17) for an operational definition from Joseph LeDoux. Since this section was written I read Stanislas Dehaene on Consciousness, and he applies a similar philosophy to the treatment of subjective reports as raw data which, together with the approach of Dream-Science to dreams creates a triple confirmation of this revolution in scientific method.

o make too much of the development, perhaps partly because of the barely-concealed scepticism emanating from their more conservative colleagues. However, his project does not hesitate to come out unequivocally in favour of the development, and to the extent of hailing it as a revolution in scientific method.

The Anti-Science tradition

A further characteristic of the thinkers behind Film Theory was what seemed rather like a distaste for and disinterest in science. Christian Metz put it that Science is a big word'.[44] The contention here is that Language, in contrast, is a small word. It seems quite extraordinary that a whole intellectual tradition could ignore the advances in science, and particularly in neuroscience, as though they did not exist. It is as though Kant gave a license to philosophy, in his declaration of its independence, to turn decisively away from science in the firm belief that the autonomy of philosophical truth was a sufficient protection. While a certain autonomy is reasonable, as the discourse of philosophy and that of science are not coterminous, the result in many cases has been that tumbling ground for whimsies William James described, the 'Fantastical learning' decried by Bacon. The failure to engage with science would seem to be a significant intellectual failure, virtually a dereliction of duty, and hardly credible seen from the outside. The contrary fact is that most scientists appear to regard 'post-modern' varieties of philosophy at best as utterly ineffectual, at worst as a downright fake, as in Richard Dawkins view of Lacan,[45] the psycho-analyst.

As one educated in the Humanities and working in the Arts, broadly defined, I shared that guilt. It was only in realising how helpless Film Theory was at providing a fundamental account of Vision that I turned to science. Over the course of this project I have developed enormous respect for the scientists whose patient and rigorous work suggested certain parallels with my own instincts about Cinema, and that amplified my reservations about Film Theory to the point where it appears to me to be essentially idealist rhetoric, serving no purpose external to itself, academic in the worst sense of the term, and quite unwilling and unable to answer questions of any wider relevance than its internal concerns. As I recall Colin McCabe once asked 'A theory of what, exactly?'.[46]

---

44   Quoted in *Downcast Eyes*, Martin Jay. op. cit.

45   Richard Dawkins' comment on Lacan's discussion of science: 'the author of this stuff is a fake', in a review of Alan Sokal, Jean Bricmont (1988) *Intellectual Impostures*, London, Profile Books.

46   If that isn't false-memory syndrome it was a wry comment on a social occasion rather than a public pronouncement.

Viewed from my perspective on science, it seems a terrible waste of intellectua
effort to see so much scholarship spent in the fruitless pursuit of the Castles i
the Air that Film Theory has left as its inheritance. If that effort had instead bee
turned towards the formulation of ideas capable of being tested and with the goal
for example, of contributing to knowledge about how the brain works, usin
Cinema as a concrete cultural instance, a remarkable archive with which to furthe
our understanding of the relationship between Vision, the brain and Cinema
that would seem to be far more worthwhile, a substantial contrast to the cultur
and achievements of what has gone before.

The advances in the areas into which I have delved, namely neuroscience an
evolutionary biology, seem to hold out not just a real understanding of Visio
and with it Cinema, and the potential for making a constructive contribution t
greater understanding of how the brain works, but also the possibility of a prope
basis for a Science of Culture, that would finally bring back together Art & Scienc
through a depth of analysis quite simply unthinkable with Language-base
analysis.

Vision, Emotion, Cinema: Summary

Vision:

Of the trinity of Language, Consciousness and Reason, the most grievous effect
can be laid at the door of the Word, and the most deleterious of those is th
reduction of Vision.

Vision is King, as everything we really know we see. Up to three-quarters of word
describe Vision or sound. The wisdom of Vision is our only wisdom. We see s
much more than we are aware of. The Tragedy of Vision is that we do not realis
the complexity and intelligence of what it tells us. This project aims to turn th
tables upon the Word and to restore Vision to its pre-eminence.

The opposition is also set between Consciousness and Reason on the one hand
and the Automatic and Emotion on the other. Consciousness is normally oppose
in Language to the Un-Conscious, implicitly denying the latter its larger role ir
the workings of the brain. To remedy that sleight of hand, it is proposed t
introduce the term The Automatic to denote those areas of operation of the brair
that are beyond the resources of Consciousness. Likewise, Man's noble aspiration

to Reason has a tendency to both obscure his subjectivity and deny the importance of Emotion in the workings of the brain. The Matter of Vision is Emotion.

Emotion:

Emotion is the heart of the matter. The importance of Emotion is such that the proposition put forward is that the brain is Emotion. Emotion is created as a response to the body/brain system sensing a threat to Survival (however distant or indirect, it is always linked). Survival is the prime engine of Evolution. Vision evolved as the most efficient medium for the identification of threats to survival. Emotion is a matter of survival.

Emotion has entered the paradigm of scientific method, a change so substantial as to constitute a New Scientific Method with Reason finally holding hands with Emotion. In neuroscience and evolutionary biology, Emotion has come to the fore, and together these three elements constitute the approach outlined here: *Affective Neurobiology.*

In contrast to the emphasis on the affective, cognitive approaches are in thrall to the word. Cognition is predicated upon thought. Thought is conceived as occurring mainly within Language. The proposition here is that thought does not occur in Language, but in Vision, and indeed only in Vision.[47] Apprehension of the Matter of Vision is only possible through Emotion – the affective. Affective Neurobiology starts from the perspective of Emotion and traces its operations through neuroscience and biology, through the operations of the brain and evolution, seen as inextricably linked, working hand-in-hand.[48]

Cinema:

Cinema is, in a word, Emotion. Since its inception, analysis of Cinema has been reduced to the word. The restoration of Vision is necessary for a proper understanding of Cinema. Cinema is a Matter of Vision.

Vision, the Automatic and Emotion complement our understanding of the world as they enhance our understanding of the brain, and can transcend the limitations that the ideologies of Language, Consciousness and Reason have imposed. The

---

47 For those born blind, again it is suggested that the brain provides alternative circuits for the processing of Vision which the sighted also possess but become relied upon exclusively by those without sight.

48 The sense intended here is that evolution has developed the brain's functions and thus those functions are always the product of evolutionary pressures.

laboratory in which these conceptions can be tested is a complex cultural artefact whose paths to nature can be traced – Cinema.

In bringing science to bear upon art a route may be glimpsed that overcomes the gap between Art and Science. The two cultures become one. Art can *only* be fully understood through science.

Where the word inevitably reduces art, science has the potential to reveal its real complexity. For example, neuroscientists have found parallels between brain function and expressive techniques like metaphor and narrative.[49] Where science was once an unwieldy tool to unlock the subtleties of art, progress in neurobiology – and in particular the inclusion of Emotion within scientific method – has transformed its potential for a reach far deeper and fundamentally more intelligent[50] than the word.

An expansive materialism is in sight that can offer a deeper analysis of a work of art than anything that has gone before. Scientific method, revolutionised by the inclusion of Emotion in neuroscience, twinned with evolutionary biology, forms the basis of a potential Science of Culture. That notion of culture is itself biological, founded on the twin pillars of survival and reproduction, the basis of evolution, the Logic of Nature.

The Matter of Vision and Philosophy

The task this project set itself, many years ago, was to try to understand the real basis of the power of Cinema. The reason the task was set that nowhere within the prevailing framework of Film Theory was there anything remotely sufficient to that task, which seemed to me to be among the first questions to be answered about Cinema.

The two instincts that set me off on this pursuit were that Cinema was much more powerful than it was given credit for, even by its strongest adherents, and that much of that strength could be accounted for by the notion that we take in much more unconsciously from Cinema than consciously, and therein lay its secret power.

That led me to look at Vision, the unconscious – for which I propose the positive

---

49   See Commentaries section on 'Art & Science' p. 127 for discussion of these developments that help to suggest the depth of analysis ANB can bring to an understanding of Cinema.

50   Intelligent in the sense of providing more and better-quality analytical information.

and independent term, the Automatic, and Emotion – which was the one-word definition of Cinema put forward by Sam Fuller in Godard's *Pierrot Le Fou*.

Against that trio I concluded were ranged Language, and its ideology of Logocentrism, Consciousness, with the common view that it was the peak of being human, and Reason, which had the enormous successes of science to its credit, and the gradual encroachment upon superstition and irrationality that Bacon set as its task in the late medieval period, reaching a ferment in the Enlightenment.

In terms of philosophy, there is a view that nothing of importance has been said since the 18th Century, and with Spinoza and Leibniz, Hume and Kant to contend with, that is not entirely without justification.

Science has sometimes been accused of a certain naiveté in moving from laboratory experiment and results to the interpretation of those results, which tends to move to the terrain of philosophy, with its porous boundaries between the physical and the metaphysical, between the materialism of science and the terrain vague where the material no longer holds.

That is why Leibniz and arguably Spinoza are if anything more relevant today than they were in their own time. Physics today is still confirming the insights of Leibniz about some of the most basic questions, whereas Spinoza's anti-theological propositions hold more appeal for me, as despite Leibniz's genius he was irrevocably wedded to theological rationalisation at the expense, I would suspect, of a wholehearted rationalism. The meeting of three days when Leibniz went to visit the older Spinoza in Amsterdam, a liberal refuge, in 1679, is a fascinating moment in history of which unfortunately there is no direct record, only imputations of how Leibniz's views changed after his visit to the Master. There is little sense of a similar change in the views of Spinoza. Leibniz appears to have edged towards the thoroughgoing stern materialism of Spinoza, but could not or would not free himself of his debt to the theology department of his life.

Kant, regarded as the greatest modern philosopher by many, reacted against both Leibniz and Hume, and yet in so doing, and despite his enormous achievements in philosophy, it could be argued that seen from today's perspective, Kant in fact moved away from science and his Critique of Pure Reason ended ironically as a dangerous endorsement of it, claiming a certain autonomy for Reason that laid the fateful trail of German Idealism away from science and scientific materialism, betraying Bacon despite his dedication to him in the first Critique.

The Matter of Vision: Summary

- The key to understanding Cinema is through a scientific analysis of **Vision**, the **Automatic** and **Emotion**.

- **Vision** is the prime sense, but its extraordinary depth, breadth and wisdom has been the subject of a constant campaign of denigration by the ideology of **Language**: logocentrism.

- The **Automatic** is the term proposed for the 'un-conscious', flagging up how the ideology of Consciousness has used Language to reduce the importance science now shows it has.

- **Emotion** is seen as the driving force of the brain, the result of the perception, by the body/brain system, of a potential threat to **survival**.

- Moving pictures engage our emotions as movement is registered by the eye, for example, as a potential **survival** threat.

- All is **movement**. Cinema is movement. Photography is stasis. Stasis is death. Movement is life.

- Cinema is **Emotion**, as Godard had Sam Fuller declare in *Pierrot Le Fou*.

- **Emotion** has moved from the irredeemably subjective to the objective realm, as part of a revolution in scientific method that has also been successfully applied to consciousness and dream-science.

- The emphasis upon the **affective**, that is upon emotion, is the starting-point of this analysis of Cinema, in contrast to the cognitive with its implicit emphasis on Language and Thought.

- This project in one sense looks back to David Hume, who declared in 1739 that **Reason** is and must always be under the control of **Emotion**.

- **Reason** is a noble ambition of man, but inevitably becomes rationalisation rather than pure Reason. Reason is contingent upon Emotion: you can have Emotion without Reason, but not Reason without Emotion.

- **Consciousness** is an epiphenomenon of the operations of the brain, every subjective experience is produced by those operations and by no other element,

34

and is now accessible through laboratory experiment able to distinguish the conscious from the Automatic in great detail.

- **Consciousness** is an effect not a cause, an epiphenomenon of brain function, whereas the Automatic (unconscious) processes vastly more information and arguably directs consciousness to where its minute resources may be best used in the cause of survival (and then reproduction).

- **Consciousness** rationalises the few stimuli it can manage as an aid to survival strategy – hence *narrative* as the native medium of the brain.

- **Narrative** is the native medium of Cinema as it is the native medium of the brain: it is a survival strategy to make sense of the handful of stimuli consciousness can manipulate at any one time. A story links diverse stimuli from the environment to make sense of them in the cause of survival.

- **Language** opposes itself to Vision, and constantly demotes and denigrates it, while in reality Vision is at least a million times more powerful in numbers, and similarly superior in depth, breadth and wisdom – more intelligent as it has far greater resources at its disposal.

- **Affective Neurobiology** is an approach that starts from the primacy of Emotion rather than the cognitive, and emphasises the fundamental base of neuroscience in the historicity of evolution.

- The combination of contemporary **neuroscience and evolutionary biology** in the tradition of Darwin now offers material historical examples of how thoroughly science can illuminate the way Cinema works in the brain.

- Science is now capable of an understanding of Cinema **qualitative**ly deeper than any other analytical framework (An Expansive Materialism).

- **Science and art** can be reunited as neurobiology based in emotion has the capacity for a comprehensive and expansive understanding of art that qualitatively exceeds any other framework, and in particular, that of the dominant status-quo based in Language.

- The passage from science to interpretation necessarily crosses into the realm of theory and philosophy.

- This project proposes a return to Bacon's aspiration to scientific method for philosophy, tracing a tradition from Bacon via Newton and Hume that develops scientific method, in particular following Hume in subjecting Reason to Emotion and turning the subjective into raw data for objective analysis, as in Dehaene on Consciousness, LeDoux on Emotion and in Dream Science.

- The last fifty years of 'Film Theory' has been a dead-end, unscientific and merely rhetorical instead of properly scientific.

- The philosophical elements behind Film Theory are derived from 'Continental Philosophy' which itself took a fatal wrong turn with Kant's aim of a certain autonomy for Reason. As Hume rightly put it before Kant, Reason is and must always be at the service of the passions.

2

The Matter of Vision: Aphorisms

T his section is composed of aphorisms as a stimulus to thought – in vision of course. There are rhythms that will require perseverance. They may be more like shots than words, a poor sort of film that you can improve. 'The aphorism never covers itself with truth, it is either half-true, or one-and-a-half-times true.'[51]

I. Propositions

i

The history of hitherto existing societies[52]
has been the prisoner of three stern gaolers
Language, Consciousness and Reason.

The imprisoned are
Vision, the Automatic and Emotion.

Language
confines
Vision

Consciousness
effaces
The Automatic

---

51 Karl Kraus, *Werke*, Vol III, p. 161.

52 The emphasis is on modern societies

Reason
corrals
Emotion[53]

ii

Emotion

Emotion is the key
The brain is Emotion
Emotion is the brain[54].

Emotion ignites the brain.
Emotion fuels the brain.
Emotion is the motor of the brain.

The brain works through Emotion
Emotion is the raw-material of the brain
The brain thinks Emotionally.

Emotion is the function of the brain
Emotion is the reason the brain exists[55]
Emotion is the reason the brain adapts.

Emotion is the matter of life and death
Emotion is the motor of evolution
Emotion is the motor of survival.

Emotion is survival
The source of Emotion is survival
survival is Evolution[56]

Emotion is nature

---

53 It is an important distinction that it is not LCR themselves, but their 'ideologies' that are the issue.

54 All the (externally oriented) functions of the brain are movements (of blood, electrical synaptic connections etc), that are the substance, as it were, of Emotion.

55 in the sense of created through evolution.

56 Emotion is an effect whose cause is the external world, external to the body, a response to the threat of a predator – or the opportunity to be that predator.

Emotion is not Reasonable
Emotion has its Reasons

The Logic of Emotion
Is the Logic of Nature
The Logic of Nature is Emotion

Emotion without Reason
No Reason without Emotion

Emotion within scientific method
a revolution

iii

The Automatic

The Automatic is what is not Conscious

The Automatic is the un-conscious[57]

The Automatic is outside the Conscious

The Conscious is a pin in the Albert Hall
The Automatic is the Albert Hall

The Automatic merits its own term
The Automatic is a positive
(un-conscious is a negative)

The Automatic is the brain[58]
The brain is the Automatic

The Automatic is three hundred million billion connections

57   A useful distinction between the Automatic and the non-conscious could be with the autonomic nervous system as the latter – perhaps internal regulation v external orientation as a boundary, with the Automatic more externally-oriented.

58   The area outside consciousness is the major part of the brain. Consciousness is the minor part, an effect of the major part.

The Automatic is eleven million bits per second

(The Conscious is ten bits per second[59])

iv

Vision

Vision is the noblest of the senses

Vision is the prime sense

(Language is translation)

Vision is Automatic

(Consciousness is Non-Automatic)

Vision is Emotion[60]

(No Reason without Emotion)

The Tragedy of Vision
is that we take it for granted

What we know of the World comes from Vision

The world we see
Is the only world we know[61]

Vision sees everything

---

59   The raw figures are from Information Science in the 1950s. For caveats, see Consciousness in Commentaries.

60   Vision responds quickly to threats and opportunities - which create emotional responses.

61   We have only representations in our brains, as against the idea of a real world that we can perceive as a whole.

iv (a)

Vision and Language

Vision is the major sense

(Ten million bits per second)

Language is the minor sense

(Ten bits per second)

The brain operates through Vision not Language

Vision sees more

Vision sees better

Vision sees faster

Vision sees further

Our wisdom
Is the wisdom of Vision

The Matter of Vision is Emotion

iv (b)

Vision and thought

Vision is the medium of thought

Thought occurs in Vision

Thought occurs only in Vision

(Thought does not occur in language)

Thought is produced in Images
Thought is not produced in Language
Thought does not originate in Language
Thought is translated into Language

Thought exceeds Language

as

Vision exceeds Language

Language aspires to the condition of Vision

Vision sees into another's mind
– Automatically

Empathy is Automatic

Empathy is unavoidable

Empathy is unconscious

The ineluctable modality of the Visible

Thought through my eyes[62]

Thought is Vision

I see therefore I am

iv (c)

The Articulation of Vision

_____

62 Joyce's famous phrase, followed by the less-known follow-up, which might be interpreted as thought occurs in Vision.

Vision is Automatic

Language is a retreat

Wordless storytelling is natural[63]

v

Language

Language the enemy of Vision

Language puts itself above Vision

Language wants to forget its evolution

Language evolved from warning cries[64]

Language translates Vision

Language translates Vision

Language approximates Vision

Language always fails Vision

Language has ten bits per second
Vision ten million

Language should serve Vision

Language is contingent

---

63 Damasio, *The Feeling of What Happens*, Vintage, New York, 2000. p.188.

64 Language, in common with everything human, evolved only for survival. Sound as survival alarm, as with Vision, suggests that concern over the sighting of a possible predator would use the help of sound over distance to warn others.

vi

Consciousness[65]

Consciousness an effect not a cause[66]

Consciousness a pin in the Albert Hall
(William James)

Consciousness the tip of the iceberg
(Freud)

Consciousness (as we know it) does not exist[67]

Consciousness serves the Automatic[68]

Consciousness handles at most 50 bps
and averages 10 bps
(Vision has 10 million)

Consciousness an effect of the brain[69]

Consciousness is material
(anything else is mysticism)

vii

Reason

Man rationalises
he does not Reason

---

65 Of the LCR trio, Consciousness is particularly about its image rather than its reality, see Commentaries discussion.

66 Consciousness is suggested here as an epiphenomen of brain function, rather than strictly a causal agent in itself. Part of a chain of causation and therefore with a causal role, but a contingent rather than autonomous one.

67 Although this is my view, I have had conversations with well-known neuroscientists who I was surprised to find took the same view.

68 I tend to this view, although the interconnectedness of the pair makes it a difficult call.

69 That is an effect of the operations of the brain.

Reason is never autonomous
(Kant's Categorical Imperative)

Reason is always dependent upon Emotion
(Hume 1739, Damasio 1994)

Man is never reasonable

The brain is emotion not reason.

Reason is a noble ambition
(but never achievable)

Reason v subjectivity

Science is founded in Reason

Reason + Emotion = New Science

vii (a)

Reason and Nature

Nature has its reasons

Nature is not Reason

Nature has no plan

Nature is not teleological

Nature has direction but not ends

Nature is not rational
(in Man's terms)

Man has too often turned his back on the Logic of Nature

The logic of evolution
is the Logic of Nature

viii

The brain

The brain selects the Conscious[70]

The brain selects survival from information[71]

The brain directs Consciousness to survival[72]

The mode of the brain is Emotion

Emotion concerns survival

Survival motivates the brain

The Brain evolved as survival
Ne plus ultra

viii (a)

Narrative

Narrative is the native mode of the brain

Narrative is the gods' perfect engine of meaning

Narrative is not truth but representation

70   Again this is suggesting that the role of consciousness is less active than we assume, more on the receiving end.

71   That is to say the brain creates Emotion as a sign of a survival-threat contained in information perceived.

72   The notion here is that the brain utilises the resources of consciousness for the primary aim of avoiding threats to survival.

Narrative interprets information for survival

ix

Evolution

Evolution is nature

Evolution is survival

Nothing in Neuroscience makes sense outside evolution

ix (a)

Cultural evolution

Culture is nature

Nothing is beyond nature

Culture is evolution

Everything in culture comes from evolution
From culture to nature:
Cinema

ix (b)

Art & science

Science explains art via Emotion

Neuroscience shows art is material

The Two Cultures are one

A science of culture

x

A Short History of Philosophy

Hume declared Reason dependent on Emotion

Kant declared Reason Categorically independent

Kant's Idealism licenses Hegel's Castles of Abstraction

France abandons Port Royal for German Idealism

Philosophy has turned its back on nature

The 'unreasonable ineffectiveness of Philosophy'
results

Reason is contingent upon Emotion

(Damasio)

Reason has no independence

x (a)

Philosophy & science

Kant declares Philosophy has an equal truth to science

Philosophy turns its back on nature

If every idea is testable in principal

Philosophy returns to nature

The superiority of science to (an autonomous) Philosophy

Testing is no panacea

No Testing is 'a tumbling ground for whimsies'

x (b)

Instinct & knowledge

Unwritten knowledge exceeds written knowledge

Informal knowledge exceeds formal knowledge

Tacit knowledge is concrete

Infinitely more wisdom
in tacit knowledge
than in the Academy

II Extensions

i.

*The history of all hitherto existing societies
has been the prisoner of three stern gaolers*
Language, Consciousness and Reason

These pillars of being human
evolved ideologies
reducing their opposites

Language demotes Vision
Consciousness masks the Automatic
Reason condescends to Emotion

Verbal and 'Non-Verbal'
Conscious and 'Un-conscious'
Reason and 'Un-reason'

We are aware of the 'non-verbal'
even as we deny it a name
We are aware of the un-conscious
even as we deny it a word of its own
We are most aware of Emotion
but demote it opposite Reason

Man can have Emotion without Reason
But not Reason without Emotion.
Reason is in fact contingent upon Emotion
The opposite of the ideology of Reason

Emotion is the primary fact
of our existence
It surrounds Reason and Consciousness
and suffuses Language

Emotion is the heart of the brain

ii

Language, Consciousness and Reason

The trinity think themselves the foundations of civilisation
but hold back man's development.

It is not LCR themselves that is the problem
But how man sees them.

Each has developed its own Ideology
to protect it from the threat
perceived in its opposite.

Each has become a
thing in itself
an artefact
(of ideology)

with a boundary to protect

Each one reacts like an animal
feeling a threat
to its territory.

iii

Language

Language is a chimaera.
Language is blind.

Vision is so much older than Language
The upstart attempts to usurp the veteran
waging ceaseless war against its superior
claiming hegemony against the odds.

To grasp the full depth of Vision
can encourage Language to place itself in its service

Verbal and 'Non-Verbal' intelligence.
Visual intelligence is not on the agenda
not recognised as a thing in itself
Only a negative form.

With Consciousness
There is the Conscious
Opposed to the Un-conscious
Merely the negative form

As though the Conscious
Was the dominant mode
And the rest of minor significance.

iv

Consciousness & The Automatic

Consciousness is perhaps one millionth of the senses*.
The Automatic is the million – minus the one of consciousness.

(*Trincker 1965 "only one millionth of what our eyes see, our ears hear, and our other
senses inform us about appears in our consciousness"[73]).

Until we grasp the scope of the Automatic
we will remain imprisoned within Consciousness.

Consciousness

processes around 10 bits per second of information

The area beyond Consciousness
Here called the Automatic

Has perhaps
three-hundred million billion connections in the brain

Consciousness
the tip of the tip of the iceberg

v

Reason

---

73   Dietrich Trinker, *Aufnahme, Speicherung und Verarbeitung von Information durch den Menschen*, Veroffentlchungen
      der Schleswig-Holsteinischen Universitatsgesellschaft, Neu Foge, nr 44 (Kiel: Verlag Ferdinand Hort, 1966), p. 11.
      quoted in Norretranders op. cit. p. 126.

Reason is a noble ambition.
Mankind is unreasonable.
Man is inevitably imprisoned in his own subjectivity
Not reason but rationalisation.

Reason can be opposed to unreason

Or to Emotion.

Emotion can exist without Reason
Reason cannot exist without Emotion

Yet the Ideology of Reason
Deems it superior to Emotion.

vi

LCR ideologies

In each case
ideology
sets out to conceal
reality

Each of the trinity
has a lesser role
in the mind of man
than they would have you believe.

Language believes itself the medium of thought
Consciousness believes it runs the brain
Reason believes it is objective.

None are true.

Language is not the medium of thought, but Vision
Consciousness is a millionth of brain activity, the rest is Automatic

53

Reason is (and should always be) at the behest of Emotion
(David Hume[74])

Language is inferior to the Visual

Culture protests the opposite.

Consciousness is a tiny part of brain activity.

Man's ego cannot believe that to be the case.

Reason needs Emotion.

Emotion does not need Reason.

Reason is unthroned.

Language, Consciousness and Reason

as we presently conceive of them
conceal rather than reveal
the truth.

vii

Vision

Knowledge is Vision

Show not tell

Knowledge is Vision

---

74   David Hume, *A Treatise of Human Nature*, 1739.

All true knowledge resides in Vision
and in Vision alone.

What we cannot see we cannot fully know

Vision can exist without Consciousness

The eye sees more than Consciousness knows

We see more than we know

viii

Thought

Vision is the medium of thought

Thought is produced in images
Thought is not produced in Language
Thought does not originate in Language
Thought is translated into Language

Thought exceeds Language
as
Vision exceeds Language

Poetry aspires to the condition of Vision

Language is specific to man
But man existed without Language
(And perhaps will so again)

Vision is not specific to man
But man cannot exist without Vision

Vision sees everything

ix

Emotion

Man's attention is captured only by Emotion.

Man grants significance only to what arouses Emotion.

Emotion is the dimension of survival.

The survival instinct is a continuum
from life or death, love or hate, to like or dislike ...

The raw material of the brain is Emotion.
Emotion ignites the brain, sets it in motion.

Motion/Emotion.

The brain and the body are set in motion only by Emotion.
The brain and the body respond to threats to survival, near or far, with Emotion.

Without Emotion man's interest quickly wanes.
Emotion is the motor of fascination, the engine of interest.

For Spinoza, mind and body are one.
Against Descartes, who has them (mainly) distinct.

Man is a system that integrates mind and body
through the fuel of Emotion.

Their common element is survival.

Survival is Emotion.

The narratives of meaning in the mind are wordless.
They are images, visual mainly, but not solely.
Sound comes next, and some distance beyond
taste and feel.

Wordless storytelling is natural
Language is not necessary for the self [75].

The self is pre-language, composed
of images,
memory, reason.

Language is not required.

Objects of attention become subjects through the magnet of Emotion.
Without Emotion man does not pause but passes on.

From all possible object of attention
Man selects only those with affect (with Emotion)

Objects without Emotion are without meaning.
Meaning and Emotion are one.

Meaning is Emotion

Without emotion we don't care
the emotion-engine is not engaged.

Care is subjective.

We care about what has engaged our Emotions.

Emotion is life in motion.
Motion is the founding moment of Life.
Life seeks survival.

Emotion is the reflection of that desire.

We care about things only insofar as they are related to survival.
Disinterested caring does not exist.

Selflessness is selfish as mutual interest aids survival.
Altruism has evolutionary purpose.

75   see Damasio, *The Feeling of What happens*, Vintage, New York, 2000, pp. 188, 198.

We are altruistic only better to survive.

Morality cannot be superimposed on evolution
nor extracted from evolution.

Evolution is disinterested.
It is.

Emotion is the engine of life[76].

x

The Automatic

Consciousness handles ten bits per second[77]
The brain absorbs eleven million

Eleven million minus ten
with no word of its own.

Conscious and unconscious
ten v eleven million.

Un-conscious not just not conscious
but automatic all the time.

Automatic.
We are not aware of it.

Without our knowing
a billion tasks a second.

The Automatic.

---

76 Emotion – blood flow, synaptic connection etc – is movement – a form of drive in that it ends by producing physical
     movement in our muscles and limbs, but also psychological, producing thought as part of processing Vision. But
     Emotion is also an effect whose cause is the external world, external to the body, a response to the threat of a predator
     – or the opportunity to be that predator.

77 Said to be an average for conversation, with an effective maximum of 45 bps in silent reading. Norretranders op.
     cit.

If most of a film enters the brain
outside consciousness
enters the Automatic.

Then
Cinema a treasure-trove
of the Automatic.

experimental design
untangles

Conscious from Automatic
a priority for
Affective Neurobiology
& Cinema

III. Cinema

i

Cinema is nature

Cinema is a matter of Vision

Vision is a matter of Emotion

Emotion is a matter of survival

Survival is a matter of nature

Nature becomes Culture in cinema

Cinema is nature

Nature becomes culture

Cinema is culture [78].

ii

Movement I.

Cinema is moving images
Movement is fundamental to existence
Movement of a predator.

Life is movement
Death is no movement.

Vision captures movement.
Evolution favoured Vision
The eye is the first sense.

We follow the hero
As we follow the predator
A matter of life and death.

iii

Movement II.

Cinema is Emotion

Classical Hollywood made Emotion visible
The movement of Emotion became visible[79].

We follow Emotional movement on the screen.

---

78 Cinema is a development of Culture. Everything in Culture evolves from Nature, therefore Cinema is Nature
    Culture here means evolution exaptated from genetic to cultural evolution. It is salient to be reminded of the lineage

79 See Cinema section for more discussion. I would see that as a major achievement, largely unrecorded.

The fortunes of the hero/ine carry our attention

We watch their fate as it were our own.

iv

Movement III.

Movement attracts Emotion
Movement generates Emotion
Movement creates Emotion.

We are moved.

Movement of the hero across the frame
extended in time and space
by metaphorical movement
of emotions around him.

We care about the fate of the hero
Only because we care about our own.

The mechanism of Cinema
arouses the same processes
In the human brain

We follow the fate of the heroine
New information all the time
Adds to our knowledge about her.

Stars suspend a negative conclusion
Even when the hero is a baddie
(Hitchcock's Uncle Charlie[80])

The trajectory of the fate of the hero attracts us
As our own fate at the hands of a predator.

---

80   In *Shadow of a Doubt* (1943).

The graph of his rise and fall
attracts our attention
as he stands in for us.

Like and dislike
Love and hate.
Life and death.
An unbroken continuum.

Cinema is Emotion in motion.

v.

Empathy I

The brain and the body are one[81]

Our brains inhabit the bodies of others

Our brains imitate the Emotions of others

Imitation is the mode of attachment to another.[82]

We see more than we know

We *cannot avoid* knowing the mind of another
None conscious, all Automatic

opposite to the wisdom of philosophers.

A hero in jeopardy puts us in jeopardy

Emotional identification/intuitive harmonisation[83]

---

81 automatically aping them.

82 see Christian Keysers, *The Empathic Brain*, op. cit. Keysers discovered *Shared Circuits*, which move empathy from the physical, as in Mirror Neurons, to the emotional, a crucial discovery in terms of the themes here.

83 A phrase from McGilchrist that echoes Christian Keysers' themes (McGilchrist Ch 3, p. 122. op. cit.)

We become the hero

sharing what s/he feels.

Light from the dark

Illumination.

vi

Empathy II

The fate of the hero.
Ninety minutes
to watch a predator.
A short time
When life is at stake.

Cinema adds to our fascination with movement
fascination with the fate of the hero

Our own fate at the hands of the predator
is turned into a fascination
with the fate of the hero

Involving the same emotions
transferred from ourselves

To her or him
On the screen.

vii

Cinema dramatises Vision

63

The *quality* of Vision
exceeds our view

Everything we know
we know from Vision

We see more than we know
(than we are aware)

Cinema taps into this power
and intensifies it.
Cinema dramatises Vision.

Emotion keeps our eyes on the hero/ine.

But of what we learn
we Know only a fraction

The iceberg effect

The realm of the Automatic.

To bring the Automatic to light
Is a matter for experiment[84].

viii

A film is not a text

A film is not a piece of literature

Non-sense[85] to refer to a film as a text.

---

84   The design of experiments to recover what enters the audience's mind outside consciousness would be a key task for an *ANB* approach to Cinema.

85   cf. Wittgenstein's attitude to what does not make sense.

Only under the hegemony of Logocentrism
does such reduction make sense.

Cinema is not structured like a language

Cinema is structured like the brain [86].

ix

Historicism:

Classical Hollywood

from *Stagecoach* (1939) to *Marnie* (1964).

Defining characteristic of 'Classical' Cinema

It made emotion visible.

In *Mildred Pierce* I know where I am.
I feel that I know the emotional status of the heroine.

I am *shown* how she feels.
Not 'literally' through the actor's anguished facial expression.
But dramatically:
the narrative sets up dramatic situations
which force to me to project
onto her ambivalent expression
her emotional status

Kuleshov – as understood by Hitchcock:

We see a character's action
We see another character watching that action
And that character's reaction to it.

The reaction expresses a particular reaction

---

86   see Cinema section for discussion of the eye, narrative and empathy in this context.

Not the only one possible
But one to guide us in the labyrinth of possible meanings.

The crying baby
The sad man

The crying baby
The laughing man

The sad baby
The sinister man

The sad baby

The syllogism looking/looked at/reaction figure
ignites the narrative movement

Add to this sound and
a character never says what s/he means

Dialogue is a game of chess
Not a telling of the story.

Bogart tells Ingrid he hates her
But we know he loves her.
Cinema!

x

Film Theory

The eye evolved to track motion
We follow motion because of survival

Emotion arises from survival
The arc of a film
is the trace of Emotion

The brain follows Emotion
as the eye follows motion
(Neither are conscious)

We cannot avoid empathy
(Neither is that conscious)
The body/brain shadows the hero
we go through what s/he goes through
(Shared Circuits)

The brain connects diverse stimuli
to survive.

It is not a question of reality
but of representation.

The least unlikely explanation
for the co-presence of the various stimuli.

A story
is making the best of what we see.

Narrative is the native mode of the brain.

The Classic Hollywood Cinema
created a perfect engine of meaning
The Ideal Narrative

Each scene changes
the emotional status of the hero

Cinema is change
as life is change

The ideal script
has one change after another
scene after scene
Marnie.

From Culture to nature
reverse-engineering Cinema

Cultural evolution
(after Darwin)
from nature to culture

A science of culture
The Logic of Nature
The logic of culture
Cinema

3

Commentaries

This Section fills out the propositions put forward in the aphorisms and sketched in the opening chapter in order to set out an overall framework, the basis of a paradigm to analyse Cinema.

Life/Change/Movement/Cinema

A basic factor in biology is that life is change. Life itself is a process of change – a cycle of growth and decay. Change is also movement. Without change there is no movement, and without movement there is only stasis, and stasis is the absence of life. In Death there is no change, no change in life. Death may feed life in other forms, but the object that has no life can no longer grow, change in the sense that life moves by its own force. Life is dynamic, founded on change. The tale of the seasons in nature is one of constant change and it is the same with all life. Life is constantly in movement and never at rest.

Change is fundamental to Cinema. Change equals movement, and Cinema is all movement. The images move, the eye moves to follow that movement, the characters' fate moves and our emotions follow theirs in the sense of tracing them, our attention is devoted (by Cinema) to their emotional status. Moving pictures move us. Movement is change and change is life. No change, no life. Cinema brings us to Life.

Movement and the Eye

The eye is attracted by movement. The reason is biological. Movement is the most effective way the body/brain system of Man has of registering an external stimulus that may potentially be a predator, a threat to survival, or an opportunity, prey, food. The eye developed quickly in biological terms in order to deal with a

69

new situation in which Vision was suddenly at a premium. The terms for survival changed. Imagine the Earth seen from space, wreathed in mist. The mists dispersed and Vision was at a premium. In the mist vision was of only local significance, at short distances, like seeing in front of yourself in fog. When the mists began to disperse distant prospects came into view, and therefore that capacity to view became relevant for survival. It was possible to see the approach of a predator at a distance, giving creatures more time to react, to plan their escape, to increase their chances of survival. The other side of the coin was that it was also possible to see prey at a distance, to plan for food, pursuit, killing.

It was at that point in geological time that Vision ascended to become the most important sense. In the biologically brief period of a million years the eye developed at a rapid rate. Scientists have recently confirmed the evidence of the geological record with experiments showing that the eye of a fish (unconcerned as it may be with mist) for example, can develop to the degree required over a period calculated at 400,000 years.[87]

The dominance of the eye among the senses, dating back those 542 million years, was confirmed numerically by Information-scientists in the 1950s who estimated that the eye absorbs around 10 million bits per second of information. The next most powerful sense is touch with 1 million, then hearing and taste with 100,000 bits apiece, and finally smell, relatively undeveloped in humans, with 10,000 bits.[88]

The raw numbers are only part of the story of the dominance of the eye, but that fact and its interest in movement are significant factors in the birth and evolution of Cinema.

I learned from film-making that the eye is attracted to movement on the screen, in the editing process. In the long hours of editing a film one's attention may wander. There was a founding moment when my attention was suddenly alerted by a movement in my peripheral vision. It was then I realised that movement always attracts. It is the first thing that attracts. Our eyes react to movement immediately. The source of that attraction has a history of 542 million years. The attraction of physical movement is one of the foundations of Cinema, a biological foundation. The matter of Vision is basic to life, in both biological senses of

87   Andrew Parker, op. cit.

88   Manfred Zimmerman, 'The Nervous System in the Context of Information Theory'. In R.F. Schmidt and G.Thews eds. *Human Physiology*, 2nd ed. Springer Verlag, Berlin, 1989, p. 172. Quoted in Norretranders *The User Illusion* op. cit. p. 143.

genetic evolution and, taking Cinema as an example, cultural evolution – seen in biological terms.

Survival and the Brain

The relatively speedy evolution of the eye came about as all things come about in biological life, in nature, that is as a matter of survival. The eye was selected and adapted by the process of evolution solely in order to improve chances of survival. Evolution is not teleological but it is said to have direction. That direction, that movement, that change happens in the cause of survival and survival alone. Survival is the prerequisite of reproduction. The law of evolution might be thought of as survive in order to reproduce. There is no reproduction without survival.

Neuroscience, the study of the brain, has made substantial progress in the last century. When Freud developed the ambition to create a scientific psychology, in 1889, he was frustrated in his attempts by the lack of knowledge of the brain. As a result he was forced to abandon that path and retreated to the pre-scientific practice of interpretation, effectively abandoning scientific method. Freud's achievements were eventually recognised with a Nobel prize, but in literature not science. Neuroscience after Freud, in the second half of the twentieth century, made great advances, although still on what might be regarded as the foothills of knowledge about the brain. The growth of neuroscience is one of the striking features of science in the twenty-first century.

Rooting that knowledge in a historical framework is a key task in orienting this knowledge to a wider context. It seems to be a consistent factor that neuroscientists have turned to biology to do that. Without a historical sense, even where the time-frames of biology are on a large scale, there is a danger that neuroscience becomes facts in search of a system or to put it in philosophical terms, Idealist. Evolutionary biology provides that material history, providing the 'why' to the 'what' of research data. There is a well-known quote about Biology by Dobzhansky to the effect that 'Nothing Makes Sense in Biology Except in the Light of Evolution[89]'. Here it is suggested that nothing makes sense in neuroscience outside evolution. To see everything in the brain as oriented to survival (& reproduction) provides a broad framework for both understanding how individual elements evolved and their relations to each other. In the light of survival, the

---

89   Theodosius Dobzhansky, *American Biology Teacher*, volume 35, pp. 125–129, 1973.

complexities of the brain, about which we are getting increasing information, make sense.

Survival is a consistent theme here as it seems particularly important to ground discussions of the brain in the biology of evolution. Time and again, researchers find a touchstone for understanding particular features of the brain & its operations in survival. It is the baseline connection that always needs to be the reference for why something developed as it did. Without survival as a constant reference it would be puzzling to understand how and why anything in the brain developed as it did.

I would also suggest that the application of a similar approach to Cinema would yield the same benefits. Although Cinema is evolution in the cultural sphere rather than the genetic, the basic features of the eye, for example, that I draw attention to are deeply based in genetic inheritance. But it is the application of evolution and survival to what we might otherwise think of as cultural in a sociological or strictly anthropological sense that I feel will yield a new approach and attitude. Every film is a 'moment' in evolution, bearing in its every element the traces of survival. Techniques in Cinema survive or disappear according to the same principals, as the proscenium shot of early Cinema gave way to the close-up – so the audience could follow the action more easily, identify the main characters, and focus their attention on their fates. The development of Cinema, seen from the point of view of survival, is a case-study in evolution. It is that case-study this project proposes.

Emotion and the Brain

The one particular development in neuroscience which is key for this project is the attention lately paid to Emotion. Traditionally, Emotion has been regarded as the enemy of reason and therefore of science. Likewise, reason has been traditionally regarded as the lodestone of science, the foundation of scientific method from the time of Newton. Over the last generation or so that situation has changed. Emotion has not just been brought onto the stage of neuroscience, but arguably pushed to centre stage. To bring Emotion into the golden circle, to admit the enemy to the party, has all the threat of the Trojan horse to scientists of traditional views.

On the other hand to my mind it opens a new continent, enormously expanding the reach of scientific-method. It is almost as though the study of hemispheric lateralisation, the functions of the two hemispheres of the brain, had alerted researchers to the missed potential of the approach of the right hemisphere for science, and had decided to remedy that by admitting Emotion, often but not exclusively associated with the right hemisphere's approach. The two hemispheres of the brain are today regarded as both dealing with the full range of issues with which they are faced, but in substantially different ways and with substantially different emphases[90] which, when both hemispheres function fully, are valuably complementary (an echo of how evolution has seen brain functions handled in general by numerous overlapping systems that deal with the same issue from different functional perspectives. That also suggests how evolution is not a design-process in familiar human terms, but how functions evolve to deal with different issues over time, producing this overlapping element, which does not necessarily involve redundancy, but different angles on the same problem). In broad terms, where the 'left' is local, the 'right' is global, where the 'left' is oriented to the word, the 'right' is oriented to Vision. Science without Emotion can be argued to be more 'left' than 'right'. With Emotion inside the walls there is the potential for that valuable complementarity. The 'left' brain, in dealing with all the issues, cannot be thought of as lacking the ability to address certain problems, but it is the way it addresses those problems that is different.[91]

The difference is graphically illustrated in an experiment with split-brain patients, in whom the normal connections between the two hemispheres have been damaged in some way. The 'right hemisphere attends to the entire visual field, but the left hemisphere only to the right'[92]. The result is that 'Because the concern of the left hemisphere is with the right of the world only, the left half of the body, and everything lying in the left part of the visual field, fails to materialise'. Drawings of a clock, a house and a cat were copied by such patients – but only the right side of the drawing was copied. The left side was missing. 'So extreme can this phenomenon be that the sufferer may fail to acknowledge the existence of anyone standing to his left, the left half face of a clock, or the left page of a newspaper or book, and will even neglect to wash, shave or dress the left half of the body, sometimes going as far as to deny that it exists at all[93]'.

90 A summary of left/right brain experimental results can be found in McGilchrist. op. cit. Ch 2. For a more nuanced view it is worth following up his extensive references to papers of the original experiments.

91 Strictly speaking, it is problematic to talk of 'left' and 'right' as though the balance could be changed. What we have is the product of evolution and begs the practical question of the wisdom of fiddling with nature.

92 An experiment by Berlucchi, Mangan and Gazzaniga, 'Visuospatial attention and the split brain', in *News in Physiological Sciences*, 1997, 12 (5), pp 226–231. Quoted in McGilchrist op. cit. pp. 44–45.

93 McGilchrist op. cit. p. 45.

The implications of that narrow focus, compared to the wider focus of the 'right brain' approach, for scientific experiment and interpretation which sees the whole picture, literally and metaphorically, makes an interesting parallel with the recent inclusion of Emotion within the paradigm of scientific method. What science has been missing is perhaps not just literally half the picture, but the broader overall implications that a 'whole picture' view would make available. A similar point could be made about the 'formal' knowledge of the Academy as a whole, for example in philosophy (to which I return in the section On Method).

A point of departure for this study was the notion that "Cinema is – in a word – Emotion[94]". The context of that claim, spoken by Sam Fuller in a film by Godard, unites the Classic Hollywood Cinema with the *New Wave*, although Fuller was something of an outsider as in his own way was Godard. To my mind the Classic Hollywood Cinema was particularly focussed on Emotion, certainly between around 1939 and 1964 (see the Section on Cinema), and therefore that claim is particularly pertinent.

Joseph LeDoux, in *The Emotional Brain*, takes a robust approach towards definition: ' "Emotion" is only a label, a convenient way of talking about aspects of **the brain and its mind**'[95], and he views 'emotions as biological functions of the nervous system'[96]. The literature suggests that Emotion is critical to absolutely every function of the brain, and again usually linked to the question of evolution and survival.

My interpretation is that **Emotion is the reaction of the body/brain system to any external stimulus that it perceives as a potential threat to survival**. Survival is also the precursor to reproduction in evolution, threat and opportunity yoked together, as it were. The external emphasis is not absolute[97] as internal functions are maintained, e.g. body temperature, in much the same way, and with critical and direct implications for survival, but it is external stimuli that are relevant for the case of Cinema.

It is an alarm-system, but one that has evolved from the original genetic function – is that a Tiger over there? – to a cultural one (again seeing culture in a biological sense). Something as superficially remote as shopping arouses our Emotions in the same way, but in a different context, an adaptation or 'exaptation' of an

94 Said by Sam Fuller in Godard's *Pierrot Le Fou*, 1965.
95 p.16. Weidenfeld and Nicolson, London, 1998.
96 p.12, op. cit.
97 Dehaene emphasises that 95% of brain activity is internal, only 5% is external. Dehaene op. cit. p. 186.

original direct survival mechanism for virtually every personal and social situation that we experience in our everyday lives – the cultural inheritance of the original genetic function.

Our Emotions can reach fever-pitch in the Sales almost as much as when spotting a Tiger in a jungle-clearing. The underlying point is that the same functional system has evolved and adapted to, for example, everyday life in a modern urban society.

The survival issue may seem remote, but fighting for a handbag in the Sales rush is not too remote from more primitive conflicts. Road-rage is another such, not in itself life-threatening, but the Emotions involved can and have led, in extreme cases, to homicide.

Superficially more remote again are issues about self-image. With regard to shopping, where buying clothes more obviously relates to self-image, so does a mother choosing cereal in a supermarket shopping aisle. Choosing between Choco-Flakes and Eco-Grains cereals may involve all kinds of mental battles of feeling and emotion: am I the sort of mother who insists on healthy food despite my childrens' resistance, or am I the sort who gives them a treat with what they like? Is the treat a bribe or do I think one cereal is as good as another health-wise? Am I too tired to argue about healthy food and will give in and buy what I know they like etc etc? Images about the self are attached to every decision, no decision of that kind is merely a mechanical one. The good-mother/bad-mother battle is in its own way an exaptation of the original survival impulse, translated into the question of self-worth. That is then linearly related to a version of the life/death situation with a Tiger – to whit – Do I Deserve to Live? Do my children love me? It is easy to see how the latter question relates to happiness/unhappiness, but it is only a matter of degree before one might imagine a situation in which a depressed person is so unhappy that they question their desire to live, and in extreme situations again that could potentially lead to self-destruction – suicide. Shopping is a more dangerous activity than we might realise.

What originally evolved for the life and death priority of avoiding predators (or on the other side of the coin of searching for prey) has been adapted to meet the needs of every situation that we face every day of our lives. The link between life and death and appraising the face of a stranger who we are forced into close proximity with on the tube may appear at first glance to be non-existent, but the speed with which we reach a view about that face is directly related to the need for fast decision when, in the state of nature, a remote ancestor saw a new face in a jungle clearing. Fight or flight is thus visualised as a linear relation of the almost instant like/dislike decision we make, for the most part unconsciously, bracing ourselves against the rolling of the tube-train in the rush-hour and right up against a new face. A man against a man has himself unconsciously ask 'Will it kill me/can I kill it? A man against a woman may ask 'Can I mate with it?' The 'it' is the animal factor irrespective of politesse. Our actual feelings, insofar as we are aware of them, and in the urban transport situation, will probably be as mild as the very slightest positive or negative feeling about that face. We will have negative or positive feelings of which we will be unconscious, and those feelings of which we are unaware will probably be the great majority, whereas on the surface, in our conscious minds, in our awareness, we will have had no discernible reaction – should we be asked at that moment for a reaction. However, the body/brain system knows better and will have been quietly getting on with its job, whose roots are buried millions of years in the evolutionary past.

Emotion, in this interpretation, is ubiquitous as the raw-material of the brain, the fuel that drives it, virtually the dynamic material of which it is made. It is behind everything the brain does, as the new connections the brain has made that constitute evolution in the cultural sphere represent adaptations to the requirements of man living in ever-greater groups growing into cities around ten thousand years ago. Emotion as the alarm, the early-warning system that alerts the body/brain, while evolved for the priority of survival, has evolved to deal with every situation that man has to face in the subsequent context of cultural evolution.

Genetic to Cultural evolution

There is a view among neuroscientists (e.g. Ramachandran[98]) that genetic evolution slowed thousands of years ago, perhaps coinciding in broad terms with the Great Leap Forward that man is said to have made around 50,000 years ago, beginning to make clothes, jewellery, art and tools. One date for the origins of language roughly coincides with that era, at 40,000 years ago. From that time, accelerating as man's settlements grew in size, cultural evolution is seen as taking over from genetic evolution. It would make sense that the evolution of man's emotional responses to face the new challenges of social life in larger and larger settlements also dated from around that time.

---

98   See V. Ramachandran on Metaphor in *The Tell-Tale Brain, Unlocking the Mystery of Human Nature*, Heinemann, London, 2011.

The move from genetic to cultural evolution is highly significant, not least as it allows evolution to take back the phrase from its appropriation by other disciplines – without the context of biological evolution. There is a looser sense, in sociology for example, of 'cultural evolution' than the one to which I refer for this project. The notion here is that the migration from genetic to cultural evolution must always be seen in the context of genetic evolution. Culture in this sense is a product of exaptations, the adaptation to a new purpose of an evolved form from its original function. The eye jumping to spot a moving predator becomes our following the hero/ine across the screen. Recent discoveries about the plasticity of the brain suggest that exaptations have vastly increased the range of situations that emotion has evolved to deal with, and Cinema would present many such situations.

Every film in its every moment, using that term in both its literal and metaphorical sense, bears the trace of evolution and the impetus to survival. Each film has a visible and invisible history of its evolution, which covers everything to do with its conception, production and exhibition. An invisible element would be the work involved in the writing of a script (to which I return later – the idea of 'logical depth' p. 277). Some of that work is left out but forms the background (back-story is the film term) to the characters and is thus immanent in the script although not actually there (an example from later in the book is the opening scene of *Psycho* where the tensions between the lovers has a history).

Emotion & Survival

When a human meets another for the first time s/he makes up her/his mind about the other person in a fraction of a second. That process of deciding whether we like/dislike, fancy/don't fancy, is a highly complex one completed in a fraction of a second by the body/brain system. The way it does that is an echo of the life/death decision of Will It Kill Me. There is a hierarchy, with life/death at the top and like/dislike some way down, based on the intensity of emotion experienced. Although there are often a lack of conscious reaction to others, experimental result tend to suggest that unconsciously we always react, we always as it were make up our minds positively or negatively, even in that judgement makes no appearance in our consciousness.

A sociopath may feel less emotion when killing someone than a sensitive soul shopping for groceries when faced with a choice between two cereals. In the

THE MATTER OF VISION

non-sociopathic population we would expect to find a similar distribution of emotional arousal depending upon the proximity to the extreme of life/death. Emotions are obviously aroused in a fight or argument, less obviously when are feelings about ourselves are involved. The key point about the 'founding moment' of the life/death scenario is that ultimate scene sets the pattern for the mode of operation of the brain/body system as a whole. As it was the effective way of dealing with the highest risk, the idea is that it also became the mode for all choice-making (a speculation as the whole pattern of responses to stimuli might have all been set by that moment, rather than developing over time, or it could have been adopted during evolution as the response that serviced Survival, or perhaps more likely a combination of the two).

The point remains that all our responses to stimuli bear the traces of the founding life/death moment. Whether we are choosing cereal on a supermarket aisle or fight or flight in a jungle clearing, Emotion is the matter of the brain/body system's operations: galvanic skin response, blood coursing around, synapses connecting etc. Today we can see the dynamics of response in the brain through fMRI scanning. We can measure the brain's response to stimuli, and see which parts of the brain are activated. Speculation can be replaced by measurement, observation and experiment, at increasingly accurate levels and greater depths.

My conception of Emotion is however a speculative one, a hypothesis of how the brain works. It provides a conceptual hierarchical framework in which all brain responses and body/brain activity make sense and devolve from the single fact – of Emotion It provides a framework to understand what is going on and more importantly, why. It proposes a model of the brain that relates back to the most fundamental aspect of evolution, survival. Emotion is, as it were, the raw material of our lives. It is what drives the brain, and how the brain drives the body. It drives the body and the body sends signals to the brain. All in the cause of survival.

Emotion and Reason

From twenty years' work with brain-damaged patients, Damasio concluded that Reason cannot exist without Emotion[99]. In other words, Reason is dependent upon Emotion, and Emotion is independent of Reason. Reason is therefore contingent on Emotion.

99   see Damasio *Descartes' Error* op. cit.

The view that Damasio reached of the contingency of Reason in relation to Emotion overturns the common idea of the relationship, not to mention the view of the majority of philosophers and scientists through the ages. The common tendency is to think that Reason is superior and Emotion is irrational and unreliable, but neuroscience has arguably shown that Emotion has its own rationality, one derived from evolution rather than man's logic. Emotion is not subject to the regime of Reason. In that sense it is 'unreasonable'. Emotion may not be 'reasonable', but as Pascal famously put it the heart has its reasons, of which reason knows nothing. Emotion is seen here as largely unconscious or Automatic, and Reason as largely Conscious. The traditional view is that Reason is there to control Emotion, to mediate its excesses. That assumes the Conscious is in control of the unconscious. The suggestion here is that the reverse may well be the case, and the reach of Emotion is greater than Reason can control, it is unreasonable partly in that sense. Emotion has its reasons, but they do not follow classical Reason. Arguably Emotion's reasons have a greater objectivity than Reason, a different economy based in evolution and the priorities of survival.

Language, Consciousness and Reason

There are two basic factors in the view taken here of the trio. The primary one is a concern with our ideas *about* them, the ideology they enshrine, rather than the things themselves. There is no question that each has played an important evolutionary role, and it would be senseless to attack them in that context. The problem I want to point to is that the cultural status they have is to some degree at the expense of their opposite numbers, VAE.

The secondary factor is to do with their actual roles biologically rather than ideologically. The prime target is clearly Language in its relationship with Vision, with the sense that it inhibits the latter in a left-brain/right-brain context. It is important there to draw a line in terms of why it happens and what can be done to correct the perceived imbalance. This would be seen not as a biological issue but as a cultural issue. Evolution has done its work, but arguably the balance between the hemispheres is not itself immutable and there is a sense that we may be seeing a shift between Language and Vision for example on the net, with more of an emphasis on Vision as a better sales tool than language.

Consciousness is the complex question as its relation with the Automatic is a matter of fierce debate that may perhaps be coming towards evidential conclusions as neuroscience increases its knowledge about more and more brain functions. But that situation does not yet obtain and the field of discussion remains open. While neuroscience can arguably show certain theories of consciousness are erroneous it is not yet at the stage of being able to nominate one theory as demonstrably superior. This project takes an instinctive line about consciousness, but it is only speculative, and may be proven to be erroneous. Is consciousness a cause or an effect? The debate is far from settled.

Reason is discussed as both the thought-process and the Enlightenment cause as well as the foundation of science. There is a question of should Reason be thought of as conscious? There is a notion in current debate that the reasoning process can only be partly conscious and always involves the Automatic. That ties in with the view from Damasio that Reason is contingent upon Emotion, rather than being autonomous. The implications of the shift away from an autonomy to Reason are still to be fully explored, but the fact that the conclusion was drawn from clinical study rather than abstract philosophy promises a reliable base from which to make that further exploration.

Language, Consciousness and Reason are also conceived here as historical in the evolutionary sense. The timescales involved make that difficult to accept at first glance, but with consciousness as probably the longest-standing of the trio there is an evolutionary argument that it emerged from the Automatic, selected for survival-advantage, but of course hundreds of thousands if not millions of years ago.

The idea that there was a time when man did not have these three apparent staples of being human challenges our normal assumptions. Language may be only about 40,000 years old. The idea of Consciousness can be traced back to the Greeks[100], two thousand years ago, although its material origins lie in the evolutionary development of the 'higher faculties' in man's brain. The idea of Reason is of similar vintage, but the practice would seem logically to belong to a later phase, man is conscious and only later does he begin to reason. There is a view that man is rather poor at reasoning on an individual basis but that it evolved socially, in order to persuade others in a group, reason as argument[101]. Because they seem ubiquitous in our everyday lives, it is hard to imagine man without these three staples of being human. Before Language there were grunts and other vestiges of communication that became Language. Before the *idea* of Consciousness, what

---

100 See Julian Jaynes *The Origin of Consciousness in the breakdown of the bicameral mind*, Houghton Mifflin, New York, 1982.

101 See https://sites.google.com/site/hugomercier/theargumentativetheoryofreasoning

we might call the birth of *self*-consciousness, Men undoubtedly were conscious and sometimes aware of being so as part of being in society with others. In evolutionary terms Reason seems to be about problem-solving for survival, such as the idea of tool-making to crack nuts.

While on the one hand the very existence of the triumvirate may be instructively thought of as having a history, of not existing at one time and therefore making a difference, having an evolutionary function for Man, on the other hand is the question of the image we have of them. It is the ideologies attached to Language, Consciousness and Reason (LCR) that are most relevant in this context – the argument being that LCR have an exaggerated status conferred upon them in Western Culture in particular. Part of exaggerating their importance is the demotion of their opposites, and in this context it is the battle between LCR and VAE, Vision, the Automatic and Emotion that is of most interest here.

The existence and evolution of LCR is not the problem as they each perform invaluable functions every moment of our waking lives (and Consciousness plays an invaluable role in sleep, during dreaming, if in different ways and at different levels, due to the simple fact of the change in inputs from having our eyes closed and various chemical changes appropriate to the sleeping and dreaming modes). It is in the battle of ideas – and their effects upon other ideas and upon actions resulting from them – that the issue lies. The argument made here is that in effect LCR is in a constant battle with their opposite numbers VAE, and a part of the form of that argument is to praise themselves and to denigrate the opposition. One result is that we know little about Vision, the Automatic and Emotion in comparison. Yet, the argument goes here, they are much more powerful and important than the opposing ideologies would allow. LCR try to pull the wool over our eyes about the reality of power in order to protect themselves and preserve their privileges as exalted aspects of the nature of being human.

It would be an interesting task to identify how that situation came to pass, but for the present enquiry the matter of most urgent relevance is in the impact of this quasi-ideological struggle. Language has been given an exalted status and an exaggerated importance at the expense of Vision. Consciousness has been praised to the skies as the glory of humanity, but at the expense of the Automatic (or unconscious), and Reason has been planted at the pinnacle by philosophers and scientists alike at the expense, until very recently, of Emotion. And it is in this battle that the first sign of a breach in the defences of the triumvirate has been made of late, with the release of Emotion from its negative image to take a seat at the table of scientific method. That innovation is seen here as of great significance as it breaks an ancient taboo, and opens the door for the similar liberations of the Automatic and the main focus of this project, Vision. The contention is that VAE are in fact superior, quantitatively and probably qualitatively, in their contributions to the workings of the brain and that it has been the active role of the ideologies of LCR to deny that and to minimise their contribution.

In broad terms it is comprehensible that man would promote Consciousness, as in the famous doubts of Descartes, edging away from despair with the one thing in which he could be certain – that he possessed consciousness as revealed in the ability to think. Likewise the assumed association between thought and Language, to the effect that Language is the medium in which thought takes place, and between thought and Reason, in that reasoning is seen as a process of thinking that takes place in consciousness, all simply cement the triumvirate of LCR at the peak of what it is to be human, a part of that ideology that is anxious to identify the uniqueness of man and mark out clear blue water between man and animals.

Darwin increased that anxiety with his second great work *The Descent of Man*, (1871), famously showing man as evolved from the apes, to the horrified and/or amused reaction of his Victorian contemporaries. It was also Darwin in his third and last great work, *The Expression of Emotion in Man and Animals*, following a year later (1872), that opened the door to the scientific study of Emotion in which only the recent generation of neuroscientists have been able to make substantial progress.

To conceive of LCR as limits upon man rather than instruments of his liberation is somewhat counterintuitive. Reason has produced the incredible advances of Science, which in turn would not have been possible without Consciousness and Language. There is no question that we owe so much to LCR that the world would be a much poorer place without them, from skyscrapers to motorways, from medicine to nuclear physics, from Shakespeare to the internet, the whole of our modern world and its cultural inheritance would be inconceivable without the triumvirate.

There is an interesting relationship between the left brain/right brain debate and the battle between LCR and VAE. While early research identified that the two hemispheres had rather different abilities, the later emphasis has been on the nature of the complementarity between the two sides. Left and right both deal with the full spectrum of issues that the brain addresses. Where it was originally thought that the left hemisphere was good at language, analysis and reason and the right was more concerned with broader, intuitive and spatial qualities, later work showed that language, for example, is not only located in the left-brain, as the right-brain adds intonation, rhythm and other 'non-verbal' qualities, its melody or *prosody*.[102] In fact, it might be useful to see notions about the two sides of the brain as a metaphor for two different sets of values[103] in conflict, quite a different matter from how evolution has developed the different approaches of each hemisphere as properly bringing different emphases to the solution of the same problem.

That pattern follows one remarked upon more generally in the logic of evolution, that functions are often doubled or carried out by several parts of the brain, but not in a simple matter of redundancy. It is not that the brain simply has failsafes that allow functions to be carried on by other parts of the brain, although that is certainly a feature as shown in brain-damaged patients where even certain functions of vision are carried out by other parts of the brain when sight is damaged or lost. The apparent redundancy is often revealed through experiment to be the same things done in different ways, ways that are complementary rather than simple repetitive. The left/right example seems likely to indicate the same kind of complementarity that probably exists between LCR and VAE, between Language and Vision, Consciousness and the Automatic, and Reason and Emotion.

A further aspect of the issue of complementarity is related to the major philosophical debates about the very notion of reality. For Kant, for example, there was the reality we know and the reality that is beyond ourselves and is unknowable. The reality we know is the one in our heads, the reality that we cannot know is the reality out there of the world. For Kant that was not just a matter of seeing more, a matter of quantity. It was importantly the notion that reality could not be known by or accessible to us, a qualitative matter.

Richard Gregory's work on Vision led him to conclude that we do not see reality but what he called a 'hypothesis', a simulation of the world, a representation of reality rather than reality itself.[104] Even the richness and depth of information of which Vision is capable of providing is only a selection from 'reality' rather than the thing itself, which cannot be known, as Kant was perhaps the first to declare (Berkeley was arguably the first on this point if in a more theological context). It is popularly known that Consciousness has limited resources, for example in only

102 Quoted from Norretranders, op. cit. p. 278.
103 See Left brain/Right brain entry in this section.
104 From Norretranders, op. cit. p. 186.

being able to register a maximum of seven things at any one time (in working memory). These factors point towards a sense that our relationship with the external world is a construction, a representation, a cartoon, a sample as it were derived from some larger if inaccessible reality, selected in some way, but clearly an image rather than the impossible thing itself.

It is not as though the brain lacks capacity. With something in the order of three hundred million billion connections, it is said to be the most complex thing in the universe. That suggests that reality is not a reality, if I may put it that way. What we know is some kind of sample, based on some principle of selection. That is what constitutes our 'reality'. It would be an article of faith for this project that the answer to the question of what is the criterion for that sample would be 'survival'. For evolution reproduction is the driver and survival the pre-condition. The selection, the reality of which we are aware, even of which the body/brain system is aware – and that largely excludes conscious awareness in the sense that most of that awareness is outside consciousness – is chosen according to the strictest possible criteria of biological-value, that is of relevance for survival (& reproduction). What we know is only related to survival. We know nothing else. By definition.

The problem with the conflicts between LCR and VAE is that the 'ideologies' of LCR tend to prevent us, in one way or another, from bringing into consciousness the scale of awareness about VAE that would create a complementary balance between the two sides. Does that simply mean that is how humans are and that it is pointless to question it? Or is the case that different cultures, in the anthropological sense, have different priorities, so that Eastern culture, very broadly conceived, shows examples of a greater appreciation of such complementarity? Is it perhaps the case that Western cultures, again very broadly conceived, have passed through a period in which 'left-brain' approaches to problems yielded solutions efficiently, but the implied imbalance eventually exacts a price that – by dint of evolution in the cultural sphere – leads to pressure for correcting the balance.

The battle in such a case would therefore be not to dismiss LCR in favour of VAE, but to identify what the relatively unknown aspects of VAE bring to the brain. Both are necessary and have been selected for by the evolutionary process. The current imbalance in our knowledge and appreciation of VAE in contrast to LCR is not just a need for more information but a qualitative aspect that can contribute substantially to our understanding of how the brain works.

The implications of the imbalance go beyond neuroscience as a discipline to the big social and political questions, the elephant in the room in understanding our own species. When reason has made such advances possible in science, people often ask how is it that we seem quite unable to solve the ever-present problems of war, prejudice and poverty? The battle between Reason and Unreason is not academic. Our current understanding of how Vision, the Automatic and Emotion work lags far behind the attention that has been given to their opposite numbers.

A final thought about the relations between LCR and VAE again goes back to the Left/Right brain debate. Before Roger Sperry's Nobel-winning work in the 1960s the Left hemisphere was traditionally known as the Major hemisphere and the Right as the Minor. That characterisation was based primarily upon the fact that language skills were seen to belong to the Left brain. There could hardly be a better example of what I suggest is the ideology of Language in operation.

The fact that Reason turns out to be dependent upon Emotion, in Damasio's experience, whilst overturning the traditional conception of the relationship begins to suggest something more. Firstly, if we take the view I propose here, that Language should also be seen as dependent upon Vision and unable to be independent of it, there is a parallel. Secondly, if we also take the view that Consciousness may be dependent upon the Automatic (or unconscious), again as I would suggest, then a pattern emerges. In all three cases of LCR, the traditional precedence is overturned in favour of the 'Minor' partner. In that situation the reverse of the 'ideological' view may be confirmed through scientific experiments. It would not only be that the 'Minor' partner turns out in fact to be the dominant one, but the partner formerly the Major, is not only inferior – but actually dependent upon its opposite number.

Language, the Word and Logocentrism

The issue with Language for this project is twofold. Firstly, the exaggerated status given to the word due to what I call logocentrism, and secondly, the attitude towards Vision that is engendered by that ideology. There is of course no question how useful Language has been in the evolution of man, to the extent of kindly facilitating this attack upon itself. The case for the word has been made so often and with such passion that it is hardly necessary to even remind ourselves of the fact. Arguments against the word appear to be most uncommon and that is partly because the influence and prestige of the word is so pervasive and hegemonic as for criticism to be almost literally unthinkable. Why bite the hand that feeds you? The very idea of taking on the word would seem to put David and Goliath in the shade, an almost inconceivable undertaking. The word has got under our skins to such an extent that we can hardly separate ourselves from its presence in our lives, we and the word are one. Why, indeed, would we even want to take a distance from it?

Seen from the point of view of Vision, the terrain looks rather different. The word constantly seeks to criticise Vision. It takes an attitude towards it that is disparaging, viewing itself as a far superior medium. Language is claimed to be more subtle, more sophisticated, so much more able to express the depths of human feeling. On the other hand, Vision can only produce images that are obvious, vulgar, crass, superficial, on the surface. Profundity is said to belong to Language, whereas Vision tends to the trite. Language is so articulable, with it you can put your finger on something. Vision is vague, general, unspecific, floating over the surface rather than penetrating the depths and fixing it with a word.

All this is true in its own way and more than that, understandable. Language is hard work. Finding the right word is quite a task. There is a universe in that short sentence. My own experience is that it is often difficult to find the right word. Sometimes it is just there, and I don't notice the effort. It is when it is not there that the difficulties begin. The word may not be there at all or it may be hovering in the back of my head or on the tip of my tongue. Then I may distract myself and return to the thought and there it is. It has popped up into my conscious mind. As this, at least for me, is a common experience I began to wonder where it was coming from, this correct word? The answer was from my unconscious mind. If I was not aware of it, then it must be coming from somewhere beyond my awareness, beyond consciousness. But how was it getting into my conscious? Something was serving it up for me, a dumb-waiter of the word. Even that brief account is a glimpse into an unknown land that manages to deliver the right word when my poor mind struggles to find it. There must be a huge store down there somewhere, an Amazon warehouse with fork-lift robots grabbing the right word and delivering them efficiently up top to my struggling consciousness. Sometimes I can't find the right word and juggle between words that are in the right territory but not quite what I want. I know, somehow, what I want, but I can't exactly find it. It's a bit like this word, but not quite right. I tried the Visual Thesaurus but it is currently rather limited and not up to the job, much as I like the idea. The connections it presents don't help. I need to make my own, and in the end

I always do. It might be a matter of a split-second or a day and a night, when that word escapes me, annoying the hell out of me, not even showing up before I go to bed, but next morning there it is.

I would think that sketch is not untypical, perhaps even universal, but its point is that there is a certain work involved in the word. We respect the word not least because every day we are aware of the practice required to find the right word. On the other hand Vision seems easy. No practice required. It's only natural to value what we have to work for, and not to value what comes easy.

When Information Scientists began to design new telephone systems in the 1950s, they asked how much information phone lines needed to carry. The answers that came up were counter-intuitive. The maximum information Consciousness could carry was around 45 bits per second, and that was for silent reading. Counting objects produced only 3 bps. An average conversation might handle around 10 bits. Language and the word had a ceiling below 50 bits and an average around 10 bits. Vision, on the other hand, processed around 10 million bits per second.[105] Whereas we might think the word is more powerful than Vision, the opposite turns out to be the case. Vision would be, in crude numbers, around a million times more powerful than the word.[106]

Language has not always been with us. As noted above, current estimates vary between 40,000 years and 100,000 years old, but man is broadly thought to be around 2.4 million years old. A lot of debate around figures like this depends upon definition. When is Language truly itself, is it syntax or grammar that defines it? The evolution of language is a matter of some debate, but the approach that makes the most sense for this project sees language as developing from warning cries. The issue is again one of survival. An ape seeing a predator approaching his group would warn them through making noises with his vocal chords. In that conception, language evolved by exaptation to accommodate the much broader range of communications with which we are familiar today. What was originally evolved as an alarm-system (and later music) became Shakespeare. One of the rules of playwriting is that drama is about putting the hero/ine in jeopardy. One writer described it as putting your hero up a tree and then getting him down. If we take the licence of imagining the hero has sought refuge up a

---

105 See Norretranders, op. cit., pp. 136–141.

106 The crude numbers from that period have to be taken with a pinch of salt. Raw 'information' numbers change dramatically with changing variables or, for example, seeing Consciousness as a switch that itself needs little power but controls much more. Consciousness as information-processing is only part of the story. The only element I might be able to leave intact after that fusillade would be a comparison of scale, but I would probably have to look elsewhere to justify that. What remains is the instinct that Vision is much more powerful than Language.

tree because of an approaching Tiger, then we are in familiar Survival territory. Drama is not only about Jeopardy but it is a necessary if not sufficient condition of its existence. No Jeopardy, no Drama. What we learn about the human condition immeasurably enriches our experience with Shakespeare, and the Drama may fairly be seen as a pretext for the pearls of wisdom that accompany the journey, but it is the journey, the getting up the tree and the getting down, that keeps our attention on track. No other journeys qualify as Shakespeare but the form is not immaterial. Alarums have their place.

Thought takes place only in Vision

Language is seen here as a medium of translation. Language is not autonomous. Language is dependent, contingent, contingent upon Vision. Language does not originate thought. Thought does not take place in Language. Thought takes place in Vision. Thought takes place only in Vision[107]. The task of Language is the attempt to capture the wealth of Vision in its own medium. Those poor words that try to be adequate to what Vision has shown us will always be inadequate. The word strives after Vision. The word aspires to the condition of Vision, of seeing everything through trying to say everything. Vision escapes the word. The word is always following in the trail of Vision, always in its wake, always in the dust as Vision speeds on ahead.

Ask yourself the doubting question. Could it be possible that every thought I have in some way belongs to an image, descends from an image, is dependent upon seeing? I rather think that may be the case. I didn't believe it myself at first. Sometimes an idea will come that is shocking, that shocks me myself. Where does that idea come from? I have got used to the idea that it comes from somewhere rather valuable, and should always be given at least temporary residence. Surely there are many moments when we are turning ideas over in our heads, turning thoughts around? They surely cannot be dependent upon Vision? As I thought further about it I began to see how it just might be the case that, despite what seemed at first sight to be unlikely, as I prodded the thought further it gave up the possibility that in fact there were always images involved somewhere, that

107 The statement is counter-intuitive and may set readers' minds spinning to disprove the assertion. I was wary of it myself when it first came to mind, but the more I thought about it the more it set about convincing me that it was true.

Vision was in fact ubiquitous. You may wish to try that for yourself. Schopen-hauer put it that ' thoughts die the moment they are embodied by words'.[108]

Do the blind not think? Those who have gone blind[109] have been shown to have what is called *blindsight*, wherein the brain shows its flexibility in having paths for Vision that are not dependent upon the eyes. As with many brain functions, this is an example of the overlapping processes that evolve and, where one function is lost or damaged, other processes are able to take up that function.

For those born blind the visual cortex still plays a key role in the blind's mental mapping process. Their brains use echoes to generate spatial maps, which are sometimes so detailed that they enable for example, mountain biking, basketball and safely exploring new environments. Scans with fMRI show activity in areas of their brains associated with visual processing. In other words, brain scans of the blind resemble those of a sighted person identifying an object in a photo.[110]

I suggest that what has traditionally been called 'thought' is a case of the Automatic shooting things up to the vulnerable nest of the conscious mind for a mere moment, all that consciousness can afford, and that moment is a moment of Vision.

Logocentrism

The utter dominance of the word in British culture is so marked that would seem impolite even to point it out and extraordinary to conceive of challenging it. The Word enjoys an unparalleled prestige among the educated, after all this is the land of Shakespeare. In my experience even those that work in the film and television industries share this assumption, which is just so pervasive as not to be worth remarking, an assumption, something taken-for-granted to such a degree that it would be hard to think of how it would even be possible to raise it as an issue. The firm assumption is one hundred percent that the word is superior to Vision, so much so that it is not even an area of debate. When a few years ago the government of the day decided that a campaign on Visual Literacy was in order it seemed clear that no one had the slightest clue what that was, or could be, including the staff working on the campaign. They naturally shared the same easy

---

108 Quoted by mathematician Jacques Hadamard in *Essay on the Psychology of Invention in the Mathematical Field*, Princeton University Press, Princeton, NJ, 1949.

109 Those who have gone blind, that is, as against those born blind.

110 http://www.livescience.com/23709-blind-people-picture-reality.html

assumptions that the word was all-powerful, even if something should be done about the profusion of images in a modern society. There can hardly be any set of ideas, any world-view as pervasively successful as the ideology of Language and the word.

Logocentrism is the view that Language is much more powerful than it is in reality, and is based on the widespread reification of the word in Western culture and a concomitant aggressive demotion of the status of Vision. These attitudes are so thoroughly pervasive as to constitute an Ideology, a view of the world that gives precedence to the word in particular in relation to Vision. Logocentrism asserts the autonomy of the word when in reality the word is contingent upon Vision. Logocentrism is antagonistic to Vision, claiming Language is the more powerful medium when, in terms of information, it is substantially inferior (ie at a millionth the processing-power). Language is constantly on the attack against Vision, being derogatory about its expressive capabilities and contrasting it unfavourably with the richness of the word. For example, Language talks of verbal and 'non-verbal' tests instead of verbal and *visual* tests, as though the idea of Vision is being repressed. The left and right hemispheres of the brain used to be known as the Major and Minor hemispheres, the 'Major' hemisphere identified by its capacity for Language. The left hemisphere is known to 'inhibit the affective responses activated by the right hemisphere'.[111] Extensive research on the qualities of the two hemispheres demonstrate radically different qualities associated with the asymmetry of the left and right brains, so that in broad terms the left-side qualities involve a narrow focus on particulars while right-side qualities involve a holistic view. Even with words, 'the left hemisphere actively narrows its attentional focus to highly related words while the right hemisphere activates a broader range of words'[112]. There would seem to be a connection between Logocentrism and the dominance of the 'left-brain' mode which comes down not to the use of words, per se, but way in which they are used to close options down, against the more 'creative' mode of the 'right-brain' approach.

An executive, a former-journalist I came across appeared to believe that asking for something was the same as achieving the action. For him there was no gap between the word and the action. The word was not a medium but the thing in itself. It was quite an effective misapprehension as when a gap opened up he would get angry and could not understand why the word had not instantly become the

111 Joseph. P . Hellige, *Hemispherical Assymetry*, Harvard University Press, 1993. p. 338.
112 McGilchrist *The Master and his Emissary*, op. cit., p. 41.

action, and so his employees would rush to close the gap to confirm his world-view in order to protect themselves from his wrath.

The operation of logocentrism can also be seen in that virtually all analysis of Cinema begins with the reduction of the medium to the metaphor with language, as in the classic statement that 'Cinema is structured like a language'.[113] A significant part of that denial of Vision is that one might identify it with a 'left-brain' as against a 'right-brain' use of language. Reducing Cinema to Language aligns with the 'left-brain' feature of narrowing down options. Seeing Cinema in broader terms including those of Vision aligns with a 'right-brain' approach that has a more holistic view.

While a different use of language is possible, as mentioned in the letters of Cezanne and by Rilke on him, the question has to be asked whether there would be the slightest interest in exploring that potential, let alone seeing it as in any way a priority? There are two answers to that question. The first is a no, and that answer would come from virtually anyone who was asked, in government or education or the man-in-the-street. If you don't see a problem you will hardly be interested in solving it. The second is a qualified yes. Web-Marketing gurus are widely preaching the notion that we are at the edge of a whole new generation of web-sites. The predominance of text, the sales letter, the text 'video' are becoming old hat. The next generation is moving away from Language. The web is evolving and dealing with the relative efficacy of Language and Vision in its own way [114]. The role of language is changing and the Internet seems likely to play a major role in those changes.

Consciousness

The figures that compare the information-processing capacity of Consciousness to the Automatic may be reasonably accurate but the question over them is what story are they telling and is it the right one? They perhaps have a symbolic role as a caution against giving Consciousness too much credit, but Consciousness is more than information processing. In *The User Illusion*, Tor Norretranders makes a detailed case that Consciousness has been overrated in its importance and quotes extensively from the information-science work in the 50s and 60s that set out to quantify the amount of information that consciousness could handle, and in the

113 Christian Metz op. cit.
114 See the penultimate paragaph of *The Quality of Vision* p. 104.

context of how much the brain as a whole absorbed. That view was both influential in my early thinking about consciousness and useful in putting figures to the feeling that consciousness was less important both than the unconscious and than the popular image it has. However, there is a danger in reducing consciousness to information-processing, which is perhaps why Norretranders' rediscovery of the quantitative data seems to have gone largely without comment in neuroscience.

There is an interesting analogy between film and video, that is between celluloid and the digital format. Fans of film feel strongly that video misses something that film captures. It is not the amount of information that is captured but a certain quality to the feel of film that is felt to be missing with digital. It may be subjective rather than objective, a sentimental attachment to the old medium over the new, but certainly early video was less able to resolve detail and have the range of colour of film. Today, digital formats can arguably exceed the performance of celluloid objectively, but also begin subjectively to look less different as manipulation of the image becomes more sophisticated with the help of software programmes. It is possible to imagine video becoming like film but more so, but that would be unlikely to satisfy fans of celluloid. There is a similar argument to that between vinyl and digital formats. Audiophiles claim that digital reproduction is inferior to analogue in the form of vinyl. They would say that mp3 files carrying 256k bps are not as good as vinyl records. The digital reproduction misses something present on vinyl. In both cases people talk of the 'warmth' of the analogue medium compared to the 'coldness' of the digital. There is an objective and a subjective element in both cases, but the sentiment is about the 'quality' of information rather than just the crude statistics, and that involves its meaning to us which in turn involves emotion.

However, the fundamental argument against judging consciousness on the numbers is about evolution. Consciousness is a product of evolution, a process that selects for advantage. Consciousness plays the role it does in the brain because of its contribution to the old pair of survival and reproduction. There are many examples in both organisms and machines of elements that involve relatively small amounts of energy but play a vital role, as in a man's heart or a motor-car's battery. There is evidence that the brain excludes a lot of information, behaving like a reducing-valve, and only uses relatively small amounts, with a large amount discarded altogether through neurons being inhibited from processing much of the available input. In this light the question of capacity is irrelevant as Consciousness evolved to do a certain job, it does that and is useless for other functions. There may not be many neurons involved in consciousness but they are not unimportant. Brain-activation that correlates to conscious experience is about appreciation of that conscious experience, not the strength of the original signal. Talking of arithmetical limitations on Consciousness may be like bemoaning the fact that a car battery can't drive – it does certain things and not others – according to how it has evolved[115]. Perhaps the only role left for the raw numbers is in relation to the ideology surrounding Consciousness, in that they suggest that the relative workloads of the Conscious and the Automatic are almost diametrically opposite to the popular imagination.

A second fundamental argument against the numbers is to do with the integration of brain functions, another outcome of the evolutionary process. While it is tempting to talk of one aspect or another being dominant or subservient as in the left/right brain debate,[116] there is a tendency to do a disservice to the reality that brain functions broadly evolved together and are integrated, so that it is not a case of Consciousness dominating the Automatic or the reverse, but of the integration between elements and what that tells us about the nature of the relationship between them. Co-evolution of left and right hemispheres suggests a functional specialisation that is essentially complementary rather than usefully conceived of as in conflict or a matter of precedence. An attempt to correct an imbalance, as between the images of consciousness and the Automatic, should not be merely to replace one King with another, but to understand the mutuality of the body politic, as it were.

A further question is the status of consciousness as causal. Is consciousness a cause or an effect, an epiphenomenon of brain function? There is a view among neuroscientists that consciousness is an effect[117], and it is that view towards which I would tend myself. In my mind it seems more likely to be an effect as so much work is done 'unseen' by the Automatic, as LeDoux has said. If it seen as a cause the amount of information consciousness handled would arguably be less significant than if it were an effect. The notion of consciousness as a switch, for example, would not consume much energy or information, whereas carrying out active tasks would appear to consume more.

However, thinking about consciousness in terms of its evolutionary origins and the fact of its interdependence with the Automatic makes attributing a control

---

115 I owe these observations to Simon Raggett (see Acknowledgements).

116 See McGilchrist, *The Master and his Emissary* op. cit.

117 Two scientists of my acquaintance in separate conversations, one English, one American, both strongly took that view.

role between the two problematic. Virtually from conception in the womb their connections are inextricable so it would not make too much sense to say that one or the other is the driver.

In sum, the notion that consciousness is aware of around a millionth of the information that the brain is dealing with at any one time may well be factually correct, but the problem comes in turning that fact into a useful interpretation of the relative power of the conscious and the Automatic. The mechanistic arithmetic of information-processing is not a reliable guide in the context of evolutionary pressures and relationships. The quality of information is a strategic question – as with the simple idea of the switch that controls a whole system in its hinterland.

We might, on the other hand, be able to suggest that consciousness is an effect of brain function rather than a cause. In its relations it will inevitably have causal elements, for example as part of the feedback loops through which consciousness is connected to the Automatic. However, the sense that I would like to suggest is that it is the Automatic that is causal in the sense of it prompting consciousness through feedback loops. The speculative picture that occurs to me is where a threat or opportunity is sensed by the body/brain system and consciousness is alerted to its presence through Vision. Vision loops that information back some via consciousness but mainly via the Automatic, that requests Vision and consciousness to keep a watching brief on the developing situation and provide updates – all this in reality via constant feedback loops operating at high speed. It may be that the Automatic sifts feedback information and acts as an intelligent system, as it has been said that the eye is – something like a non-linear video-editing system that has criteria – always survival/reproduction oriented, that act as the basis of the request/instruction to consciousness to provide information upon.

This speculative model has consciousness as effect in the sense that it acts at the behest of the Automatic. Inherent in that conception is the notion that the Automatic is carrying out multiple complex processing and assessment of incoming information and intelligently sorting that information as the basis for further requests, like a back-room controller out of sight of the survival/reproduction situation but operating an information centre, something like a military ops room.

The important element in this discussion of possible models for consciousness is to, on the one hand, depart from a mechanical notion of consciousness as dominated by information-processing figures, which would ignore the relevance of evolution, but on the other hand to focus on what this project is centred on in relation to consciousness, and that is not the real operations of the brain, but rather the question of the image of consciousness in the public mind and what I would suggest is an ideology around it that bears even less relation to the realities than does the information-processing model.

It is this *ideology* of consciousness which is a cultural artefact, that takes its place alongside those of Language and Reason in the trio of gaolers nominated here. But that, again, is not to say that consciousness is regarded in the same manner as the latter two. While their ideologies have in common what looks rather like a desire to promote themselves at the expense of their opposite numbers suggested here, what is seen as a turning upside-down of the real relations in order to render the Major minor and the Minor major, consciousness is clearly the most fundamental of the troika and therefore requires more consideration of its complexities.

Consciousness and the Automatic are inextricably linked and complementary due to their evolutionary history. A more global question would be why would the Automatic appear to do so much and Consciousness do so little? Perhaps Consciousness is at the sharp end, the awareness tasks, whereas the Automatic is the back-room boy, responding with substantial resources to the few resources, but critical, of Consciousness out there on the coal-face. Can we see Consciousness as autonomous or is it more likely to be contingent upon the Automatic? My subjective feeling is that consciousness is contingent, driven rather than driving, as it were, but that should be seen in the context of an evolved mutual dependence.

Although neuroscience has made substantial progress in defining the parameters of such a discussion, not least with inherent references to evolution for every brain function, the variables are so massive that a clear theory of consciousness would as yet be speculative. Here it is merely my own instinct that suggests the Automatic is the driving force, but that can only realistically be seen within the contact of the coterminosity that evolution produces, so a relative autonomy at best for the Automatic, and a relative contingency to consciousness. However that is defined it still moves away from the traditional conception that consciousness is king and the unconscious is merely a negative, rather than something that might possess a degree of autonomy. It reverses the order of how Consciousness and the Automatic are thought of in the public mind.

The view proposed here is that the power of the Automatic is such that within it the majority of mental operations are carried on, with only brief flares that illuminate the Conscious mind. The Automatic is seen as the source of light, with Consciousness mainly in the dark and only momentarily seeing the light when the Automatic focuses its slim resources on the most important stimuli? In reality that is a constant process, but the idea here is that the Automatic is effectively making decisions as to what is important and what is less so, and choosing to dedicate the miniscule information-processing capacity of Consciousness only at the very very tip of what is important to get the best return on the investment of those slim resources. The wisdom of the Automatic is in the accuracy, the relevance of those choices in relation to the criteria of survival. What is most important for Survival is what the Automatic focusses the Conscious mind upon. The feedback it gets may or may not be accurate, but it is constantly updated so that it becomes more accurate by dint of the active feedback loop that is making decisions constantly and at high speed. When we are faced with a fight or flight choice we need to be able to determine that is the choice in the first place and then to confirm it to shift the focus to a flight strategy. Any one of such decisions requires a dynamic process of feedback that potentially involves millions even billions of pieces of information that are focussed by survival criteria into a developing strategy to guide us away from danger.

An alternative view of Consciousness could be that it calls upon the hidden resources of the Automatic in order to make critical decisions on survival issues. Its leadership role at the sharp end, closest to the external environment that it apprehends, exists precisely because it is the nearest thing to 'reality', and that gives it priority. The body/brain system hands over leadership to Consciousness because it, uniquely, is where the action is and has the capacity to apprehend it and interpret it, while the Automatic is its information and resource back-up. As a Chief Executive doesn't have to do all the work himself, but only to make the key decisions, so it is with Consciousness.

However, to extend Damasio's 'question', if Reason cannot exist without Emotion, is Consciousness in a similar position – does it need the Automatic as Reason needs Emotion? If Consciousness is not independent but dependent upon the Automatic/unconscious, does that suggest its role is unlikely to be causal and more likely to be an effect? We have some difficulty in demoting Consciousness as it is our most intimate contact with the world – the channel that appears to us to be closest to reality. Can it be really a product of other processes behind the scenes, merely a servant of those processes, the end of a chain rather than the beginning?

Where this relates to Cinema is in one of the originating impulses for this project

– a sense that we take in most of the meanings of a film unconsciously. If that is so then there is a lot of processing going on outside consciousness, which Joseph LeDoux and Stanislas Dehaene for example, state.[118] But what does it mean beyond the simple observation? If we absorb information without being aware of it, where does it go and what functions does it perform? I would suggest that in Cinema it orients us towards the characters and the story in much more complex ways than those of which we are conscious. As Ledoux put it – we see more than we know[119].

But what is it we see and what does the brain do with it? If, in a Hitchcock film, we take in far more information than we do in a 'non-classic' film (which has some experimental backing from Hasson[120]) then that might function as a measure of depth. It might help to explain the longevity of his classic films, as they tap in to something in the brain that is a profound mechanism (suspense). Measuring brain-activity (as Hasson did) is helpful to be able to compare films and achieve greater objectivity in assessing their qualities, something which has bedevilled film study since its inception.

By depth one is indicating the volume of information that the film is 'smuggling' into the brain outside consciousness. The information absorbed by the brain during a film outside consciousness could be seen as revealing the depth of that film, a depth that has been built into it in some way, conscious or unconscious, in the process of its making, through the agency of the key figures in its making – script-writer(s), director, editor, producer, and actors. It is important to include the element of unconscious information instead of the more traditional idea of the conscious agent entirely in conscious control of the meanings in the film. The intention may be present at some level, but it may not be conscious, history and society operating through agents intimately involved in the making of the film in specific ways. The idea is that we are not only seeing what is on the screen but gaining a feel for the characters and their lives off-screen through, for example, discussions that went on when the script was being written. This is not simply 'back-story', but more the process of creating characters on paper, modifications in discussion, what is left out as much as what is put in. This leads to an idea later in the book – assembling an 'archive' for each film that makes concrete the notion that we 'see more than we know'. Studying a film closely makes more information available, as there is always more to see than we register on a single viewing.[121]

---

118 See Joseph LeDoux, *The Emotional Brain*, Weidenfeld & Nicolas, London, 1988; Dehaene op. cit.

119 In *The Emotional Brain* op. cit.

120 Hasson et al (2008) op. cit.

121 See section on Cinema for more details.

The image of Consciousness proposed here is a little like a battle, with millions, perhaps billions of warriors vying for attention. The brain has perhaps 300 million billion connections and if we assume for the moment that they are all involved in the 'shop front' of Consciousness, the process whereby a stimulus reaches the attention-watershed that would qualify it to enter the Conscious mind is immensely complex and involves those billions of transactions and communications. It is a bit like a non-linear editing system that deals with huge information input and output in order to select those few items that Consciousness has the capacity to pay attention to. The idea of 'paying' attention is an interesting one where Consciousness has very few resources, in terms of information-processing at least, and the price of attention is very steep in terms of the numbers involved. There is a battle for attention and only a maximum of seven winners at any one time in working memory, more likely one or two on average. There has to be a criterion for selection – and this is where, in this model, survival comes in. Attention is devoted to stimuli most relevant for survival.

Did Consciousness selects those stimuli or the Automatic? If Consciousness does not have the resources to select them as well as report back on them, then something points Consciousness at the stimuli, and the leading candidate would seem to be the Automatic. Stimuli can be selected by the body, that is the body is aware of stimuli, as indicated in the studies by Benjamin Libet and others. (Libet identified a half-second gap between the body reacting to a stimulus and consciousness becoming aware of it – his methodology has been extensively criticised, but other researchers have noticed gaps of varying lengths that suggest the basic point retains validity.) So a combination of the unconscious mind and the body may be doing the work of identifying critical stimuli for the Conscious mind to pay attention to. Is a hidden body/brain dualism involved in this formulation. Is the homunculus that something that points consciousness to stimuli? The idea here is that it is the body/brain system, excluding Consciousness, that carries out that task and according to the criterion of survival. Survival is not teleological but it is concerned with the live issue of maintaining life and it acts through chemical motivation rather than moral principle. As bacteria are attracted uphill, as it were, then biological value asserts itself in the process of the individual's interaction with the external environment. The chemical becomes biological through survival, the impetus of time and movement. As time passes, movement occurs and that movement is chemical, which over time becomes biological via evolutionary processes.

A more radical statement again of Consciousness-as-effect is that Consciousness does not exist. There are some neuroscientists who take that view, perhaps more in the light of 'not as we think of it' than denying its existence completely. From what I understand of that view, it is partly the unitary notion of Consciousness that is at question. Certainly, from introspection I do not see Consciousness as anything like unitary but more like a bunch of partly unrelated shots in a trim-bin that I have to edit together to make some sort of sense. The Consciousness-effort is the making sense, the joining-up, which takes me back to this overriding sense that what I call 'narrativising' is a major mode of the brain across many functions.

Another aspect is to deny that there is a 'hard' problem with Consciousness in explaining our subjective experience. I take a fairly thorough materialist view that everything in the brain is the product of physical processes – and nothing else. There are some materialist-oriented philosophers, like Nagel, who appear to find that an insuperable problem for no reason I can ascertain apart from the fact it is a real block, a matter of belief. I have no problem in believing that the sum can be greater than the parts, and that tends to dissolve the 'hard' problem. Consciousness as we think of it my not exist, but whatever intercedes between the brain and the world seems to me a matter of fact, of physical processes, rather than anything metaphysical. That would be my statement of belief.

The reason it is so difficult to tie Consciousness down is that scientific method relies on reductionism to reduce the many variables to the key few which then act as a predictive guide to change. With the brain, despite the great progress made in the last generation or so, we are dealing with something that has 300 million billion connections. We are perhaps on the lower foothills of knowledge about the brain, so we cannot be surprised that making sense of Consciousness may take a little longer.

Consciousness and the Unconscious

Stanislas Dehaene writes extensively about the unconscious in 'Consciousness and the Brain'[122], explaining in detail how cognitive neuroscience since the 1990s, and his own lab over the last fifteen years since about 2000, has been able to devise simple laboratory experiments that distinguish between conscious and unconscious states (inspired by Francis Crick of DNA fame). The book's title privileges 'Consciousness' and therein lies an interesting paradox revealed in the text. There is a sense that Dehaene appears wedded to the ideology of Consciousness in paying tribute to its importance, despite most of what he talks about being

122 Dehaene, op. cit.

ascribed to non-conscious activity. There is a symptomatic moment where he quotes William James to the effect that Consciousness looks like "an organ added for the sake of steering a nervous system grown too complex to regulate itself" (p. 167). That seems like the driver being added by the car. The logic fails. Consciousness comes not from nowhere but is an extension to the Automatic evolved over the eons of evolutionary history. Consciousness is contingent upon the Automatic.

There is a certain irony in huffing and puffing about Consciousness whilst effectively portraying it as the icing on the cake, the shop window of a huge store, the footlights of a very large stage. It is as though Dehaene has broken his own invaluable rule - that introspection is crucial as raw data but inappropriate as a research method. We think subjectively that Consciousness is King as it is what we are aware of. He himself shows that the theatre is a bad analogy, as the audience is the Automatic. Dehaene has dedicated fifteen plus years to effectively defining the Automatic only to fall prey to the Consciousness industry.

On the other hand he brings considerable clarity to a field that has hitherto remained in the mist. In progressively defining, through laboratory experiment rather than rhetorical philosophy (Dehaene is based near Paris), the threshold between the Automatic and Consciousness, he and his colleagues have provided a notable service exemplified in the declaration by his collaborator Lionel Naccache that "the unconscious is not structured as a language but as a decaying exponential" contradicting Lacan (p. 104). The corollary of that notion is that 'Only consciousness allows us to entertain lasting thoughts'.

My interpretation is that the Automatic selects the priority stimulus, a bit like a Pop chart, and consciousness pays attention to it until the combination of feedback loops and competing stimuli prompt the Automatic to shift Consciousness to another Hit as it tops the charts. As Dehaene points out 'a staggering amount of unconscious processing occurs beneath the surface of our conscious mind ...' (p.13) and 'Because of its limited capacity, consciousness must withdraw from one item in order to gain access to another' (p. 21). He admits that 'Oblivious to this boiling hodgepodge of unconscious processes, we constantly overestimate the power of our consciousness in making decisions - but in truth, our capacity for conscious control is limited', as '... consciousness is only a thin veneer lying atop sundry unconscious processes' (p. 50). He agrees with Maudsley (1868) that 'the most important part of mental action, the essential processes on which thinking depends, is unconscious mental activity' (p. 51), that 'Freud was right: consciousness is overrated ...' (p. 79), and declares that 'unconscious processes are more objective than conscious ones' (p. 98) and 'act as fast and massively parallel statisticians, while consciousness is a slow sampler' (p. 99), through which 'we are fundamentally reduced to just about one conscious thought at a time' (p. 20), although one thought can be 'a substantial "chunk" with several subcomponents, as when we ponder the meaning of a sentence'. However, that is in comparison to the operations of the Automatic, 'synapses, numbering in the hundred thousand billions', as 'within our unconscious lies an unimaginable richness waiting to be tapped' (both p. 195), and 'Because our unconscious operations elude us, we constantly overestimate the role that consciousness plays in our physical and mental lives... By forgetting the amazing power of the unconscious, we over-attribute our actions to conscious decisions and therefore mischaracterise our consciousness as a major player in our daily lives'.

Dehaene presents the image of consciousness much less often, and against the grain of his other declarations, as 'a "free willing" machine' (p. 15), 'an elitist board of executives' (p. 171),'at the top, a select board of executives examining only a brief of the situation ... a single conscious decision-maker ... a dictatorial process' (p. 93), 'like a spokesperson in a large institution' (p. 99), asserting that 'we need to be conscious in order to rationally think through a problem' (p. 108).

The view here includes none of those things. No free will, not executive nor rational. A spokesperson speaks the words of others, so that may be closer. The executive image is the opposite of mine – the Automatic chooses, Consciousness carries out as best it can, a servant not the master. Consciousness is not independent but contingent and has no executive powers – as Dehaene's logic might be thought to suggest in much of his book.

Dehaene is a thoroughgoing materialist, believing that 'Once we clarify how any piece of sensory information can gain access to our conscious mind and becomes reportable, then the insurmountable problem of our ineffable experiences will disappear' (p. 10). He boldly and importantly claims that subjective mental experiences 'defined the very phenomenon we aimed to study', 'by definition, in consciousness research, subjectivity is at the heart of our subject matter' (p. 41), and that in fact '... introspection ... *defines* the very essence of what a science of consciousness is about ... an objective explanation of subjective reports' (p. 42), and is 'the perfect, indeed the only, platform on which to build a science of consciousness' (p. 43).

The 'masked' title of the book is 'Unconsciousness and the Brain', and his materialism traces its antecedents back to Hippocrates (460–377 BC) 'from the brain, and from the brain alone, arise our pleasures, joys, laughter and jests as well as our sorrows, pains, grieves and tears. Through it, in particular we think, see, hear and distinguish the ugly from the beautiful, the bad from the good, the pleasant from the unpleasant'. Despite that impulse his, perhaps cultural, desire for a theory propels him into the arms of Idealism in the notion of the Global Workspace, which seems to abandon the historicism of evolution for an Idea floating in its own ether. My own conclusion from this summary of laboratory work over fifteen years would be that consciousness adds value to the Automatic as its function is to enable us to hold a thought as long as it remains the priority for survival, and then can be moved on at great speed to the next, always with the criterion that the next is not 'arbitrary', but wholly determined by the twins survival and reproduction.

Automatic/Unconscious

The majority of the brain's operations take place outside consciousness,[123] and for information-processing only a millionth of it takes place within it. With Consciousness handling such a small proportion, it would seem anomalous to give only a negative term to the rest – the 'un-conscious'. It therefore seems to make sense to propose an independent term for that larger area, on the grounds that it surely deserves a word of its own. We function automatically, in the sense of beyond Consciousness, and a term in common use in neuroscience. The main mode of existence of man is Automatic.

An Independent Term

To use the term Automatic is also a statement of intent in the battle against the ideology of language. The negative term un-conscious suggests the Conscious is the Major player and the unconscious the Minor player. Yet, as Trincker put it in 1965 "only one millionth of what our eyes see, our ears hear, and our other senses inform us about appears in our consciousness"[124]. There is an argument that Language is deliberately obscuring the truth. The terms Conscious and Unconscious reinforce a view that the Conscious is dominant and that which is not Conscious is inferior, the negative term only. The much larger area beyond

123 LeDoux op. cit., p. 64.
124 Dietrich Trincker op. cit.

Consciousness has no word of its own. As nearly all of those functions are reliably carried out without our cognizance, according to the needs of survival, I propose the term Automatic.

How are we even aware of the Automatic? We are familiar with the notion from psycho-analysis that the Unconscious 'irrupts' into Consciousness in dreams. When we recall a dream or a fragment of a dream, we are delving into the realm of the Automatic. It is one thing for us to be conceive that the Automatic is dominant and the Conscious a more minor player in terms of the overall activity of the brain, but where does that lead? Consciousness has arguably proceeded like Language – in obscuring its minor role.

The reason for the Automatic is Evolution. The logic of what the Automatic dictates is the logic of nature, the process of evolution. We are driven to do what we do in the interest of the species but at the level of the individual. For example, a man leaves a woman because she wants children and he says he doesn't want children. Then almost immediately he has a child with the subsequent woman. Is that a conscious decision or the Automatic, an unconscious decision that selects a different partner for reproduction working through him almost independent of his will?

In Cinema we are familiar with the idea that there can be a gap between what the character thinks they are doing and what we observe them doing, or rather between why they think they are doing something and why we see them doing it. That is also the gap between their conscious mind and our awareness of their Automatic motivations. This is one small example of how we have access to the Automatic. It is not an unknown continent but one which lacks a comprehensive language to express it.

Freud and the unconscious

While Freud is owed a debt for having brought attention to the Unconscious, there is an opposite characterisation of the Automatic, as revealing rather than concealing. Freud's conception of the Unconscious as concealing a mass of writhing forbidden desires appears in the 21st Century a reflection of the Viennese culture in which Freud began his work. Sexuality as unmentionable is a common image of the Victorian and Viennese worlds and served a useful purpose for Freud after he was forced to abandon his attempt to develop a 'scientific psychology'. When he began that effort, in 1889, there was insufficient knowledge about the brain for him to continue. Not only was he forced to abandon the effort, but the choice that he made was to turn instead to the pre-scientific practice of interpretation – the interpretation of dreams. Today that choice is viewed by some as turning psychology back to the middle-ages in creating a cadre with exclusive claims on the ability to interpret dreams – akin to a priesthood, and essentially a religious role rather than scientific[125].

Dream Science

The development of Dream Science has seen an alternative that both attempts to apply scientific method to dreams and through its findings has decisively rejected the notion of the unconscious *concealing* in favour of a rather more straightforward view of dreams *revealing* what is going on in our minds during sleep. In addition, Dream Science has tended to see dreams as a state of consciousness rather then unconsciousness. The difference between sleeping consciousness and waking consciousness is also simple – our eyes are closed and therefore the brain loses the input from the eyes that characterises waking. Dream Science is a branch of neuroscience and has pursued the analysis of the chemical changes that occur in sleep, and in so doing has begun to account for something of the nature of dreams. Dream diaries tend to show that there is a limited repertoire of dream-forms and dream-content. While Dream Science has tended to be stronger on form than content in general, it has become clear that the role of dreams is more to do with a biological role of housekeeping waking experience and brain-input than the more forbidden roles in the Freudian conception. Putting experience into memory as a reference-library is one important role, while the forms of content of much dreaming can be ascribed to the simple facts of chemical changes in the brain and our eyes being closed. '… all of the features of dreaming that Freud wanted to explain with his wish-fulfilment, disguise-censorship theory, are explained in just the way he hoped might ultimately be possible – by the physiology and chemistry of the brain.'[126]

The errors of Freud and his followers may today be seen as partly the result of a fundamental failure to follow the most basic of scientific rules – that of observation. Even in the analytic situation the analyst eschews visual contact with the patient, who faces away from the analyst, whether on a couch or not. There could hardly be a stronger indication of the rejection of Vision and embracing the word

125 See J A Hobson, *Dreaming, a very short introduction*, OUP, Oxford, 2005.

126 Hobson op. cit., p. 102

– the 'Talking cure'. Every pillar of Freud's speculative theory seems by now disproved,[127] as Dehaene puts it: 'The ideas that are solid are not his own, while those that are his own are not solid',[128] something for which he cannot be strictly blamed as the state of neuroscience in his day meant that philosophical speculation was his only option. However, he may be more open to criticism for turning away from basic scientific procedure, despite his training, and that would go rather more so for those following in his footsteps as knowledge of the brain increased.

The conception here of the Automatic owes more to Dream Science, which has access to the unconscious through its analysis of dreaming. The Automatic plays a massive role in waking, but our access to it is currently largely through introspective accounts. What could increase our knowledge of the Automatic and its operations would be research along similar lines to those followed by Dream Science, and as pursued by Dehaene and his colleagues re Consciousness, which takes subjective accounts of our individual sense of instances of the operations of the Automatic as they appear in Consciousness in order to build a library of repertoires that could be pursued by fMRI and other techniques in order to link chemical changes in the brain to our sense of the Automatic in operation.

However, the Automatic remains largely an unknown continent, but as LeDoux and Dehaene state, as most of what the brain does is outside Consciousness it clearly merits further investigation.

My consideration of the Automatic began from a sense that the viewer takes in most of the information in a film unconsciously. If that instinct is correct the question arises as to what the Automatic does with that information. Why would we take in most information unconsciously and what do we do with it when it is absorbed? The first response would be that there is a biological reason, an evolutionary reason related to the survival question at the base of it. We take in such volumes of information Automatically probably partly because the information-processing capacity of Consciousness appears to be small. If we assume that the 11 million bits of input goes somewhere else than the Conscious mind, then the Automatic is the leading candidate, perhaps the only candidate. If we imagine that the body/brain system is monistic rather than the dualistic version of traditional accounts of Descartes then the Automatic may be taking its 11m

---

127 See Hobson op. cit., Ch 2. Dehaene, op. cit. goes further than most in listing five categories of unconscious processing. His final category 'Latent Connections' notes 'Cortical synapses, numbering in the **hundred thousand billions** in the human brain, contain dormant memories of our entire life' (my emphasis) (pp. 190–196).

128 Dehaene, op. cit. p. 52.

(minus 10) bits into the body/brain system and distributing it around both elements. Even in denying dualism it is a temptation to think of the body and the brain in some ways separately. But, for example, with Galvanic Skin Response and the experiments of Libet, we know that there is potentially some degree of independence of the body – at least from Consciousness. If the body does 'sense' external stimuli without input from the brain, then it would make sense that it both sends that information to the brain and perhaps receives information back which may be requests for further information, demands for action etc. In that conception the body and brain are both part of one indivisible feedback system. And perhaps the bulk of those activities occur within the realm of the Automatic.

At the output end my own introspective experience is derived from the kind of moment when one searches for a word and suddenly it pops into my consciousness. I have no idea where it came from or how it came, just that I was consciously scanning for it, not finding it and then, at an interval that might be less than a second, after a visit to the loo, or upon waking the next morning, the answer pops up. And it is always the right word. Whatever process of scanning below my Consciousness that has occurred, it is highly effective. As Dehaene puts it 'unconscious processes are more objective than conscious ones'.[129]

Darwin's List

When a decision has to be made, for example at its simplest, a purchase, many of us balance the pros and cons. A famous example is Darwin's list for and against marriage. Here we are trying to be rational, using our consciousness to think of all the relevant criteria. It is one of the glories of Consciousness that it allows us to think of things that are absent from our vision. We are not limited to what we can see, but we can summon up thoughts of what is invisible but lodged in our memory. We rack our brains and may return to the subject when a new thought pops up (from the Automatic again), but we reach the point of decision one way or another, even where it has been delayed, rethought, recalculated several or even many times. Something pushes us to decide. It could be circumstances, such as we arrive at the shop, or it could be emotion as we think this has gone on long enough, it's time to decide. Whatever the deciding factor, we decide. I can only speak personally on this process, but I would say that I am aware that in the end, at least for me, it is emotion that decides. Rational calculation is never enough. There is always one more factor to consider or reconsider. Reasoning is tiring and

---

129 Dehaene, op. cit. p 98.

ever reaches an end-point. In the final analysis it's not reason but feeling, instinct, emotion that decides. I want to do that, or I really don't think I should do that. It's not really good value, but I want it, or therefore I won't get it. Our decisions in every waking moment are made of thousands of such calculations, a few of which we are aware of consciously, but if the same scale applies as with the pin in the Albert Hall metaphor, then there are billions of operations in the Automatic that contribute to our every decision.

Survival

Now, why would that be? What would require such exhaustive processes? I rather take the view that only survival has enough clout to make such demands. In neuroscience and in philosophy, when it considers such matters, there is often an 'idealism' that considers such matters in the abstract. It seems to me that is always wrong. Only survival is such a demanding master to use every tiny bit of energy to contribute towards our continued existence. Survival is a material matter – up to a point[130] – and seems to me to be the (pen-) ultimate cause for our brains to do what they do.

So what does the Automatic do? To reiterate, it contributes to survival. The slim resources of Consciousness leave it a lot to do. In this conception the Automatic does the rest of the job. The glimpse we get of its myriad works, when we get a word popping up into consciousness, or an idea, or when we finally reach a decision, are the only visible elements of it that appear in consciousness.

An interesting experiment would be to assemble an archive of the information around a given film and then compare the extent of that archive with individual responses to the film. What appeared in the subjects' consciousness and what did fMRI show of their brain activity? Individuals will be different, perhaps not very different[131], but nevertheless there would be differences – and how would their accounts relate to the archive that attempted to list as much information as possible?

130 This small qualification indicates an awareness that behind the physical ultimately lies the metaphysical.

131 The Malach experiment found substantial unanimity between audience reactions, using fMRI. Malach: Perception without a Perceiver, Rafael Malach (in conversation with Zoran Josipovic), Journal of Consciousness Studies, 13, No. 9, pp. 57–66 (2006). Also see Uri Hasson, Malach et al. 'Intersubject Synchronization of Cortical Activity During Natural Vision', *Science* 303, 1634 (2004).

Survival and shopping

What has survival to do with a decision to buy a computer/car/clothing and choosing a lover/partner/one-night-stand? Survival's first port of call is to preserve life. The second port of call is reproduction. It is easy to see that we might choose lovers on a biological-fitness basis, that is a familiar idea. But a computer? A symbol of a kind of rationalism, science, technology, objectivity of the machine. What do we consider in buying a computer? Specification, price, relation to the tasks we expect to carry out with it. And image. A Mac or a PC? A cheap PC or an expensive branded one? We might identify two separate tasks in making a choice. An attempt at a rational assessment of technical specifications and the question of image. The problem with the former is that most of us don't understand the full implications of technical specifications. We are not really familiar with a specific task that spec A will fulfil and spec B will not. One spec may not play games too well, or show movies without pausing. But we probably won't know say the movies thing until we have the machine or have tried it in a shop. But trying to watch movies in a shop is a rather forced procedure and may not give us a clear idea of differences between machines. Even the exhaustive comparison of technical aspects may not satisfy us, as some will be more relevant to the key tasks we know we wish to perform, and others may tickle our fancy as things we might quite like to do but have not yet done. Experience may tell us that a machine may be able to do things that are technically impressive, but in fact we probably won't do them, or do them a couple of times and then go back to our more familiar rota of tasks we perform many times a day. In other words, image plays a part even in balancing the apparently neutral technical specification issue. When will I watch movies on my laptop? I don't go on many long journeys and have a blu-ray player attached to my forty-inch HD TV anyway. I'd be better off waiting for 4k TVs or projetors to come down in price and spend my money on that – as far a watching films goes. But that may be ages away and it would be quite nice to have the possibility of watching movies on my laptop as I might be taking more long journeys in the near future, etc etc.

Rationalise & Reason

The point is that we tend to rationalise rather than strictly reason. Rationalise in what terms? What do we mean by rationalise? We let our emotions make the decision. We want to do something so we find reasons for doing it. We want to watch movies on our laptop so we buy a machine that does that better than another machine. That's leaving aside whether the advertised spec really does make me feel it is better when I am actually watching a film on a train, or whether in that situation I could tell machine A from machine B, despite it costing £200 more. And do I really want to watch movies on the train, when I could be working on documents or reading a book or a newspaper or talking to the person next to me, or having a snooze? Again, the point is that most of this process occurs outside Consciousness, perhaps only appearing in Consciousness at the beginning and/or end of the process.

Self-image & Survival

What does any of this have to do with survival? We tend not just to do things, but to have reasons why we spend our time doing them. And those reasons are often related to self-image. Am I the kind of person who watches movies on the train for pleasure or the kind that works on the journey? Do I work so efficiently in the office that I can afford to take time for fun when travelling? Or could I do that thing I don't have time to do in the office, and use the time more profitably? Images of different selves may jostle for attention. The Man Who Works on the Train. The Cool Guy who Watches Movies. The layabout who wastes time watching films. Which one am I? Some people feel that they are the same person all the time, but many experience that jostling for self-image. Am I fat/thin, attractive/plain, bright/dull, successful/unsuccessful? As arguably with everything it is a dynamic process. It changes depending upon our mood, how happy/energetic we feel. A tired man may give up working on the train and watch a movie and then feel bad about being tired and lacking energy. An energetic man may watch a movie and feel good that he can do that and also do his work around it. That may also be the same man on different days.

We may be intermittently conscious of much of this process of decision-making, but what drives us to make the final decision is likely to at the very least involve the Automatic, and most probably be dominated by it. Desire has its day, but desire is driven by self-image, and self-image is an important element of Survival. We do more than we know. We are driven by the Automatic and the driver is survival.

The Automatic is perhaps a much larger area than Consciousness. If Consciousness is an effect, the Automatic is a cause. There is a theory that Consciousness emerged from the unconscious. Neuroscientists often refer to Consciousness as part of 'higher mental processes', which may have two connotations – higher in the sense of more sophisticated, and higher in the sense of evolved from 'lower' processes. The first bears something of the marks of the reification of Consciousness. The second could include the Automatic.

My simple example of words appearing from nowhere suggests that there is a strong memory element to the Automatic. Consciousness does not have the capacities to store much information. We should perhaps thus see Consciousness as the active shop-window, the thing that gets our attention and possesses our attention, but as it skits from one thing to another the more mature (in the sense of evolutionarily older) Automatic is doing the lion's share of the work. Why does Consciousness skit around? Perhaps because its attention-resources are pointed in particular directions. Is this a homunculus thesis? It is not. The image of the brain is of a massively complex feedback process, driven by Survival and intrinsically part of the body. The Automatic has the resources, the complexity – for example to relate fully to the body, whereas we know that our Consciousness can only manage the occasional awareness of our bodies, such as when we have a pain:

'A considerable amount of data indicates that as compared to consciously controlled cognition, the nonconscious information-acquisition processes are not only much faster but also structurally more sophisticated in the sense that they are capable of efficient processing of multidimensional and interactive relations between variables'[132].

'Most of the "real work" (both in the acquisition of skills and the execution of cognitive operations such as encoding and interpretation of stimuli) is being done at the level to which our consciousness has no access. Moreover, even if the access to that level existed, it could not be used in any way because the formal sophistication of that level and its necessary speed of processing exceed considerably what can even be approached by our consciously controlled thinking. The "responsibilities" of this inaccessible level of our cognition are not limited to the "housekeeping" operations such as retrieving information from memory or adjusting the level of arousal; they are directly involved in the development of interpretive categories, drawing inferences, determining emotional reactions, and other "high-level" cognitive operations traditionally associated with consciously controlled "thinking".'[133]

In other words, the Automatic is so much faster and more sophisticated than

132 Lewicki, Hill, and Czyzewska: Nonconscious Acquisition of Information, see: http://cogprints.org/722/1/ LEWICKI. HTML 1992.

133 Lewicki et al., op. cit.

Consciousness that it cannot even be approached by the conscious mind. That fact may itself be a valuable clue to the nature of the relationship between the Conscious and the Automatic. If it has these capacities does it seem likely that Consciousness leads rather than the Automatic? One has to be wary here of slipping into language that goes around evolution in talking at all of leading or following as there is a danger in so doing of denying the mutuality of their relationship, something that they share with all brain functions as products of evolution. If the Conscious mind cannot approach the Automatic, that makes it harder to ascribe a leading role to Consciousness, but sounds instead like a contingent position. The Automatic has no difficulty in approaching Consciousness, as I know subjectively from having the words pop up into Consciousness when they are required. In that sense the Automatic 'serves' Consciousness, but even that simple example is perhaps worth dismantling & reverse-engineering. Mutuality is the rule of evolution – Consciousness and the Automatic are tied together for no man to put asunder. I have a vague sense of the word I am looking for, usually with related words that don't quite capture the meaning I 'want'. But what is doing the wanting, is it Consciousness putting out a request in the hope the Automatic will respond? That is what it feels like. Consciousness is asking a question and in some way I am not clear about, the Automatic responds. It is not a simple matter, like taking a word off a shelf courtesy of the Automatic, there is a process involved of matching the feeling I have with the word nearest to it. It doesn't feel as though Consciousness is doing that. It tries out words, but doesn't feel to have the resources to do the work of matching, pulling different words out of a void. Even when it tries out words, where do they come from? Are they too pushed into Consciousness by the Automatic? There would seem to be several processes involved but what they seem to have in common is that they are not present in Consciousness, or at least are only temporarily there for a brief second before Consciousness moves on. In this context, Consciousness feels like a shopper looking at things in a window, but it doesn't own the store or organise the window-display, man the shop or supervise deliveries, etc etc. That would all appear to be Automatic territory. It was the Automatic that decided Darwin to marry, not the conscious list of pros and cons that he drew up. Consciousness cannot be denied its immediacy, where would we be without it? But the amount and quality of work that seems to be the province of the Automatic confirms my instinct that is where most of a film goes, and reclaiming that material would tell us a lot about this still largely terra incognita.

Research to-date has largely been in the area of 'cognitive psychology', and it just might be that treating the archive of Cinema as a resource might offer new ways into the Automatic by finding out what viewers absorb, how it varies according to conditions and individuals, and how and when it finds its way into conscious ness.

'Unconscious knowledge is claimed to be qualitatively different from consciou knowledge and acquired by means or cognitive pathways distinct from those tha produce conscious knowledge (e.g., Greenwald, 1992; Reber, 1989, 1992 1992b; Schacter, 1992)'.[134]

'UTT (Unconscious Thought Theory) merely tries to account for the existenc of what it calls "the" unconscious in the empirically observed fact that peopl seem to make better decisions when they leave it to "the" unconscious to do th job'.

'Perhaps, in the name of a sacrosanct rationalism that still equates reason an other "higher" cognitive faculties with consciousness, the objective of many though obviously not all – critics seems to be the straightforward refutation c the hypothesis that there is unconscious knowledge.'[135]

The Automatic/unconscious still arouses great controversy over its extent an even its very existence. The resistance to it is perhaps partly a matter of th negative sentiments attached to Freudianism, but if the figures are accurate the only one part in a million of the information taken in by the brain is throug Consciousness. It would be odd for science not to interest itself in the rest.

Reason

'Reason is, and ought only to be the slave of the passions, and can never preten to any other office than to serve and obey them'. (David Hume, 1739). That i an unusual view of Reason which finds an echo in this project. I am rather dow on Reason, which seems a bit unfair, since espousing science and scientifi method seems at first glance to sit uneasily with an attack on it. Reason is bot a noble ambition, as I have said, and also the foundation of the achievements o science. However, the question here is rather more to do with what might hav been lost in drawing a cordon sanitaire between it and its opposite number, th passions, or Emotion. Where Emotion was declared beyond the pail the concern was with infection, the infection of unreason and the struggle, in an inhospitabl

---

134 Luis M. Augusto, 'Unconscious Knowledge: A survey', *Advances in Cognitive Psychology*, Review Article, 2010.

135 Both quotes from Augusto op. cit.

world of unpredictable nature, to keep irrationality at bay. The simple answer, but one that has only a relatively recent history, was to apply Reason – and scientific method – to Emotion. Dream Science and neuroscience more generally have bravely stepped in that direction, despite the resistance among the scientific community to compromising the cordon sanitaire. After all, it is always a huge task to keep both eyes on Reason even with the boundaries of blind testing under laboratory conditions of a well-designed experiment to rely upon.

Hume was noted for his distinction between 'is' and 'ought' yet is careful to include both in his exhortation above, making his statement all the stronger. To suggest that the subjective, the passions, are in fact in control seems quite advanced for 1739. Man's lot may be ineluctable subjectivity, but the fears associated with it, and the bulwark that science has tried constantly to erect against superstition and the like, make such a declaration seem rather brave.

On an everyday level we are perhaps all familiar with the quandary implicit in Darwin's List. Balancing pros and cons for any action is an exercise of reason in the everyday. But it is just such an exercise that a little insight, a little emotional intelligence reveals that scoring is no infallible guide to any decision, let alone to marry or not. The strictest adherence to Reason may produce a score upon which certain persons would be happy to rely, but as with the concept of Economic Man it takes a certain blindness, a certain autistic quality, what has been called a 'left-brain' attitude, to believe that is all there is to be said about the matter.

As with LCR tout court the question is less to do with the plusses and minusses of the individual ideologies in themselves than in their relationship with their opposite numbers, in this case of Reason with Emotion. The issue is about complementarity and balance. Hume put his head in the lion's mouth by his declaration in favour of the Passions, but his polemical intent, as mine, was perhaps to enter the lists on the side of the under-regarded side of the pairing. That was especially wise as he was a partisan of the experimental sciences and thus of experience, part of the challenge that he unknowingly set for Kant. While that position one would expect to involve a strict adherence to Reason and against any challenges to it, Hume was not so narrow.

The marvellous thing about science is how it can overturn centuries of our myth-making with sober investigation – I am thinking of Damasio's conclusions about Reason and Emotion. Who would have thought that Reason would turn out to be contingent upon Emotion? That goes against the most fondly-held beliefs many have, in fact completely contradicts what a straw poll might well

come up with as an answer. The small information-processing power of Con
sciousness compared to the Automatic is another case of overturning what migh
well be the assumption in the popular mind.

Science arguably shows reason at its best, but again it is not the thing itself tha
is questioned here but the ideology that has grown around it, that has oppose
itself to Emotion. The application of Reason to Emotion, as has happened i
neuroscience, is still regarded sceptically by some researchers – as noted above r
the unconscious. As with the left/right brain debate it is a question of comple
mentarity. Instead of an opposition between Reason & Emotion, understandabl
in an earlier age when the wilderness felt like a constant threat to civilisation, i
is their mutuality that is valuable. If Reason is contingent upon Emotion then i
is the ideology of Reason that needs to come to terms with that. The applicatio
of Reason to Emotion is underway in neurobiology, it is the application o
Emotion to Reason that has been left behind. There is an echo of the lef
brain/right brain in this too, the combination of focus and a holistic view tha
their potential complementarity can provide. *Affective neurobiology* is such
statement of intent in approaching the analysis of culture (Cinema) from th
starting-point of Emotion.

Vision

If there is one thing this project would like to achieve it would be to contribut
to increasing confidence in Vision. The issue is not the capacity of Vision, eithe
in quantity or indeed in the quality of what is actually seen, but in the ideolog
that seeks to dismiss, demote and denigrate Vision. It is not Vision that is th
problem, but again our beliefs about it. The strange thing is that those belief
would seem to be an odd combination of elements that might best be describe
as cultural, but using that word in the sense discussed later in relation to Cinem
that is cultural evolution in the biological sense, and not in the sociological o
anthropological sense. A large part of those attitudes would appear to come at th
behest of the element that sees Vision as the enemy, that is to say Language an
the word, expressed in a way that appears rather like an ideology, and for whic
I use the term Logocentrism.

At one time seeking an explanation for a prejudice against Vision and in favou
of the Word would have resorted to Sociology, History, Psychology, Anthropol
ogy etc. It would not be expected to look for and find an explanation in Biology

However, the research in hemispherical lateralisation, or right-brain/left-brain as it became known, came up with some surprising facts about how the left-brain 'inhibits' the wider sweep of the right-brain in order to focus narrowly upon solutions. To think of part of the brain having an 'attitude' is counter-intuitive, but experiment after experiment detailed the dimensions of such an attitude[136], one that did not only have its own way of doing things, as both hemispheres have, but – unlike the right-brain, the activity of the left-brain includes 'inhibiting' the activity of its opposite number. There are good evolutionary reasons for such behaviour, helping to achieve smooth and efficient operations, but the designs of evolution have different criteria to what may be to man a desirable outcome. In this case the holistic approach of the right-brain to issues being inhibited by the left's desire for a focussed solution.

The issue becomes clearer with the concrete example of drawing[137]. A left-brain drawing of a man is a stick-man – effective to communicate and fast to do. A right-brain portrait has the disadvantage that the detailed observation required for a portrait can take an hour or longer, but on the other hand there is vastly more detail and the potential for a lifelike representation. Klee called drawing 'taking a line for a walk', and a portrait is a long walk where a stick-man is a single step. The value we might place on a Leonardo sketch compared to the stick-man gives an indication of the nature of the comparison. Yes, both show a man, but if we were to look at art by that criterion alone, how much poorer would we be? The modern world is often on the look-out for stick-man solutions in many spheres of activity but what suffers comes under the heading of Quality of Life.

My campaign for Vision has the belief that we see everything but know almost nothing. Descartes declared Vision the noblest and most comprehensive of the senses and it is the implications of that notion this project pursues[138]

We see what is in the minds of others (the *Shared Circuits* of Christian Keysers), something centuries of philosophers have confidently claimed was impossible. We see so much, all the time, without effort or conscious awareness, that we cannot possibly keep up with it or even realise that what we are taking in through our eyes is perhaps a million times greater than that of which we are aware.

The heart of the problem is that we do not realise what Vision does for us. We tend to think it, a matter of surface whereas the Word is a matter of depth. The

---

136 McGilchrist op. cit., Ch 2 has a useful overview of recent research findings.

137 Suggested by *Drawing on the Right Side of the Brain*, the inspiring book by Betty Edwards, Fontana, 1983.

138 Rene Descartes, *Discourse on Method, Optics, Geometry, and Meterology*, 1637, tr PJ Olscamp, Indianapolis, 1965. p. 65.

opposite is true. Language is, in reality, merely a servant, an inefficient translator of Vision that can at its Shakespearean best only intermittently manage to scratch the surface of the depth of meaning we sense in Vision.

Meaning comes via Vision. The depth of meaning that comes via Vision is not just a matter of quantity but of quality. We don't know what we are seeing when we look – in the sense that the volume of information is too great for us to accommodate within consciousness.

To return to basics – when we see a new face in a social situation our brains work overtime to provide us with a judgement about what we are seeing. The baseline are Will It Kill Me and Can I Mate With It, but beyond that there are a range of responses such as Like/Dislike. The dimensions of like/dislike are substantial – do we trust that face, are we attracted to it, is it like me, how are they reacting to me etc? Even in those simple situations the brain is processing vast amounts of information – both physical and more importantly, meaning-based, that is the kind of information that allows us to come to a judgement, make a decision, form an opinion about the face we are seeing. This is less psychological than biological activity at base (most of it being not conscious). We are deciding how to relate to the person and the criteria involved include things like symmetry of facial features, the size of eyes, whether the person is smiling etc, and at base these are all 'biological' factors in the basic sense that they relate to our instincts for Survival.

Vision produces information of the highest quality (depth, breadth, and intelligence – in the sense of mediated by Survival) and at high speed, and we are largely unaware of both. We know the world through Vision. I see therefore I am.

In the service of Vision

The contention of this project is that the proper role of the word is in the service of Vision.

Language tends, courtesy of the Left-Brain approach, to inhibit the activities of the broader vision of the Right hemisphere approach, there is 'a more diffuse functional organization in the right hemisphere compared with a more focal functional representation in the left hemisphere'[139], and the left hemisphere tends

---

139 See: 'Emotion Processing in Chimeric Faces: Hemispheric Asymmetries in Expression and Recognition of Emotions' Tim Indersmitten and Ruben C. Gur, *Journal of Neuroscience*, 1 May 2003 23(9): 3820 –3825.

o impose its 'functional'. In terms of Language that means a tendency to minimise or deny Vision. In IQ tests there a questions for 'verbal' and 'non-verbal' skills. It is like the terms Conscious and the un-conscious, the latter being denied term of its own. In the IQ case what is being denied by a certain ideology of Language is the importance and relative autonomy of Vision. We are not used to thinking of 'visual' skills. Visual articulacy[140] is not a skill on the curriculum. There is a kind of repression of the opposite, as with conscious/unconscious presenting them only as the negative side of the term rather than allowing them term of their own. The proposition is that instead of Language militating against Vision it is possible for it to serve Vision. It is not impossible to achieve that shift, does not require much of a change in the Word, but only in the ability to see Vision as valuable and therefore worth the effort of articulation, in other words question of attitude.

Take the exercise of trying to describe a painting. It would be less trying to describe your impression of the painting, what it means to you, than trying to work out what the painter is trying to do, what his aims were, why he was using particular effects. It is a question of mode of thinking, as in the experience I had of students trying to describe a scene of jealousy for a film. Their initial response was silence. How do we go about doing this? You could see the question going round in their heads. They were a small group and broke the deadlock by coming up with dialogue for the man & woman involved. They were not thinking how to *show* jealousy but were falling back upon *telling* through dialogue, putting the emotion into spoken Language. If you recall, I stopped them and forbade the use of dialogue. Silence again. I suggested ways they could think of what jealousy would look like in the behaviour of the man and woman – how they might stand in relation to each other, where they would look, what they would avoid looking at. They took to it quickly and were soon in the swing. It didn't take much, like flipping a switch from 'Left-brain' to 'Right-brain' mode. It didn't require new learning, just a small shift in how they were approaching the problem. Their inexperience in articulating visually was very evident, but not a crippling problem, merely a matter of habit. They were using the same skills of Language, but just in a different way. Show not Tell is the basic commandment in writing (including the novel). The skills were already there, it just needed that shift in thinking, a difference in attitude.

Language has a tendency to ignore or replace the Visual with its own mode, its own narrow focus. When it is asked to articulate the visual it is perfectly capable

140 See note below on Visual Articulacy.

of so doing, changing mode almost immediately, almost like switching a light o
in a room. It is perfectly possible and practical for Language to articulate Visio
– and in so doing to serve it, to move from trying to master it, to dominate an
inhibit its mode, to becoming its servant, using its resources to attempt to t
adequate to the expression of Vision.

The irony of Vision is that we take it for granted. With Language we constant
practice the search for the right word, working to bring it to consciousness. W
are often aware of the gap between the meaning we are trying to grasp and th
poor imitation that is all that the Word is able to serve up. Language is a practi
that fills our waking hours. With Vision we are not conscious of learning to s
as we are conscious of finding the right word. Vision does the work for us, main
beyond our consciousness. Because we are not aware of that work for the mo
part, the practice of vision is by and large not part of our conscious lives, whi
constant labour is required to produce the right word. It is only natural that w
appreciate that effort, one that is always with us, always playing in our consciou
ness, whereas Vision just gets on with it and is rarely rewarded with a place in th
scarce resources of the conscious mind.

The quality of Vision

The suggestion here is that Vision is both vastly older and vastly wiser than th
word. As we are largely unaware of the practice of Vision we are also unaware
the quality of information that the eyes take in every second of our waking live
It is also possible that our non-waking lives, the hours of sleep and dreamin
whose key difference is the lack of visual input from the outside world, that is ou
eyes are closed, have the major function of a down-time sorting of the massiv
visual input from the waking hours of Vision-on, a housekeeping functic
including sorting through imagery for storing as memory. In other words, slee
exists for warehousing Vision. 'Shut-eye' is so important that around a third
our lives is devoted to stopping visual input and sorting that which comes fro
the other two-thirds. That fact alone suggests the substantial significance
Vision in human existence.

The scale of operations of vision is demonstrated in a paper entitled 'One pictu
is worth at least a million neurons',[141] which concludes: 'A careful estimate show

141 Levy, Hasson, and Malach, 'One Picture Is Worth at Least a Million Neurons', *Current Biology*, Vol. 14, 996–100
8 June 2004.

hat at least a million neurons in object-related areas and at least 30 million neurons in the entire visual cortex are activated by a single-object image (e.g. a photo of a face*). This estimate has important implications for theoretical models of object representation, since it implies an enormous cortical storage capacity'(*my addition).

The simple question for the experiment was how many neurons participate in the representation of a single image? They found that 'a single face image activated between 30 and 300 million neurons in the entire visual cortex ... A single house image activated between 40 and 400 million neurons'. The paper concluded that the results are compatible with a recent study showing that the brain's normal energy consumption allows a ceiling of about 30 million concomitantly active neurons'.

The founding instinct for this project was that we take in much more from a film than we realise, 'we see more than we know'. In other words the amount of information of which we are conscious when watching a film is but a fraction of the real amount that is going into our brains. As a film viewer there are times when I am aware that there is much more information coming to me from a film than I can grasp, the feeling that it is slipping away from me even as I watch, but it is there if I could put the process into slow-motion. That might possibly come from a greater attention to what a film is doing in a narrative sense than most viewers would be conscious of, as a film-maker, but it gives an inkling of how much more information there is, in *Mildred Pierce* for example, than my conscious mind can deal with at any one time. It was that feeling, that I also had with *Vertigo*, *The Searchers*, and more recently with an episode of the net-drama *House of Cards* (2013) as further examples, that confirms my conviction that Cinema[142] is vastly undervalued in both the amount and quality of information it has the potential to communicate.

The contention here is also that information is likewise inevitably vastly greater in both quantity and quality than the word can possibly manage. In other words Cinema is a superior medium to Language, despite all the cultural prejudices to the contrary.

It can certainly be argued from the science that the quantity of information is far greater in Vision than the word, but what is the argument for quality? That depends on a further instinct, that the depth and breadth of information we automatically absorb through Vision reflects the quantitative superiority that

142 That *House of Cards* episode was directed by Cinema director, David Fincher.

information-science has long-claimed. In other words not only do we see more but we see deeper than we realise, both much more and much deeper.

When we meet a person for the first time, we make up our minds about them in a fraction of a second. Survival and reproduction. In that split-second decision imagine how many variables are involved that result in the judgement. It is said that we gain something like 90% of our information about the world from faces. The human face is a magnet to us, something we search for information automatically, unconsciously. What is the nature of that information that we derive from looking at a face? At base I would suggest it is emotional information that we seek, and by emotion I mean simply information relevant to the kill/mate basic options. Liking a face can mean all sorts of things. This person is like me, not like me. S/he is friendly, attractive, untrustworthy, hostile etc etc. There are many nuances in how we react to another face, but the argument here is that they are all connected, proximately or distantly, to the basic pairing of kill/mate.

In contrast if you look at a cow you may not be sure what to think. Does it look friendly, sweet, nice or the opposite, just like humans? Cows are perhaps less rewarding than dogs, about which famously we can endlessly speculate on their 'human' attributes. When human qualities are present we gravitate towards them, when they are absent we tend to superimpose them without strict regard to reason. We are primed for human faces because so much depends upon it. The city is a jungle of human faces that we negotiate daily. Every face we notice is a challenge to our judgement. And that process of judgement never fails to operate, to process large amounts of information in order to deliver a decision related, closely or distantly, to Will It Kill Me or Can I Mate With It?

I feel sure that the information we gain from faces is no simple matter. Making up our minds in a fraction of a second is not an easy process. Neither is it, for the most part, conscious. What we are doing when we come to an almost instant judgement is using the part of our brains beyond the conscious in order to process the information that informs that judgement, the criteria of judgement. The brain is whirring away, in order to reach a summary view in that fraction of a second. We may revise that view later when we realise an attractive face is part of an unattractive personality or vice versa. That initial judgement may not be perfect. It works with what information it has and reaches a judgement based on that. Further information later may lead to an adjustment or correction. That feedback loop is how the brain appears to work in general, whether checking if the Tiger has seen us across the clearing or deciding that nice-looking person is rather nasty.

120

One of the reasons for the dominance of narrative Cinema is that it provides settings for us to carry on that activity – looking at faces. The invention of the close-up was more than a convenience, it was an echo of our biological need to inspect the faces of other humans. In the process of a film we gain more and more information about the hero/ine in particular, often from their person, sometimes from the reaction of other characters to them. Just like in life. One of the skills of film-making, one of its requirements in fact, is that we learn new information in each successive shot, and amongst the most valuable information is that we gain about the main character. We are building up a store of information about the character, their motives, their personality, indeed their character. Is *Mildred Pierce* a good mother or a bad mother, smart or a dupe, a snob or a successful entrepreneur? With each successive scene we learn more, from her behaviour, from her face, her body-language and from how Wally and Monty and Veda react to her, and how it changes. The narrative film is a ceaseless engine of change and in a film of emotional complexity like *Mildred Pierce* we have a hard time keeping up, while at the same time somehow always knowing where we are. That balance is a not an easy achievement and I argue later that it is a mark of the great achievement of Classical Hollywood, and as with Cinema in general, one still hugely under-appreciated in its complexity and sophistication.

'Vision just happens to be the most efficient mechanism for acquiring knowledge and it extends our capacity to do so almost infinitely' (Semir Zeki, *Inner Vision: an exploration of art and the brain*, 1999, OUP, Oxford).

If many times more information goes in through the eye than we know about then it is reasonable to assume that it enters the unconscious. We know from many experiments that people can recall things they have seen but of which they are not conscious. The question is what is the nature of that information? My proposition is that it would surprise us to find out both the quantity and *quality* of information that we absorb, its depth and complexity, the kind of information that leads to us making judgements about other people. Christian Keysers' experiments suggest that what he calls Shared Circuits automatically and unconsciously have us emotionally empathise with others – in social situations and with actors on the screen. For Keysers, Shared Circuits are the emotional extension of the mirroring we do physically through the earlier discovery of Mirror Neurons. It is not a question of choice, but something that happens as a matter of course as that is how we relate to others. It may well be that Shared Circuits are an exaptation of the mechanism of Mirror Neurons that evolved at a fast rate as man started to live in larger and larger settlements, leading to town and then cities. It would make sense that we adapted more basic survival skills to this new situation. While such skills would have been undoubtedly useful in the wild, as it were, meeting new faces constantly in a city means the skills involved are exercised more regularly.

My feeling is that all the kinds of information we gather about others that we assume is the product of the exercise of consciousness is in fact almost exclusively absorbed unconsciously, automatically as it were. We already know that attraction, for example, is largely unconscious, and it is clear that the amount of information involved in us coming to a judgement about whether we are attracted to someone is complex and sophisticated, involving millions perhaps billions of transactions in the brain in fractions of a second[143]. Those transactions involve things like the characteristics of the face, down to basic physical elements of line colour and shape, moving up to the size and shape and colour of eyes – a big feature in our decision-making processes – the poets' windows on the soul. The basic survival questions of Will It Kill Me or Can I Mate With It transmute into attraction/repulsion, which in turn may appear in our feelings as 'S/he is my kind of person' or the opposite. That kind of feeling is a translation of the survival issues, a soft version, as it were. When we are unaccountably drawn to someone, wish for their interest, their good opinion, their liking us in return, the information involved is neither simple nor basic – as much as it flows from basic issues of survival. To put it a little dramatically – we don't know what we know – we are not consciously aware of the information we have gathered and the decisions we have made unconsciously about the other person.

My suggestion is that those judgements are of great depth and complexity, and far more so than anything we would even be able to give voice to. The process involved, I would argue, is much more sophisticated than we normally allow. It involves a constant shuttling between the conscious and the Automatic, but with the vast preponderance of work being done in and by the latter.

Another way of looking at that as a proposition is the notion that therefore we don't know what we are doing and why we are doing it. We are creatures of the Automatic, in fact, rather than our rather romantic notions of conscious actors of free will in control of ourselves and our destinies. Our identities are likewise fragile coalitions standing on constantly-shifting ground, subject to desires and pressures that we are at best only aware of fragmentarily as our Conscious minds move at electrifying pace and with extraordinary versatility from one thing to

143 The Hasson experiment suggests up to 400 million neurons are involved in a single image of a house. op. cit. (105)

another, from one dimension to another. Consciousness may be agile in some senses but its capacities are arguably tiny, factors which may perhaps be linked.

My feeling is that almost everything we know comes through the channel of Vision. On figures alone no other input channels come near it, with touch second-best, bringing around a tenth of the input from the external environment. Quite where quantity becomes quality is difficult to identify, but my sense is that insights we commonly put down to Language, Consciousness and Reason arise unconsciously, emotionally and in Vision. In other words in reality we know the world through our eyes. Even the empathy Keysers discovered into what is in the mind of others arises unconsciously and visibly. We don't *think* about what someone else is thinking and then work it out. We sense it and know it through our senses.

It seems to me a point of some significance that the way we believe ourselves to apprehend the world is largely erroneous. Language has no generative role but is only a medium of translation – from Vision. Philosophers have generally assumed we could not know what was in the minds of others, and in a literal, 'left-brain', slightly autistic way, that is quite correct. We don't have an image of their ideas floating up before us like subtitles over their visage. We don't know in a literal way what the content of their thoughts are. What we do know, as Keysers discovered, is the emotional tenor of how they are feeling, and the medium in which we empathise is Emotion.

That shift in perspective, in mode, in *what we are looking for* is the revolution Keysers' discovery constitutes. If you look in the wrong place you don't find what you are looking for. The modest revolution is that Philosophers were perhaps looking in the wrong place. 'Left-brain' skills blind the observer to the 'right-brain' possibilities which as a consequence get overlooked. Looking for thoughts in the head is a rather literal idea.

The concrete implications of what appears to be the current imbalance between left and right modes are suggested by this example and may go some way to explaining the 'unreasonable ineffectiveness of philosophy' declared by the Nobel physicist Steven Weinberg.[144] On the other hand there are a couple of reasons for optimism. Firstly, I take the view that a modest rebalancing may well be easier than it would sound, as with the example of my film-students and visual articulacy, an easily attainable shift from elements already in play rather than anything more radical. Secondly, there are signs that current changes in the

144 Steven Weinberg, *Dreams of a Final Theory*, Vintage, New York, 1993.

Internet – specifically the trend of migration to video from text on websites, and the Instagram app (photos) capturing a market that Twitter might have thought it would inherit – both conceivably examples of the Word in retreat and Vision advancing.

The implications of this suggested quality of seeing has particular implications for our understanding and appreciation of Cinema, an issue taken up in the next section.

Left brain/Right brain

The Nobel Prize-winning work on 'hemispherical lateralisation' initiated by Roger Sperry, is relevant to the battle between LCR and VAE. Sperry discovered in the 1960s that the two hemispheres of the brain, later called 'left-brain' and 'right-brain' by Michael Gazzaniga, Sperry's graduate student, had rather different 'characters'. Popularisation of the concept led to the idea that individuals were either 'left' or 'right' brained, which was not supported by the results at the time or since. The later idea among researchers was that both sides handle all the functions but with different emphases. Both sides are in constant communication, but there was a lingering sense that the 'left' actively interfered with the activity of the right, or 'inhibited' it, as some researchers put it.

That led to a notion that left and right were two opposed world views, two conflicting ideologies, and that too much left-brainism had a range of deleterious effects[145]. Although that broadly fits with my sense of a certain aggression by the word towards Vision (Martin Jay gives chapter and verse in the context of French 20th Century culture, and indeed much further afield[146]), it would seem to me potentially dangerous to move from identifying different characteristics, even 'inhibition' by the left, to conclude there is a full-scale battle of ideologies between the two sides of the brain. Such a characterisation runs the risk of superimposing one mode, ideological views about the individual and society, on the biology of brain function, epistemologically a rupture between modes, a grid-shift.

As an analogue for my feeling that there is antagonism between the 'ideology' of the word and its attitude towards Vision, what evidence is there of a similar sentiment between the left and right hemispheres? One study suggested anger

145 see McGilchrist, *The Master and the Emissary*, Yale UP, London, 2009.
146 Martin Jay, *Downcast Eyes: The Denigration of Vision in 20th Century French Culture*, op. cit.

124

and aggression was a particular left-brain quality,[147] with that particular element apparently confirmed by a follow-up study.[148] Aggression, as with all brain-function, expresses an adaptive advantage in, for example, inhibiting fear. It is also associated with positive qualities of determination and confidence. Aggression in itself is functional, but moving from that, including resulting inhibition of right-brain functions, is a different question where that involves judging whether the left's aggression towards the right is dysfunctional. That seems to be a shift from the biological to the moral. To judge an evolved response as good or bad jumps the rails of analysis to alight in the world of ideology, reading back into experiments on evolutionary principles a political agenda, mixing Nature and Ideology.

That question mirrors the opposition I suggest between LCR and VAE, or to take the principle example, between Language and Vision. Is that making the same 'grid-shift' between the way the brain works and ideology? Language has, for example, been identified with 'left-brain' modes and Vision with 'right-brain' modes. Language is a product of evolution just as is Vision. On the other there is a clear difference between hemispherical lateralisation as a biological reality and the ideas about LCR that is the concern here. It would not be wise, as noted above, to suggest that LCR is changed through, for example, biofeedback exercises to change their nature, as might be suggested for left-brain approaches in order to stop inhibition of right-brain functions. The complexity of the ecology of left/right relations should warn against unintended consequences of that kind of manipulation.

It might be more sensible to regard these differences as analogues of important differences in our beliefs about how to approach issues of all kinds, rather than literal ideologies belonging to one or other hemisphere. The question then becomes one of balance and which approach is right in particular circumstances. For my purposes here it would be most helpful to suggest that inhibition of the left and encouragement of the right is what the world needs, but that seems to me to be something of a nonsense. While one may identify an opposition to Vision and a presumption in favour of the word, in 20th Century French culture (Martin Jay has given striking evidence of the latter), it is perhaps a confusion of modes to suggest interfering with the hemispheres of the brain to correct that imbalance.

147 Indersmitten, T. & Gur, R.C., 'Emotion processing in chimeric faces:hemispheric asymmetries in expression and recognition of emotions', *Journal of Neuroscience*, 2003, 23(9), pp. 3820–3825. Quoted in McGilchrist, op. cit.

148 Geiger A, Kaufmann J M, Schweinberger S R, 2004, 'Chimeric faces reveal hemispheric contributions to emotion processing', *Perception* 33 ECVP Abstract Supplement.

The imbalance is perhaps due to the nature of industrial societies and their emphasis on production, speed and efficiency. A stick-man drawing versus a careful portrait; the first takes moments, a portrait-drawing hours. Where results rather than aesthetics are the priority then stick-man wins every time. It is perfectly appropriate to question priorities of production, exploitation of natural resources and our relationship with our planet, but to confuse that with tinkering with the brain would seem to be potentially dangerous. Quite how industrial values influence philosophers I do not know, except that it may well be that adaptations that create the culture of an industrial society permeate other spheres of life, so that the Academy, in its own way, is infected by those values. The Academy itself, as a producer of Education, Degrees etc is tied in with industrial society, and the mirroring of factory-production by Research-production is not unfamiliar in Higher Education in Britain.

The Logic of Nature

The contrast I wish to draw here is between philosophy that largely ignores evolution and one that returns, as it were, to nature. Philosophy seems to have departed from the consideration of nature in part through the influence of Kant and his aim of asserting the autonomy of Reason. He also laid claim to a certain autonomy for philosophy, claiming its own kind of truth as against scientific truth derived from the experimental method of Newton. The contemplation of nature, its observation and the attempt to understand its laws were at the heart of both 'Natural Science' and 'Natural Philosophy', but Kant rather claimed a license that seemed to lead philosophy further and further away from a connection with nature, with deleterious effects. The gap between philosophy and science is now so great that very few philosophers concern themselves with the natural order and the laws of nature. Despite the enormous impact of Darwin's ideas, philosophy carries on largely independently and appears both blind to and unconcerned with science.

The pervasive influence of ideas about Evolution on neuroscience and the relatively recent incorporation of Emotion within the paradigm of scientific method make the gap between philosophy and science of increasing concern. When a Nobel physicist like Steven Weinberg writes of 'the unreasonable ineffectiveness of philosophy' the warning signs are plain to see.

The logic by which evolution proceeds is famously not teleological but has direction. The overlapping systems found in the brain do not just repeat functions redundantly but provide different angles of approach, a failsafe that covers all possibilities. It would seem to me, admittedly neither philosopher nor scientist, that philosophy is 'misinformed' in failing to try to understand how nature operates. It fails to address the questions to which it should devote energy and instead wastes its efforts in a variety of other directions than the essential. A certain humility before nature would appear to be long overdue for philosophy to overcome the accusation of being academic in the worst sense of the term.

Art & Science : Aesthetics & Brain Function

Metaphor

We are used to thinking of metaphor as a literary technique but it has been suggested (by Ramachandran[149]) that metaphor is also one of the fundamental ways in which the brain works. The method of comparison is not an isolated feature of brain functions and relates to Mirror Neurons and Shared Circuits, which facilitate connection by mirroring, and 'confabulation' which facilitates connection to rationalise diverse stimuli into a biologically meaningful relationship.

If metaphor is a brain-function then it is a product of evolution and historically would clearly precede the use of that method of operation adapted, or 'exaptated' as the term suggested by Gould puts it, as a literary technique. Exaptation adapts something evolved for one purpose to serve quite a different purpose, and metaphor as a literary trope would exemplify that process.

That conception shifts the perspective radically – from a local matter of literary technique to a matter of evolutionary timescales. It would also serve as an example of how genetic evolution transmutes into cultural evolution – as a biological process. What was a genetic evolution of brain function evolves within human culture as part of the evolution of Language, which some accounts put as beginning as recently as 40,000 years ago. The more things human society produces, as man's settlements grew larger, evolving into cities around 10,000 years ago and latterly into the Industrial Revolution, a matter of less than

149 V. Ramachandran, op. cit.

300 years ago, the more things there are in existence and available for Man's imagination to use to compare to novel things in the classic method of metaphor.

Narrative

The impulse towards narrative is a profound function of the brain, operating according to the biological priority of survival. It is no accident that literature, drama and Cinema adopted the narrative form and that it became in each case the dominant mode. As a formal system narrative has firm foundations in human biology, in particular in the evolutionary pressures to survival, and that connection also serves to demonstrate the non-arbitrary nature of the evolution of aesthetics (see Cinema section for more on narrative).

Identification and Shared Circuits

Shared Circuits are a recent discovery by the neuroscientist Christian Keysers, who was involved in the earlier discovery of *Mirror Neurons*, a process that began in the 1990s. Where Mirror Neurons discovered that a viewer simulates the physical reactions of a person being watched – for example in lifting a cup the watcher would internally go through similar physiological changes, only the actual movement would be inhibited by chemical inhibitors designed for the purpose.

With Shared Circuits the physical process becomes an emotional one. What Keysers discovered was that when we see for example James Bond with a tarantula dropping on his back as he lays in bed, we not only react physically but also emotionally. In other words our body/brain system mirrors the feelings as well as the physical character of the person observed.

Where theories of identification tended to suggest that a conscious effort was required to shift the audience from a passive to an active mode, Shared Circuits suggest that process goes on automatically, unconsciously and is not a conscious act of will or activation. Empathy is automatic and biological rather than conscious and ideological. (See Cinema section for more on Shared Circuits).

Each of these elements, the first in particular a literary trope, the second and third applicable to Cinema, give an indication of how neuroscience, neurobiology in particular, is revealing the kind of information about the operations of the brain that are highly suggestive about the origins and influences upon aesthetic matters that we might take at first glance to be remote from scientific analysis.

It is these kinds of advances in knowledge in what I would see as the useful combination of Emotion with neuroscience inflected by evolutionary biology – *affective neurobiology* – that suggest we are on the edge of being able to analyse art, in this case Cinema, with an unprecedented depth and rigour – brought by the application of scientific method to art – the beginning of a Science of Culture.

The key distinction is the adoption of a certain attitude – towards the testing of ideas, so that ideas are formulated in the light of the duty that the way they are formulated makes them eligible for the submission to testing.

It has been the dream of more than one approach to the analysis of Cinema, for example, to bring the discipline of science to bear upon the analysis of the medium. While the reduction of Cinema to Language presided that was effectively impossible. In freeing Cinema from the prison of Language and liberating it with the analysis of Vision, the promise of being able to properly apply scientific rigour in analysis of the arts hoves into view.

The prize of reuniting art & science, of bridging the chasm between the Two Cultures, is a notable one. I would suggest that it is now in sight, principally due to another innovation – the inclusion of Emotion within the paradigm of scientific method. That change is substantial, a key advance on the road to an effective Science of Culture and without which it would not be possible.

Art cannot be analysed in depth without featuring Emotion. With it all things are possible. In relation to Cinema, described as – 'In a word – Emotion' – the conjunction is a particularly happy one. If, to put it simply, science is Reason, and art is expression, then the perfect and necessary tool to bring them together is Emotion subject to Reason.

Similarly, without evolution analysis could not be rooted in time, as it were historically. It is the sense of evolution as a process in historical time that renders *affective neuro-biology* as a materialist project. Emotion, neuroscience, evolutionary biology – together I would suggest that they are capable of breaking down the barriers between art & science that extend back into at least the Eighteenth-Century and until now seemed incapable of being breached.

The extraordinary thing that science can do is turn our easy assumptions upside-down and inside-out. To realise that something as apparently based in

129

aesthetics, in artistic practice, in literary tropes as metaphor, in fact is not an invention of Language but has its roots before the birth of Language, in the very process of genetic evolution of the human brain going back *millions* of years, is a rather humbling experience. It is perhaps such a humility before nature that has been missing from much of human thought and in particular from philosophy. Arguably Kant's 'Copernican Revolution' turned into Hegel's 'Castles in the Air' and the triumph of a canny idealism, which in French thought of the last fifty years in particular, has clothed itself in the stolen vestments of a proper materialism, long overdue to be returned to their proper owners. I would suggest that the combination *affective neurobiology* holds out such a hope.

Art & Science: Emotion

The estrangement between art & science is about two different ways of thinking. Scientists have tended to regard art as imprecise and impressionistic and those on the art side have regarded science as narrowly rational and incapable of understanding the essence of creativity. When scientists have attempted analysis of art, it has usually resulted in generalities, categories that fail to get to grips with an individual work, let alone at a finer grain. The battle between the rational and the creative minds has produce estrangement rather than adding to our understanding.

The inclusion of Emotion within the paradigm of scientific method potentially changes that. Until very recently Emotion was excluded de facto as the opposite of and enemy to Reason, the foundation of science. It is still far from universally accepted by scientists but the example of neuroscience devising objective methods of analysing Emotion and Consciousness and also of Dream Science doing the same for dreams is not just a technical advance but potentially a revolution both in science and in its relationship to the arts.

If Cinema is, in a word, Emotion, then the significance of this development in neuroscience is obvious. The word is only the beginning. What are the connections between neuroscientific analysis of Emotion and a greater understanding of Cinema?

At its broadest, if we gain a scientific understanding of Emotion then that can be applied to understanding the power of Cinema in terms of Emotion. If we understand more about how the brain works in relation to Emotion it can potentially reveal the mechanisms of how Cinema works in our brains.

Although it is early days in the science of Emotion it is my feeling that there are sufficient indications of parallels between the way the brain works and the way Cinema works to make strong connections that suggest a new way of looking at Cinema. That approach is not merely novel but at a depth that completely transcends previous approaches. That may be symbolised in the contrast between the age of the Eye and that of Language. Language is a recent arrival on the evolutionary scene. Most analysis of Cinema has been been predicated, since its birth as a medium, on the notion that it is in some way a Language. The obvious fact that Cinema is a visual medium was put to one side as there seemed to be no way to analyse the visual, whereas the analysis of language was already established.

The rapid growth of neuroscience in the second half of the 20th Century began to change that situation and it is my contention that the arrival of Emotion on the scene is the critical development that finally makes it possible for Science to understand and analyse Art – and at a far greater depth than anything possible under an analysis derived from Language. The combination of neuroscience and Emotion potentially renders language-based analysis instantly anachronistic, the flat-earth of theory. Cinema is structured like a language as much as the earth is flat.

Our understanding of how the brain works becomes grounded in historical time as soon as an evolutionary perspective is brought to bear. While the historical scale of genetic evolution is almost unimaginable, it seems to be coming clearer that the shift from genetic evolution to cultural evolution, that is a notion of cultural evolution seen in a biological framework (rather than a sociological or any other 'social science'), also allows us to see evolution – in the sphere of culture – as something occurring at an incomparably faster rate than in an average genetic timeframe. The recent emphasis on the plasticity of the brain suggests that 'hard-wired' is a relative rather than absolute term in certain cases, and that the brain's adaptability in constantly making new connections suggests a rather different view of cultural evolution than that obtaining in the 19th and most of the 20th Centuries. When women went to work in factories during WWII their speedy adaptation to an unfamiliar rhythm meant that women were if anything better at detailed work than the men. In other words the notion that biology means determinism and is a socially conservative force now seems outdated and ideological rather than properly based on a scientific approach.

It has recently been argued that Darwin originated the move from genetic to cultural evolution in *The Descent of Man* of 1871, followed by *The Expression of Emotion in Man and Animals* in 1872. That combination of cultural evolution and emphasis on Emotion is fundamental to the ideas put forward here and, I would also suggest, offers the potential for a Science of Culture (not least of Cinema).

One of the great achievements of science is to turn our preconceptions upside down and neuroscience has a good and improving record in so doing. To see the Narrative impulse as fundamental to how the brain works begins to suggest a biological source for the dominant mode of Cinema. *Shared Circuits* and *Mirror Neurons* together suggest a physical and emotional basis for our identification with characters on the screen, and Automatically, unconsciously into the bargain.

I would therefore argue that one begins to get a sense that many of the fundamental modes in which we are discovering the brain works find their reflection in art, in literature and Cinema for example. It should be no surprise that biology underwrites 'culture' and art, but the resistance to biology based on its past reputation for sustaining a rigid social conservatism is more than enough explanation. It is perhaps the moment that resistance retreats in the current conjuncture – as Emotion takes centre stage and plasticity pits change against the rigidity of the 'hard-wired'.

There is no frame, shot, scene, sequence or film that cannot be explained with qualitatively greater depth and rigour through ANB than with any other framework, but it is not only the physical film itself but its whole ecology within a historicised neuro-biological framework that dwarfs previous frameworks of analysis. In comparison any word-based analysis is superficial. Language is a recent arrival in evolutionary terms and to reduce Cinema to Language as a precondition is a kind of ahistorical idealism. Where theorists have resisted that temptation, and there are very few of those, after that initial wisdom, it would appear that there is merely a relapse into another variant of idealist speculative philosophy – as though science did not exist – not untypical in the Arts and Humanities.

Plasticity of the brain

The recent discovery that, contrary to the traditional notion of 'hard-wiring', there is a degree of flexibility in the way the brain develops over the lifetime of the individual is important in the context of the image of biology on the left. Traditionally, biology has been accused of being on the heredity side of the old debate between heredity and environment. That led to immense suspicion that this nominally neutral science was in fact a weapon in the armoury of conservative opinion. The plasticity issue suggests that a change in that perception may be possible, resistent though such views often are to change themselves, ironically. The ability of the brain to make new connections, indeed its inability to fail to do so, has given succour to those who would like to think that society can change for the better, particularly in regard to the issue of equality between the sexes. As mentioned, during WWII women could easily adapt to working in factories when some of them had not previously worked outside the home, can easily be seen as an encouragement to social change. The idea that the plasticity of the brain contributed to that ability to adapt puts biology in a rather more positive light than it has previously enjoyed. There are many other aspects to this notion of plasticity as it suggests the brain more generally has great capacities for developing new skills – something that in retrospect seems obvious. On the other hand it would be a disservice to suggest that the matter is that simple. The relationship between nature and ideology is never going to be an easy one, at least until it becomes a greater priority to return to the view that it is more important to understand nature than to impose our anthropomorphic wishes upon it.

Emotion and the Automatic

Most Emotion is conceived here as unconscious and only fragments make their way into the scarce information-processing resources of Consciousness, and on an intermittent basis. Consciousness is constantly trying to assign meaning to the stimuli that it is handling at any one time, and that activity I have described as *narrativising*. There is a difference between the process of planning and reasoning as a neutral activity and the conception of narrativising as a survival-response. Stimuli are 'joined-up' in order to make sense of them, and making sense means deciphering them in terms of the most urgent priority, which is survival. Therefore the narrative mode is an evolved response pattern that makes sense of the stimuli present in consciousness. We make up a story that is tailored to the stimuli in sight, that makes the most of them in a biological sense of their value.

This conception assumes there is what might be called a 'cognitive unconscious', that is work of planning and reasoning that goes on outside Consciousness. My feeling would be that in fact the vast majority of such planning has to take place in the Automatic, yet again due to the limitations of Consciousness's information-processing capacity. The Automatic is wholly outside Consciousness, whereas Emotion is mainly so but refers, as it were, matters to Consciousness as part of the constant dynamic feedback process that survival requires to monitor threats of any kind, scale or proximity.

When is the Automatic not Emotion? What role might Reason (as the opposite of Emotion) play in the Automatic? If the Automatic does what researchers suggest it seems likely to involve strategy for dealing with external threats, what might be called a certain kind of reasoning. It would be reason in the cause of survival, as with Conscious reasoning, but in this case outside Consciousness. Emotion and the Automatic overlap substantially but the Automatic is never conscious, except perhaps in those momentary glimpses we get when it provides a word we have been searching for, apparently out of the blue.

4

Cinema

A. Cinema: a revaluation

Cinema as Vision plus

This project began with the feeling that Cinema was underrated, and that conviction spread to the wider issue of Vision in general. In fact, I argue that Cinema is a special case for Vision and deserves to be rated more highly than the general status I would claim for the noblest of the senses. While the same claims can be made for both the quantitative and qualitative superiority of Cinema as for Vision, the particular circumstances that Cinema brought together entitle it to special status as a particularly intense form of Vision. Audiences seated in the dark, looking at a single illuminated surface displaying Love, Hate, War, Action, Violence – in a word, Emotion, are taking part in a peculiarly focussed expression of Vision. Those facts we take for granted about going to Cinema are, viewed in the abstract, rather remarkable and a laboratory for Vision that ingeniously makes the most of its already extravagant qualities.

Cinema as Pure Sequence

A theoretical speculation[150] is that Cinema suddenly provided the first truly human art form, as it is visual sequence as representation of action. What gives man his survival advantage over all other vertebrates is the ability to catalogue the world in pure sequence. Other animals log sequence tied to space, pure sequence permits new levels of abstraction, making possible for example language & music. Man is thus not tied to the here and now of other animals, but can imagine a visual sequence from a few days ago, or one that could be acted out in the future,

---

150 Owed to Jonathan Edwards (see acknowledgements).

or relate to one that has just moments ago been on the screen before being replaced in the present by another.

Past cultural evolution leant towards language or singing, as conveying visual sequence visually is difficult. Cave paintings were static, but there is a wonderful painting of the death of Achilles, a sequence from left to right across the canvas, with successive images of Achilles' progress towards death, simply crying out for Cinema. Mime certainly brought movement, and it is still important in ballet and in opera, as often in the latter it is difficult to make out the words.

The key difference with visual sequence is that each element is otherwise a stand-alone proposition. Language has to build up propositions with strings, making it slow and limited. Cinema suddenly offered visual sequence, images strung together, succeeding one another before your very eyes. Sequence brings movement, the movement from one stand-alone proposition to the next, to the next and so on. Pure sequence marks out man from other animals, Vision from Language, and Cinema, as Vision plus, as a further advance upon Language.

As earlier sections of the book put it, the movement of Cinema is not just literal, in the sense of a physical movement at its most basic of a character across the screen, but also metaphorical in the sense of Emotional movement. That kind of movement has the potential to move us, that is move our emotions, and it is that movement which is for me a particular concern of one moment of Cinema upon which I want to concentrate.

A Classical Art

There is an instance of Cinema that can claim to have realised the combined potential of Vision and the Seventh Art to a high degree. It deserves the appellation of a Classical Art, and the description of the system that produced it as one of 'genius'. The fact that this peak of the medium occurred in a context that superficially seems highly inauspicious only adds to the ironies of the situation. I speak of the Classic Hollywood Cinema (hereafter CHC), in this case focussing on a mature period between the commercial high-point of 1939 and the end of that particular era, which I would date to around 1964, from *Stagecoach* to *Marnie* as it were. I argue that *Marnie* is the apotheosis of the Classical era, and in those ways a fitting end to that period. In a sense, *Marnie* is the end of Cinema.

136

Science, Theory & Cinema

From 1964, the year of *Marnie*, the theorist Christian Metz posed a number of basic questions any theory of film must answer, including: 'how scientific can analysis of Cinema be?'[151]. I would contend that his response led him, and countless benighted thinkers, teachers and students after him, in quite the wrong direction, right into the hands of the prime enemy of Vision and Cinema, namely Language, or to be fair to the relative innocence of Language itself, to Logocentrism – the ideology of Language. The ambition towards science was misdirected towards Saussure, an accomplice of Language, and away from the body[152], an error of substantial proportions with even more substantial implications. That Cartesian error was by the same stroke a turn away from the real materialism of science towards a King's New Clothes materialism that was in fact a variation on idealism in different garb.

Fifty years on, however difficult that may be, it is long overdue to turn that ship around, pose the question afresh and answer it in a radically different way. As Metz warily put it "Science is a big word". Indeed it is, but in the face of the 'unreasonable ineffectiveness' of philosophy[153] it is time to take on that challenge, one that can no longer be ducked and especially not in the name of the varieties of would-be-science that have held the field for two generations.

Cinema: Status v Power

Nearly all systematic attempts to analyse Cinema throughout its history have begun from the sleight of hand that suggests Cinema can be adequately understood by comparing its structure to that of language[154]. While that strategy is understandable where the analysis of language already has a place in the culture, it begs the question why it has not hitherto been possible to begin an analysis of Cinema with a conceptual framework based upon vision. The reason for that was

---

151 Quoted in *Downcast Eyes*, Martin Jay, op. cit., p. 465.

152 For an account of Saussure and the denial of the body, in what I would call an Idealist moment, see McGilchrist op. cit., p. 119. He points out the sign is not arbitrary, the baseline of Saussure's analysis, a point echoed in Ramachandran in reference to the bouba/kiki pairing. See Ramachandran op. cit.

153 'Philosophy' is used as a broad term here to include writers not obviously primarily philosophers like Barthes and the other thinkers in the tradition of 'Continental Philosophy' and behind what became known as *Film Theory*.

154 By systematic I mean to suggest quasi-scientific. Auteur theory, arguably an exception, began as a *politique*, propaganda for the Director as creator.

simply that there seemed to be no alternative basis upon which to construct such an analysis, a fact which led to my enquiry in the first place.

This reduction of the visual to the word I eventually came to see as a major block to a proper understanding of Cinema. The implications were that what was needed was a theoretical approach that could provide an understanding of the visual, something I would see as inherently foreign to theories based in the word.

The reason for that incapacity would seem to be related to the notion from studies in hemispherical-lateralisation of the different 'attitudes' of the left and right hemispheres of the brain. Each hemisphere has a distinctive approach to how problems should be solved which are potentially complementary and make a balanced whole, but has been argued that a certain reification of the word, a 'left brain' function, has led to an imbalance in western culture[155] and the result has been a relegation, even 'denigration'[156] of vision, which may be thought of as a 'right-brain' element, in favour of language. The result of that, in terms of Cinema, has been to undervalue and underestimate the visual aspect of the medium.

We are largely unconscious of what we absorb via Cinema but concomitantly aware of the rather small amounts of information going into the brain through conscious channels. We therefore tend to identify what information we are absorbing with that handled by consciousness, and that probably contributes to a sense that Cinema is an 'easy' medium that is rather obvious and requires little intellectual effort. In turn that tends to create a popular sense of Cinema as a largely vulgar medium incapable of much in the way of profundity, which is left in our culture to literature and music. Therefore, in western culture in general, and even more so perhaps in Britain, with its strong literary culture, Cinema suffers from a generally low prestige.[157]

In general, people look to other forms of expression for profundity and complexity of thought as Cinema ironically gives us so much at a glance that it is easy to take it for granted. That is partly tied in with a view of photography as mechanical reproduction. It is easy to take a photograph, most of what is in front of your

---

155 Jaak Panksepp, the leading figure in affective neuroscience, gives some support to the possibility of such a notion in evolutionary terms: 'The level of integration between brain areas may be changing as a function of cerebral evolution … ', in *Affective Neuroscience: the Foundations of Human & Animal Emotions*, OUP, Oxford, 1998, ps 426–427, n.19 – quoted in McGilchrist op. cit. p 244 – who traces such a path in Western culture (Chapter 7).

156 The term used by Martin Jay in *Downcast Eyes*, op. cit.

157 I refer principally to the commercial 'Hollywood' Cinema. In Britain there would generally be a perception that 'Continental' Cinema – French, Italian, German – is more intellectual – a sentiment that particularly came to the fore in the 1960s with 'Art' Cinema – through directors such as Bresson, Antonioni, and Bergman.

eyes is there, you have done nothing to create it, unlike the process of drawing and painting which can take many hours, days, months. The photo image is there as soon as you turn on the camera and point it at something in the world. The apparent ease of snapping a photograph without much, or indeed any, thought creates a natural reaction that what is so easy cannot have much intrinsic value.

The transformation of that mechanical ease into creation of an image that is highly expressive through light, framing, composition, the creation of atmosphere and the selection of the content of the image to contribute to an emotional reaction in the viewer is not something we often associate with photography, which is why for instance the photographs of Atget are so distinctive. Walter Benjamin described Atget's photographs of the streets of Paris as like deserted scenes of crime, with all the emotional connotations such an image creates.

On the other hand, we may take a quick photo of a friend on a night out with a phone-camera and think nothing of it – except for the face of our friend, whose memory and the memory of that evening it preserves. Faces are the way we focus our social interactions, we get that 90% of our information about the world from them, and make up our minds about someone in a fraction of a second of 'face-time'. The speed of that reaction would be even more valuable before cities existed, in the state of nature, when we met another human in a forest clearing we needed to make the fast decision is this friend or foe, a judgement that could be a matter of life or death. That hints at the idea that our visual 'skills' have a long evolutionary history, something that came to be important for this study.

The quick phone picture of a friend does not just show their face, but may have an atmosphere all of its own as the event was a party or a hen-night and we can see happiness or something else in the friend's face, other friends jammed up against her in a lively bar and she may have got too drunk a little later, etc etc. All this gives some indication of the vast amount of information that we may be processing from a simple snap, involving memory and emotion, and all that is going on behind our eyes, as it were, bringing up a whole range of meanings and feelings into our conscious awareness.

That notion is a way in to thinking about the real power of Cinema. If that is one image, remember Cinema is 24 frames per second and a film is 90 minutes or more. The potential for processing information in that time is from around 130,000 frames. The Hasson experiment quoted earlier suggested that a single (simple) image activated as many as forty million neurons, so one may imagine the scale of brain activity with all those frames in movement.

The brain is said to have around 10,000 connections for every neuron, and there are around 10 billion neurons. If we combine a sense of the scale of information input with one of the amount of activity within the brain, then we perhaps get some sense of what I would suggest is the real complexity of Vision, and thus by extension but more intensely, of Cinema.

Contrary to our cultural assumptions, one may call it an ideology, it can be argued that vision is a vastly more powerful medium than the word and that in fact the word is an impoverished medium of information in comparison. If we put it that 99.9999% of what we take in from a film is unconscious, and assume that only a part of consciousness is devoted to the word, then the scale of the superiority of vision and its dominance is the polar opposite to the dominant logocentric ideology.

Why therefore, we may ask, is it the common practice to assume that Cinema may be said be structured like a language? Deleuze is one exception among theorists who has stood out against that particular conceit, and also came out against the twin claim that the unconscious is also structured like a language[158] If that contention were true, the idea that we absorb such a high proportion of information from the unconscious would be less significant, as that information would be strongly related in its organisation to the rules that apply to language and Vision would have little to say about it.

However, it is suggested here that both assumptions suffer from the same error. One argument is concerned with the evolutionary history of the eye and language. Language is variously estimated to be between 40,000 and 100,000 years old. The geological record reveals[159] that the eye evolved between 542 and 543 million year ago.

The notion that language, of such relatively recent date – and probably evolved from visual warning signs and grunted noises – should set the agenda for a visual medium does not make too much sense. In fact, the contrary is much more likely, that language has many visual elements (gesture, body language, expression) that are key components in the communication of meaning, and came before verbal utterances. There is a notion that language is embodied vision,[160] which in this context seems to make rather more sense than other, idealist, theories of language.

The main argument is not about age but about quality, one that has been made

---

158 Despite that good start, Deleuze trod the wheel of Idealism, in another ingenious guise, in two books on Cinema.

159 From the period known as the Cambrian explosion, see Parker op. cit. (85).

160 See for example the review of such ideas in McGilchrist, Ch 3, op. cit.

above in relation to Vision in general. The point here would be that the intense focus in Cinema, the darkened room and the dramatised 'Pure Sequence' elements, added to the quantity and quality of information that Vision provides, creates a powerful experience for the audience, and one far in excess of anything of which Language is capable.

Language, Vision and the Brain

It is suggested here that Cinema is structured not like language, but like the brain[161]. The point is that Cinema as a cultural artefact (that is a product of evolution in the cultural sphere) evolved in such a way as to mirror some of the fundamental ways in which the brain works, a not unexpected conclusion when approached from a neurobiological perspective. The case is made in detail in relation to the Classic Hollywood Cinema, but suffice it to say that the precedence of existence of vision puts it far ahead of language in evolutionary antiquity. Similarly, the unconscious belongs to an earlier stage of evolution than consciousness and again would seem most unlikely to owe its structure to the recent arrival of language. In both cases it would seem to be putting the cart before the horse to give precedence to language. Language is the new kid on the block, quick and dirty, the sketch not the portrait, the stick-man against the Leonardo.

In contrast, Vision has both the 'wisdom' of age and the high volume of input, superiority both quantitively and qualitatively, and can therefore be argued to be more profound both literally and metaphorically. The question against that is why would evolution favour Language in certain ways as against Vision? In other words, if there is indeed a left-brain orientation to the current relationship between the two hemispheres of the brain[162], is that entirely a product of evolutionary forces and therefore effectively pointless to query, or does the plasticity of the brain of relatively recent discovery, suggest on the contrary that there would be no conflict between a re-orientation of the complementary relationship between the hemispheres and a broadly cultural agenda that sought such a rebalancing? In my simple experiment of asking students to stop using language to express an emotion in a scene for a film, the switch from the word to the Image was a switch waiting to be clicked rather than for example a major operation of biofeedback that could interfere with the ecology of the hemispheri-

---

161 More precisely, the body/brain system seen as one, as first expressed by Spinoza.

162 An argument made in detail by McGilchrist op. cit., with which I would broadly concur.

cal relationship, with potential unintended negative consequences. Add to that changes in the wider world such as the progressive migration of websites to video and the popularity of image-based rather than word-based apps for a new generation of smart-phone users, and a shift to Vision seems not so much unlikely, as I admit I used to think, as inevitable.

With Language more recent than Vision, would it suggest it is therefore perhaps more sophisticated, a later and therefore more advanced phenomenon than Vision? While it is a reasonable question, it is asked from the wrong end of the telescope. Evolution selects for advantage rather than design. Language has definite advantages, often the other side of the coin of its disadvantages. For example, a stick-man drawing may not be elegant or beautiful but it is quick as a communication tool. Language has certainly evolved to fulfil certain advantageous functions, but that is not the same as saying it is more sophisticated. It is a question of function in relation to survival and reproduction, rather than more abstract considerations of aesthetics or design. In other words recency is not a mark of progress but of function. It certainly adds to man's armoury in the field of survival, but that is quite a different criterion from sophistication or any other criterion of quality. The claims of Vision are untouched by the novelty of language, the mode of evolution marches to a different drum in which anachronism represents fundamentals, while novelty represents epiphenomena, effects rather than more basic causes. In that sense, Language may be twinned with Consciousness (as in LCR) in comparison to Vision and the Automatic, with Vision richer and more beautiful than Language.

B. Neurobiology and Cinema

In trying to make sense of the visual power of Cinema I kept coming up against a brick wall with the existing analyses based around Language and the word. The 'language' of Cinema is more than a mere metaphor. There is a more sinister aspect to the metaphor than it might appear. It is part of a systematic reduction of Cinema to the terms of Language, which is itself inherently unable to identify the key elements of how Cinema actually works, and thus might deserve the term literary reductionism. Searching for an understanding of the eye and how it worked soon led me to neuroscience, and the most grounded views in neuroscience inherently adopted a framework derived from evolutionary biology that brought a historical dimension extending eons before human history. This ombination of neurobiology suggested a number of parallels with Cinema that orms the basis for a new Theory of Cinema.

The eye and movement

Before the dispersal of the mists on earth, vision was of limited use, after it vision was pre-eminent. Seeing distance is not too much use in fog. But when the fog departs vision comes into its own. As a result vision developed at an accelerated rate during the relatively brief evolutionary period of a million years. In a general sense it is therefore not surprising that the eye should be so fundamental and important to humans. With such a history going so far back it would be odd if its significance was not profound.

The significance of the eye in relation to Cinema is perhaps more oriented to evolution than to plain neuroscience, if I can put it that way. One thing I noticed in film-making was how movement of any kind on the screen immediately catches the attention. Our eyes automatically shoot towards anything that moves on the screen. But why should movement be so attractive? The answer is evolution.

The reason the eye became the most important of the senses was that it was the most effective monitor of survival-threats. If it moves it might kill me. Movement is a key indicator of the approach of a predator. The importance of movement is a matter of life or death. This is not a merely physical matter where the eye responds to movement, but an issue of the most importance anything has to any creature – survival.

This analysis is grounded in survival. The matter of life or death is at the top of the food-chain of nature. I imagine a vertical axis with life/death at the top and mild-preference at somewhere near the bottom. Some issues are nearer to death, others are further away, but still connected. The other element of the image is a continuum. Death and shopping are on the same continuum. The tiger in the clearing is proximate to death, the choice of cereal in the supermarket aisle is distant – but crucially connected along the same continuum.

The eye follows movement on the screen. That might be thought of as the first moment of Cinema. Movement is not just a thing in itself, nor merely a warning of possible danger. Movement is fundamental to life, to nature. The one thing that is constant in life is movement, that is change. Natural life is about constant change from birth to death. In nature change is universal and undeniable, it is the one constant. When the train entered the station at La Ciotat in 1895, the audience may not in fact have felt fear as the myth goes – the train was not coming at the camera but alongside, as it was mounted on the station platform – but what was undeniable and new was that the images moved[163]. Movies. Moving images moving pictures. Movement.

We may be hard-wired to be alert to movement, to react to it as fast as the body/brain system is capable, but what was originally genetic evolution became cultural evolution. Our reaction to movement on the screen is a linear descendant of an ancestor's (man or ape) reaction to the movement of a potential predator in the state of nature. The significance of movement comes directly from the survival reaction, but over time it can adapt, 'exaptate'[164] to new situations of all kinds, and Cinema is one such manifestation, an evolutionary development in the realm of human culture.

Every film-editor knows, consciously and unconsciously, that movement is important. S/he can use that movement to reveal or to disguise. 'Cutting on Action' is an example of the latter. From a mid-shot of a character in the process of sitting down, we cut to a close shot, but the cut is not before or after the action but during it. The transition is calculated to smooth the jerk of cutting from one shot to another. The pace of sitting in the wider shot should try to match the pace of the sitting action in the closer shot. Cutting on Action disguises the cut, smooths it out, so that the fluidity of the storytelling rule is obeyed. Cutting on Action is one of the commandments of the Classic Hollywood Cinema, whereby a whole (local) culture evolved with the smooth invisibility of the technical sacrosanct in order to minimise the disruption to the audience's ability to concentrate on the story being told.

The brain and movement: emotion

While physical movement is a 'gut' reaction, perhaps from deep within the earliest regions of the brain's evolution, developed to respond to predator threat, my notion is that there is a parallel to that basic physicality in higher-order areas of the brain. In both cases there is the common factor of what I refer to as emotion.

I have offered the definition that emotion can best be defined as a reaction in the

---

163 The original moment seems in fact to have been in October 1888, in Leeds, from a different Louis, Louis Le Prince.
164 See Gould, S. J. op.cit.

body/brain system to an external stimulus. That reaction only occurs when a threshold is reached that identifies the stimulus as of significance, and the abiding definition of significance is biological value, that is in these terms, a survival threat of one kind or strength or another.

Emotion is thus a barometer of potential threat, an alarm-system. It should not be only thought of as external, as for example a key function of the body/brain system's internal monitoring is the maintenance of temperature at healthy levels for the body.[165] Any variation from normal temperature is a warning-sign that there is a problem. We are familiar with 'having a temperature', hot flushes, sweats etc – signs of departures from the normal temperature parameters.

The external threat is not a qualitatively different set of responses but it is crucially oriented to the body/brain system's environment beyond the body. Feeling emotional, when we see a child cry or a goal scored, are not unfamiliar feelings. They are reflections of negative or positive feelings that have their own proximate or distant connection to the fundamental pulse of energy that articulates them – life or death, reproduction, the basic forces of evolution.

Cinema is, as Godard put it, in a word – emotion. A film is a drama. Life with the boring bits taken out. A selection of moments in a story that are the most dramatic ones. The progress of a story over ninety minutes or so is a process of movement – emotional movement over time.

Where physical movement ends, as it were, emotional movement takes over. What we are attracted to in the unfolding of a story in Cinema is the fate of the hero/ine. We watch with interest, both in the sense of attentively and in the usurial sense of expecting a payoff. What we are watching is movement, change – the successive changes in the situation of the hero/ine, ups and downs, but always moving, towards a conclusion, a climax, a resolution. That is the way of the narrative film.

This second kind of movement, emotional movement, is the psychological equivalent of the physical movement that attracts the eye. Emotional movement attracts the brain, because emotion is the modus operandi of the brain. Whereas the attraction to physical movement is momentary, the attraction to emotional movement can last the ninety minutes or so of a film. That length of attraction is not remotely automatic, it has to be very carefully managed by the film-makers. That process of management was the quest that led to the Classic Hollywood

---

165 95% of such stimuli are in fact internal, according to Dehaene (op. cit.), but external threats are the focus here.

period I discuss below, an era of only around 25 years, which I identify as from 1939 to 1964, from *Stagecoach* to *Marnie*.

Emotional movement is a more complex phenomenon than physical movement but its basic condition of existence is that we are attracted to discover what is going to happen to the hero/ine. We may like the main character, but liking is not strictly necessary. Our attraction is not actually a matter of persons, but of drive we have to see what happens next to him or her.

There is an important distinction to be made here. Film Theory often talks of identification with the hero. The notion is that we suspend judgement and are drawn into a passive wish to put ourselves in the place of the hero, to be him or her. That conception was at the base of the brechtian idea that it was necessary to break that identification in order that the audience have a critical distance from the status-quo. In identifying with the hero, the audience was being drawn into complicity with the system, with capitalism and with bourgeois ideology.

The reality is rather different. We unconsciously mirror both the physical action and the emotional movements of the hero (and other characters, but to a lesser degree as classic narrative focusses on the main character). But there is no necessary sense that we suspend critical judgement in the process. We may be swept up in the story by the skills of its telling, but it is absolutely normal that we retain our critical faculties – how many films do you come out of without questions about the story or the characters?[166]

Narrative and neuroscience

In neuroscience there is a term for the tendency to create narratives from diverse stimuli, confabulation. In ordinary usage that term suggests lying and has a moral undertone. Such connotations are less certain in its neurological use, but it is possible to detect negative associations in the way some researchers use the term.

I want to put forward a radically different set of connotations for this narrative tendency, stripped of any negative undertones and in fact replacing them with positive connotations. In a number of different contexts in the brain a similar tendency to 'confabulation' appears. The basic factor is that given a number of

166 The aspiration for a critical ideological attitude from formal means is arguably another brand of Idealism.

iverse stimuli patients will tend to link them, even though there is no inherent
nk between them.

A further weakness of the term confabulation is that it suggests an activity that is
utside the mainstream, an interloper in the normal performance of the brain.
But what arguably seems to be the case is that, on the contrary, the narrative mode
s native to the whole way the brain works. This tendency to join things up is not
ccentric but central to the whole approach the brain has to making sense of the
world.

With Mirror Neurons for example, there is something similar, a mirroring activity
hat copies the physiological responses required to perform an action, but cut
hort of the actual action by an inhibiting chemical that stops us, for example
unching the person next to us in the Cinema during a boxing match on the
creen.

The narrativising tendency is not identical to what happens with mirror neurons
ut there is the evolutionary link of survival activity. With mirror neurons
opying to learn, as in learning how to feed by watching a parent's physical
ctions, has a survival function. Joining diverse stimuli to make sense of the world
lso has a survival function, we link them in order to rationalise the (highly-se-
ected) 'reality' we perceive into a form that explains the individual stimulus in a
onnected flow of meaning that acts as a guide to whether or not we are required
o take action, with the base criteria being survival, as in the avoidance of
redators.

What I suggest here is that narrative is a method of making sense of the world in
he context of evolution. It is not merely a literary technique, in fact the literary
echnique is an epiphenomenon of something more basic, the evolutionary
lement of survival. It is a literary technique second and a survival strategy first.
That is a pattern that is found in a number of elements that are thought of as
elonging to Language but in fact have much deeper roots in the evolutionary
ast.

There is also an epistemological, even metaphysical, element to the notion that
he brain works in this way. Reality is not available for our inspection and
omprehension – to the conscious mind – because the capacity of consciousness
s very severely limited – the old saw of us being able to remember a maximum
f seven things at any one time (in working memory). Out there, in the
nvironment the conscious mind focuses on those few stimuli from a vast
otential field. Its reality is that choice, those stimuli that appear in consciousness.

Reality is a representation. Actually, not quite yet. Reality becomes a representation when those seven stimuli, more often something like three or four (Consciousness can only handle a single thought at a time),[167] are handled in such a way as to make some sense of that infinitely larger field from which they have been plucked. The process of making-sense involves connecting them in some way, and that is what narrative does. Narrative connects diverse stimuli in such a way as to make sense of them. It does its best to make those few samples of the inherently ungraspable reality[168] out there into something we can use, and the prime use is survival. That is why the brain evolved in that way, in order to improve survival-chances.

It is an interesting thought, in addition, that this tiny sample from the vast field of possible stimuli that the body/brain system selects for the conscious to report back upon, belies the notion that we grasp reality, when we grasp consciously only a very small selection. Furthermore our reality is unrepresentative as sample, as it is selected according to criteria of survival, as I would propose it, and therefore a 'best guess' kind of calculation, based on a tiny number from a vast field of possibilities. Finally, it is also therefore both highly fallible in principal and wholly oriented towards survival. Our reality is a survival-reality, a conditional and contingent one.

It does not of course mean that every or even most examples are directly related to survival, because the principle of exaptation applies to this development as it does to many others in the brain. What was originally a technique developed for the prime purpose of aiding our survival becomes in time also usable in other contexts, of which Cinema is one.

Take the experiment (from Gazzaniga) where a patient is shown the three stimuli of a spade, a chicken's foot, and a shed. The patient has no difficulty in making sense of the three – the spade is for digging chicken-poo out of the chicken shed. In that simple example the drive towards narrativising, joining and bonding diversity into a coherent narrative is evident.

167 Dehaene, op. cit p. 20. emphasises this point.

168 This notion seems different to Kant's notion of the thing-in-itself, the *noumenon*, unknowable and inaccessible to our senses, as that refers to the world of ideas, which appear immaterial. Here, the sense – taken from current neuroscience – is both a material one that consciousness can only deal with a little of what is out there, and metaphysical one in that even if consciousness were to busy itself with acquainting itself with more and more things out there it would never be able to exhaust reality, not least as it is always changing. It is a nice point whether it a quantitative or qualitative matter, where the material crosses over to the metaphysical. With 'inherently' I might be guilty of suggesting a metaphysic but my assumptions are more practical – consciousness hasn't got the time.

Narrative is a native mode of the brain – and that would help to explain why Cinema developed as a predominantly narrative medium.

Not all films are narrative, but non- or anti-narrative films have yet to reach the mainstream. As a film-maker I struggled for many years with the idea of the possibility of an anti-narrative Cinema, and would not be the first to find the conclusions I have come to particularly welcome. While it is the case that most film-makers who have tried to make films outside the narrative tradition have in the end returned to it, does that mean the challenges are insuperable? In principle the plasticity of the brain and the pace of cultural evolution suggests that it is not impossible that anti-narrative Cinema will prosper, but the fundamental nature of the narrative drive in the brain suggests the hurdles are substantial. The drive to narrativise is so strong and ubiquitous that film-makers have a hard task to create alternatives with anything like the attraction that narrative possesses.

If the pressure towards narrative is so strong why have film-makers attempted to create alternatives? Art and politics are the two main reasons. Abstract artists would not necessarily resort to narrative as a first instinct and a broad ideology against Capitalism would encourage a quest for regimes outside those most associated with it through the dominance of Hollywood. A third reason, which was also partly my own, is the sense that one is limited in what it is possible to say by the narrative form. Every form has its rules, and with narrative they are particularly restrictive.

The excitement of the films of Godard in the early 60s was partly from the feeling that here was someone who shared that feeling and was putting things in films that were not permissable under the rules of the status-quo. His lightness of touch and fleetness of foot made that rule-breaking tremendously attractive. Using cartoon-imagery, words on the screen, not using lighting or anti-realist lighting, 'natural' sound in real locations, reciting poetry, adding a song where he felt like it, all those elements were so refreshing compared to the stultifying regularity of narrative, the familiarity of its tropes, the predictability of a happy ending, the claustrophobic feeling the rules created. There must be another way, summed up the feeling of the time.

Antonioni was another film-maker who came to prominence in the 60s and went against the traditional narrative model. His famous trilogy *L'Avventura*, *La Notte*, and *L'Eclisse* were perhaps less energetic than Godard, more narrative-oriented and classical in conception, but notoriously difficult for audiences to stay with, testing their endurance in the pace of the story and its lack of the thrills and spills of commercial Cinema. I strongly remember wrestling for years to find ways of saying other things than appeared to be permitted by classical narrative. These struggles were an everyday feature of my own attempts to make films in the 1970 and 80s, when the inheritance of the 60s experiments loomed large. That wa why a Godard or an Antonioni were such an inspiration, as, in their differen ways, they had found a way to go against the overwhelming dominance of the Hollywood model.

In *La Notte* there is a scene in a hospital bedroom, a couple are visiting a frienc who is ill. A helicopter is heard outside the window of his private room. The scene, not unusually in Antonioni, has a certain lethargy about it, as though the heat is too much, that life must slow down, that thought must replace action that people are uncertain how to deal with each other, what to say to each other what to do next. There is a majesty and magnificence in Antonioni, a determi nation to portray the world as he sees it rather than as the Hollywood Cinema would have it, a European independence and dignity that insists vulgar commer cialisation is a waste of the medium, unintelligent and crass. Antonioni's cinema is aristocratic rather than popular, one of those little ironies for an alternative tradition that rejects commerciality in favour of a liberal agenda that has associa tions of ideological opposition to the mainstream. But his Cinema is more a modernised Lampedusa than a call to revolution. That is not a criticism. But can I say these things? Is this tone appropriate? Does it matter if it is different from other tones in the book? Does a classical aesthetic impose the strictest rules that mean so many things cannot be said? Do I mean rules or should I say discipline A rule is something you are against. A discipline is something you respect. Such reflexivity was what was attractive about a Godard and an Antonioni.

The scene in the hospital in *La Notte* is quite difficult to watch. It doesn't provide the normal narrative pleasures. It may have pleasures of its own, but they are not immediately graspable in the context of our expectations of what films do, how they work. All the parts are there, or at least many of them, but they seem to be in the wrong order. Our conventional expectations are frustrated. What is Antonioni trying to do in the scene? His work is notoriously difficult to grasp and even where critics have tried, often they end up unable to put things clearly to really grasp themselves what he is about, instead stumbling about in explana tions historical, cultural, ideological, but not – in the end – Cinematic.

I would argue that what he is doing in that scene is clear, but from only one perspective. He is going against the rules of the Classic Cinema. The scene only makes sense as a strategy conceived in opposition to the classical model of

150

Hollywood Cinema. At each key point in the scene he does things differently from the classical model. That is what creates the disorientation in the scene for an audience, but it still only makes sense in relation to the Classic paradigm, in a kind of dialectical opposition to it.

The problem is that strategy is not easy to see, and the result is experienced by many viewers as simply boring. The fundamental problem is the doubt that it could ever not be so, that the gods of narrative won't allow it and laugh at hubris that imagines otherwise. That boredom always seems to have been the reaction to Antonioni, especially for the trilogy, and despite it being the best-known of his films. I love his films myself, but it is not hard to see how difficult they are for audiences, a difficulty that I am also of course aware of when watching the films, despite their chiming with many of my own interests.

Despite their remarkable achievements, neither Godard nor Antonioni managed to create a coherent alternative that gave rise to a 'tradition' following their example. There were influences, particularly of Godard, visible for example in films by Oshima and Bertolucci and elements in Scorsese and the 'movie-brat' generation in America, but in general they did not create a substantial-enough alternative to found a fully-fledged method strong enough to provide more than a fragmentary opposition to the classic cinema. The gods of narrative are strict masters, never able to be convinced that there are alternatives to their forbidding rule.

The difficulty arises because the narrative orientation of the way the brain works means that a narrative film is going with the flow, so to speak, working with the tide rather than against it. While narrative is a very strict discipline that excludes so many things, it has its reasons and those reasons are almost impossible successfully to contradict. Films operate over time, ninety minutes or more for a feature film. It is possible to attract the audience with fireworks for a short time, but to keep their attention over ninety minutes is just what narrative evolved to do. The task of an individual creating a coherent alternative to all that is perhaps just too much to ask of anyone. At the moment, narrative rules. With the plasticity of the brain and the speed of evolution of human culture it is impossible to rule out that new forms may arise and gain majority assent, but at the moment the power of the narrative mode and its inherent relationship with the very structure of how the brain works make it still an indefatigable force.

a. Narrativisation, Causation and Cinema

David Hume, in 1739, put forward the notion that man is primarily a creature of emotion rather than reason, and that reason holds a subordinate role in his makeup. Today, in the light of recent neuroscience (for example in *Descartes Error* by Antonio Damasio) that feels like a very modern thought. The contingency of reason has implications for our understanding of Cinema.

A central proposition of the view of the brain offered here is that it deals with diverse stimuli by spinning a web of meaning, of sense, that owes its biological value to survival. The process of creating a narrative therefore has a high biological value, hence the view here of it as a central pillar of Cinema – itself referenced as a concrete instance of Culture. Cinema is seen as nature in the realm of culture.

Arguably, there is an important step before the process of narrativisation in the functioning of the brain and that is embodied in the issue of causation – the cause and effect chain. Does causation come first, before narrativisation, and if so what are the implications for the theory?

Causation remains a big issue for science, one that famously dogged Einstein to his death. He worked out some of the basic principles of Quantum theory, but found them so contradictory to causation that he set out to disprove those discoveries, but was unable to do so before he died.

In the Kuleshov experiment (1917) the audience were said to interpret the first image (the neutral expression on the face of the actor Mosjoukine) in terms of the image that followed, for example a bowl of soup. The narrativisation that occurred was to project onto his face a feeling of hunger.

The meaning of the bowl of soup was open when viewed, only when the face came next was its meaning 'revealed', closed or determined by the audience. The face required an interpretation, or re-interpretation in order to bring sense to the two shots as a unit of meaning. The work of the brain was to provide a meaning to the first shot by linking it to the second shot in such a way as to make sense of the succession. We see the actor's face. What does that mean after seeing the bowl of soup? It means that the actor is related to the bowl of soup. The expression on the face is related to the bowl of soup. The relationship devised rationalises the juxtaposition of the two images – soup – food – face – hunger. Alternatives are possible to imagine – disgust, cold, too hot, etc etc, but arguably the simplest

152

route is taken: he is looking at the soup because he is hungry. Narrativisation plumps for what is perhaps the most direct explanation.

Survival requires the most rational solution, except the precise definition of what is rational raises an important issue. What is rational for survival is different from what is rational in the Enlightenment sense. When the criterion is survival, evolution has its own version of rationality. It is arguably *only* in that context that man is truly rational. He is driven by the Automatic and the Automatic is driven by survival. When a strategy dedicated to survival produces a reaction that best-serves that survival, that is clearly highly rational in its own terms.

However, another view of the construction of that relationship is causation – the cause and effect chain. The first shot is, as it were, a cause and the second shot has to show an effect – not quite in the conventional sense. The effect is that the audience conclude the actor is feeling hungry. The fact is that his neutral expression is the same as and indeed is the same shot as before. The audience reconstructs the image to fit in with the preceding shot – it constructs a story, or rather it constructs a cause-effect chain that operates at a different level.

To force the neutral expression to make sense in the context of the preceding bowl of soup the question here that the audience has to satisfy itself upon is why are we being shown a bowl of soup and then a man's face? The creative response of the brain is to come up with a plausible link between soup and man. Man 'looks' at soup because he wants it. He wants it because he is hungry. The solution is also an emotional one – the neutral face is interpreted as having behind it a feeling of hunger. There are a range of alternatives, as mentioned above, but hunger is a pretty straightforward solution to the problem for the brain. Even that imprecision, that vulgarity, if you will, is of significance. It is the mode of evolutionary survival, a 'least-bad' approach – in the way we humans might view it with our intellects and appreciation of design. The reason the brain does something is pretty straightforward seen from its point of view, and its point of view is always survival. The best may be the enemy of the good in that context, and survival will tend to plump for the good every time. An animal tearing the heart out of another animal in front of our eyes may be reprehensible to our finer feelings but it is the way of nature, and there also hunger is the motive. The hart has its reasons.

To go back even further let us not forget the role of the word. The audience *said* the actor looked hungry. What the audience was actually doing was searching for an emotion that linked with the soup, and came up with hunger. That mode of desire then was translated into the word. The audience drew a blank with the neutral face so had to construct a feeling, search for an appropriate feeling that plausibly linked to the bowl of soup, and 'hunger' was perhaps the most obvious answer.

In this sense narrative is an issue of cause and effect, but not a simple one as it involves a creative role on the part of the brain. It would be wrong to say that the soup caused the hungry look. The survival mechanism reached for the nearest plausible solution, a spatial analogy with Ockham's razor. But here we are some distance from the simple cause/effect relationship. The key factor is that the brain is hard-wired to look for a causal relationship, something which is also very useful for film-editors. It is the brain that 'caused' the hungry look, rather than the shot of the actor's neutral expression.

Any discussion of Kuleshov is unsatisfactory as it is a report of an experiment rather than the experiment itself. Kuleshov could be restaged to test the accuracy of the report. However, the general principle is familiar to film-editors, who are always asking themselves 'why is the audience looking at this shot?'. Give an editor the bowl of soup shot. Give her a neutral facial expression, and she will put the two next to each other, confident that the audience will interpret the link in the classic way – and this is indeed a creative input – and one that mirrors the way the brain operates. It is part of the editor's task to understand how the brain will react, and the Kuleshov moment is just such a question.

The issue is that we make sense of consecutive images as an emotional task rather than a rational one. A rational view would see soup and neutral expression and perhaps conclude that there was no particular attachment between the actor and the soup. It is only an emotional criterion, a criterion dedicated to survival, that needs to interpret that neutral expression in an emotional way, thus as a survival issue. It is that which turns neutral to hungry – otherwise there is no strong rationale linking the two images. That inflection to cause and effect hinges on the propensity of the brain to narrativise in the cause of survival. That is a significant reason for the dominance of the narrative form in the history of Cinema.

The major point that can be derived from this exploration is the suggestion that the age-old issue of causality can be seen differently through the conjunction of neurobiology and Cinema that is explored here. We can see from the Kuleshov moment that cause and effect in the brain is not as straightforward as logic, the logic of man as expressed in philosophical discussion, would have it.

154

The brain 'confabulates' a causal connection. The fundamental reason it does so is Survival. This perspective shifts conclusively the traditional 'introspective' view of cause and effect. For Enlightenment reason cause and effect is thought of as A bumps into B, thus B moves, here it is seen as we link the image of the soup and the face of Mosjoukine in a creative process that is not a fact but a fiction. It is not a rational link in the Enlightenment understanding of rationality. A cause does not produce an effect directly. The process in the brain is fed through the Survival criterion whose response is to create a fictional narrative that links the two according to its own lights. The perspective of Survival is not that of Reason. This decisive inflection arguably renders conventional notions of reason obsolete at a stroke in this particular context.

In conventional reasoning A bumps into B and B moves, therefore causality is direct and factual. In the Kuleshov moment (and in the Gazzaniga experiment referred to on page 23 above), it is indirect – in being fed through the survival criterion – and fictional – Mosjoukine wasn't hungry (or should we say showed no signs of being hungry). What Kuleshov/Gazzaniga show is that the way the brain functions is to create fictions with survival as the goal and reason. Cause and effect works in Cinema – the soup followed by Mosjoukine – because the brain interprets what it sees in the interest of survival – it deduces that Mosjoukine is hungry in order to make sense of what we are seeing – the stimuli presented to the brain. It is not 'true' in the traditional sense, it is functional for the brain's priority of survival. It doesn't matter to the brain that its interpretation is not true. Truth is not the issue. The odds on survival is the issue. The brain's job is to produce an interpretation of the stimuli with which it is presented that serves survival. Its task is life not truth. Philosophy, in contrast, has often been traditionally concerned with what is 'true' in a literal sense.

When cause and effect are thrown into doubt the door is potentially opened to a quantum view of reality. To introduce the notion of a different basis for reality parallels Einstein's tortured doubts about discarding causality – and incidentally confirms the tacit knowledge every film-editor possesses – truth is not the issue but plausibility – the fiction is truer than the fact (for the brain). With Survival as the overarching criterion it is possible to glimpse a different order of reality in nature to man's Enlightenment view. Perhaps there is something in the logic of nature, of evolution, of survival that relates to the branching realities of Quantum theory.

David Bohm, who worked closely with Einstein in the late 40s, gave an example of a greater reality (which he called the implicate order, against the explicate order of apparent reality) in the reverberation of earlier notes when listening to music. Compare that to the bowl of soup in the Kuleshov moment 'reverberating' in the brain when it is presented with the succeeding shot of the actor's neutral expression. The beauty of that moment is how concrete the evidence of the Mosjoukine shot is compared to musical reverberations. If we accept that the audience inserted into the neutral expression hunger, there is a decisive shift in factual reality that undermines the autonomy of the 'neutral' shot. That both confirms tacit film-making knowledge, that the shot is never autonomous as it is a link in a chain, and roots that relatedness (or 'implication' in Bohm's schema) to emotion. The mind of the audience inserts behind the neutral expression of the actor the emotion of hunger, for which there is no objective evidence. That is confirmed by the idea that the audience had previously seen the neutral expression before seeing the bowl of soup and that upon seeing his face after the soup, had mentally changed the emotion behind the face – an invisible emotion given the neutral expression – to one that created harmony between soup and face. What I term – locally, as it were – the narrativisation impulse, has a rather wider implication in the context of quantum physicists' philosophical questions.

A further interesting implication is that, unlike musical reverberations, shots in a film are relatively concrete and their effect upon an audience are potentially capable of forming part of an experimental design – could be tested, in line with the practice of scientific method. This is one benefit of taking Cinema as a concrete existing cultural phenomenon and 'reverse-engineering' into neurobiological questions. The opposite route of imagining how nature evolves into culture (e.g. through memes) is arguably a rather more difficult task than working back from an already existing cultural artefact with its trillions of historical & informal moments as raw material.

The brain is Emotion and Emotion is about survival. The contrast drawn here is between Reason concerned with man's (philosophical) notion of truth, and Emotion concerned with the brain's notion of plausibility in the service of survival. We see what we want to see, or rather what the brain's dedication to survival reasons it is seeing. David Hume, in 1739, and David Bohm two hundred and fifty years later were onto something.

b. Kuleshov, Hitchcock and the narrativising tendency

The Kuleshov experiments of 1917 were remarkable for two reasons for this nalysis. The first is that they betoken a scientific attitude towards Cinema, as though the Bolshevik Revolution was a liberation of the arts from subjectivity nd a desire to associate them with the modernity of science – through experiment. The second is their importance for identifying what I take to be a key lement of the new medium, the movement between images.

Hitchcock[169] took the experiment a stage further by adding the third-term, the eaction shot. With Kuleshov there are a series of double moments. We see the actor Mosjoukine, we see for example the bowl of soup, then the actor again, a rying child etc. What would appear to be happening in the reports of that xperiment is an interpretation not entirely borne out by the facts. The actor looks, we see what s/he is looking at. Cinematic logic of the moment when we eturn to the actor is that we read into his neutral expression a reaction to the owl of soup and then the crying child. But, in fact, that requires three shots – ctor, soup, actor. Only in the third term of what is effectively a syllogism do we get the conclusion – the reaction of the actor to the bowl of soup.

t is a matter of the greatest concern to the conception of Cinema that I put orward here that the actor's expression is neutral. The essence of Cinema is that ve project onto that neutral expression sentiments effectively derived from the previous shots. Actor/Soup/Actor requires that third shot in order to create a change – a response (at least in our heads) to seeing the bowl of soup. The Kuleshov story is that the audience marvelled at how hungry the actor looked. The key factor is that of the emotional movement encapsulated in that third term. Whether it is facial movement or none, we – as in the Kuleshov conception – interpret the connection between the face and the image in a second shot of the face in which it reacts to the first pairing, and there is a movement that constitutes a reaction and closes the syllogism.

t was in fact Hitchcock who saw the syllogism clearly, a building block for his conception of suspense. The classic situation is that we see two men sitting at a able. We see a bomb under the table. We want the hero of the two actors to ealise there is a bomb under the table. We would be looking for his reaction. That last part at least is the same as the Kuleshov experiment. But Hitchcock urned it into a stand-alone figure – Actor/Soup/Actor reaction. The movement, he change, the dynamism comes only in the third term.

69 Hitchcock was a member of the London Film Society in the 1920s when it showed Soviet films regularly.

c. Narrative, Change and Script

The notion here is of a relatively small number of writers developing a form, over a period of twenty years or so, whose contents lie partly in the background of theatre and the novel and partly in the ether of the commercial pressures to make films move along and show as little trace of their making as possible. The force driving them is partly conscious and probably mainly unconscious (simply because most forces are mainly unconscious).

Forward movement, change is the key feature of all scripts – the story has to move forward, and the quicker the better.

Change is basic to Cinema – it is a cultural vehicle for change – a culturally-evolved medium in which it could be argued the unacknowledged metaphysical force is change. In a script characters must develop, the story must progress, an 'arc' of change is basic to script. There is a philosophy of change about all screenwriting. While change is key to the novel and to theatre, it is more urgent because the medium is on a screen, recorded, and we either follow or we don't, stick with it or lose ourselves in the story. *The Big Sleep* famously showed that you can have an illogical story as long as the forward movement is sufficient to propel the story and the audience with it.

Change is ineluctable for Cinema as a narrative medium. While theatre has similar problems with keeping an audience's attention, it does not have the disadvantage of images disappearing one after the other, if you don't stay with it you can't go back, so the task of the screenwriter, and an abstract task it is in one sense, is to find a way to attract the audience's attention and keep it during the 90 or so minutes of the film.

This is where Cinema is tied to nature, life and evolution, which all have change as arguably their most basic feature. The screenplay is a form that encapsulates change at its heart. It is its raison d'être and all the other elements are there to serve change.

If, for a moment, we think of the screenplay in abstract terms, it is a vehicle for the management of change, and it has adapted narrative to its purposes. Narrative is a method of linking disparate things together into a coherent pattern. It is often taken-for-granted how easy it is to watch a film – for the audience. The manifold difficulties for the makers are, and must be, invisible. Think of it as this big white screen with hundreds of people sitting before it, waiting to see what will come

158

up on that screen. The task of the film-makers is to grab the audience's attention and keep hold of it for a long, long time. Not for a few seconds, or even a few minutes, but for 90 or 120 minutes or more. If there are false steps during that time, the danger is that the audience will lose the trail, their attention will lapse. A film is like the mythical thread leading through the labyrinth. The task of the script is to see that the string remains intact and that there are no breaks in it that will permit the audience to lose track and stop that relentless forward movement that ends only with the titles (and not then in their minds). That task is a very demanding one, which is one reason why there are now dozens of practical books on the topic.

Why did the Producer Hal Wallis send a list of cuts to the editor of Casablanca? Firstly, he was a hands-on Producer. Behind that neat phrase lies a wealth of tacit knowledge. Wallis knew about writing and what makes a film work with audiences, which would have been one of the reasons for his success. Did he send a list of cuts in order to show his power over the Director? That is entirely possible, but the overarching reason would have been, at least in his mind, the common goal of making the film move faster and smoother, maximising the attention of the audience upon its story. Part of the process of editing is to correct, as far as possible, any errors of construction in the script.[170] While it is limited what can be achieved by the editor, as s/he only has the material available that has been shot (on occasion re-shoots would be called for in the Studio system for that very reason) to work with, and cannot create what is not there in the first place, only ameliorate or disguise any falling away from the ideal model. Wallis's goal with his cuts list would have been to keep things moving in one way or another – to make the forward movement of the story clearer to the audience, removing ambiguities where possible.[171]

d. Hitchcock, Change and the Ideal Script

Hold, if you will, this image of the script as an abstract engine for the propulsion of audience interest via the narrative method (see Section C: 'Neurology and Narrative: Why Narrative', p. 166 on the neurobiological links between the brain and narrative). The significance of this notion is that the native procedure of the brain is also what I would call narrative[172], working to connect disparate stimuli

---

170 For comment on construction, see the notes on Woody Allen's *Blue Jasmine*, (2013) later in this section.

171 There is another story here of Producers simplifying stories against the complexities of the scriptwriter's intentions. Eliminating ambiguity might be thought to serve the commercial interest of a film, but it might well harm the

in such a way as to make sense of them. 'Sense' here is intimately related to survival[173] – making sense means aiding survival, the purpose of joining stimuli up is to make sense of the world in terms of threats to survival of one kind or another, proximate or distant, direct or indirect.

One of the rules for the ideal construction of a scene is about there not being a dull moment that will allow the audience to stop moving forward with the story. In particular, the relevant rule is to come in at the last possible moment in the scene, just as a change is about to happen, the change happens, and the scene ends.

It is well-known that Hitchcock had a tendency to set himself a different 'technical'[174] challenge with each new film. With *Marnie* the challenge was, it is argued here, related to the ideal form of the script. The idea is that Hitchcock set himself the task with this film of realising the ideal scene – with every scene. That is, to try to keep strictly to the ideal for each and every scene in the picture. Now, that is quite a task – alongside balancing plot, character and forward movement.

The result was that the *Marnie* script does indeed come in at the last possible moment in each scene, the action happens and the scene ends. The effect of that happening scene after scene is like a train-crash, straight into the scene as the change is about to happen, it happens and the scene ends, straight into the next scene, the change happens, the scene ends, straight into the next scene. *Marnie* has been called the most avant-garde Hollywood film ever made, and that by a New York avant-garde film-maker and critic[175].

The change concerned always impinges upon the emotional status of the hero, directly or indirectly. In other words, it is always linked to his or her happiness or prosperity or prospects for survival. The link may be direct, where s/he is in the scene, or it may appear to be indirect, as when Marnie steals from his company safe. Almost the first rule of screenwriting is that character is action. In that scene Marnie establishes the nature of her character as a habitual and amoral thief. The connection to Mark's happiness is that he takes her bad character as just the sort of challenge he wants in a woman, bored as he is by the conventional women of his social circle. The tragic aspect of the film is in his attempts to retrain that bad

172 This is my reading of the neuroscience literature, which tends to use the term 'confabulation' for the process. There are a number of similar processes across the functions of the brain that suggest that this connecting mode is universal in the brain, rather than an odd exception, as confabulation might indicate.

173 Survival's twin is Reproduction in all matters evolutionary.

174 In fact these were aesthetic challenges, often presented as technical so as not to frighten the horses.

175 Jonas Mekas from memory.

character, but also that for the heroine of the film, after whom it is named, she has no apparent route to happiness. The big question is – was it environment or heredity that made her bad? Is her badness unredeemable? Can Mark (Sean Connery) save her from herself, can he change her?

Hitchcock perhaps meditated upon the theme of change, in *Marnie*. She does not want to change but Mark wants the challenge of having her change. And so it is possible that Hitchcock built the theme right through the structure of every scene in the film – a film about change in both content and form.

Mirror Neurons and Cinema

Mirror Neurons, discovered in the 1990s, and thought by some researchers to be as important a development as the discovery of DNA, unconsciously ape the physical actions of others. When James Bond has a scorpion drop on him, our bodies react as his body does[176]. We physically mirror another person we are watching. When we see boxing in a film or on TV our muscles tense as though we were about to deliver a punch.

Of course, we don't actually do it. That is true, but the 'of course', is where we take for granted a particular aspect of the brain that affects both waking and sleeping behaviour. We have a system that inhibits turning the tensing actually into action. Although our bodies go through the internal motions required to prepare us for the same actions, there is a cut-off that stops us performing the action. We know the difference between fiction and reality. A similar process occurs in dreaming. Our bodies ape the processes required to prepare us for an action we are seeing in a dream, but a similar cut-off stops us turning it into action. We may move in sleep, but the movements are limited by these systems[177].

This surprising phenomenon of copying behaviour we see was first noticed, by chance, in monkeys[178], but has since been found to be a fundamental part of human behaviour, with mirror neurons found in several parts of the brain. The simple word 'see' here elides a process whereby the eyes are focussed on watching closely another person carry out a particular action. A sense of the biological necessity of this quality may be imagined in monkeys learning how to take food

176 This example is from Christian Keysers, discoverer of Shared Circuits, see *The Empathic Brain*, 2011.

177 See A.H. Hobson, *Dreaming*, OUP, 2003 for a discussion of these mechanisms.

178 By an Italian neuroscientist, Giacomo Rizzalatti, part of a team in Parma in the 1990s.

from a tree by watching their parent. The infant is learning how to carry out actions basic to the prolongation of life. That is the biological reason such skill would be selected for by evolution. It has an obvious biological value.

What began as an evolutionary process genetically has an important role in human culture, so far removed from the original as almost to test credibility. But this example is a crucial – cultural – case of what evolutionary biologists call exaptation, whereby something developed originally for one purpose is adapted for quite another purpose. The physical example often quoted is the bones in the ear that were originally part of fins for swimming when our very distant ancestors were sea-creatures, and were later exapted to help communicate sound in what became our ears.

In this case the idea is that this copying feature, originally perhaps utilised by infant creatures to learn from their parents skills basic to survival, today shows up in us squirming in our seats in Cinema. Contrast that reality with the notion that it is 'bourgeois ideology' that has us identify with the hero in a drama. cultural factors can play a critical part but unless we understand the evolutionary basics there is a danger of wishful-thinking in giving formal factors powers they do not and cannot possess.

Shared Circuits and Cinema

In the teens of the 21st Century a second discovery, Shared Circuits, extended this operation in the brain from the physical to the emotional. When we see someone undergo a particular emotional situation we rehearse the same emotions. We go through the same process. It does not necessarily mean we submerge ourselves in the experience, but we unconsciously mirror it on the physiological level.

This second discovery is arguably of even greater potential significance than the first. One of the shibboleths of philosophy has been the assertion that we cannot know what goes on in the minds of others, an assumption made by philosophers over the ages. Shared Circuits undermines that assumption with scientific evidence that on the contrary, not only do we have the potential to sense what is going on in the minds of others, but we cannot avoid doing so, such social creatures are we through cultural evolution. We live in the social world of other people by an automatic process of mirroring what they are going through.

This is another example of the amazing capacities of vision, the uses of the eye. We see what others are going through and our body/brain system replicates key elements of it. It is a classic statement of neuroscience that 'we see more than we know', and in Shared Circuits we begin to understand something of the truth behind that statement. Not only can we see what others are thinking, but we are not 'trying' to think what they are thinking, our whole system is doing it for us, automatically. It is not a literal case of seeing thoughts in others' heads, but the reality that our body/brain systems cannot help but naturally empathise with another human's experience. As it is a feature of evolution, an adaptation with biological value for our survival, it has been developed as a fundamental element of our body/brain system. I see therefore I am. The radical correction of Shared Circuits is that we don't need to know what the other person is thinking – in a conscious sense – as our body/brain system uses the information provided by our eyes to copy its key elements, so that we are going through the same processes as they are – our system knows, not merely our conscious mind, which is but a millionth of who we are. Any easy assumption that we cannot know what is in the minds of others takes a fatal blow from science.

Shared Circuits show that we cannot avoid but see into the minds of others. This is not a process of thinking, as Descartes would have it. It is an automatic process developed by evolution for its own purposes helpful to survival. The fact that we can 'know' what someone else is going through is an epiphenomenon of that evolutionary development, a kind of exaptation of a process originally developed for other purposes. And then, by extension, Cinema is an epiphenomenon, in the sphere of the evolution of culture, where we carry out very similar processes to different ends. But 'different' is not quite the truth. It is a case of similar ends in a different context – here the context of culture. What was originally a genetic process motivated by evolutionary survival itself evolves into a cultural process that is at the centre of something as superficially remote as Cinema.

The Automatic: Consciousness downgraded, the Automatic upgraded

One reconceptualisation of thought would make conscious thinking a constantly shifting process, unlike the fixed notion of a self, a constant battle between different registers and representations, in which the self is at stake, in a sense, as the attempt to create, maintain, recreate a coherent self is part of the everyday process of waking consciousness. And of course, it is not exclusively or even mainly conscious. Consciousness is merely a part of the process, in which the unconscious plays by far the major role – the pin in the Albert Hall comparison

It is a massive shift in our traditional ways of thinking to downgrade consciousness, which we know, and upgrade the unconscious, which we don't. As modern Dream Science has shown, the unconscious is completely the opposite of Freud's conception[179]. It is a revealing mechanism not a concealing one. It doesn't hide things but on the contrary reveals them. That notions suggests that accessing the Automatic in the cause of understanding how Cinema operates in the brain is perhaps more feasible than it might first appear. Neuroscientists like Dehaene have made substantial progress in untangling conscious from unconscious input, but the scale of operations that appear to take place in the Automatic make work on that task an enticing challenge in relation to Cinema. If, as my founding instinct tells me, we ingest most of Cinema unconsciously, there awaits a treasure trove to be discovered that could also throw light upon the functions of the Automatic.

C. The Classic Hollywood Cinema: a pinnacle of the medium

Classicism & Genius

Against the grain of the auteur theory that he had set off, it was Andre Bazin who recognised two essential features of Hollywood. The first was that the Hollywood Cinema was a classical art, not immediately obvious to the rest of the world in the 1950s, but more than that it was not this or that individual that lay at the heart of the matter, but what he called The Genius of the System.

The Classic Hollywood Cinema has received no lack of attention and revisionist acclaim for its achievements against the predominant view of Hollywood as a tawdry circus glorying in all the worst aspects of mankind. I would like to draw back to Bazin's pairing – in order to make even greater claims for the 'CHC' than have perhaps been made before.

The view I would like to put forward here is that Classic Hollywood, of all the most unlikely things, has been underrated, and not in a minor way. The Classic Hollywood Cinema is one of the greatest artistic achievements of mankind, truly

---

179 See J Allan Hobson, *Dreaming*, OUP, 2003. op. cit. Ch. 2.

a Classical Art as Bazin so perceptively claimed. That alone would be a remarkable fact, but much more remarkable is that it occurred, I would argue, not in spite of the vulgar commercialism, but because of it. The System of Genius Bazin identified was ironically responsible for the pressures, the cauldron, that created this Classical Cinema and without which, in all probability, it would not have evolved.

It was an inherent factor of the commercial pressures that it created both individual works that came close to realising the extraordinary potential of what Hollywood made of the new medium, but also created a shadow creature, the Ideal Film, created from the Ideal Script. The potential for Cinema to be a *Gesammtkunstwerk* at a greater scale than even Wagner conceived lies in those twin concepts.

i. Evolution, Culture and the Classic Hollywood Cinema

The controversies following the publication of *The Origin of Species* (1859) saw Darwin's side taken by Galton and Spencer, but in ways that varied significantly from his own views. When he published *The Descent of Man* (1870) Darwin took care to express those differences, but the echoes of the outcry against the earlier book rather drowned out a point of great significance in the later one, the notion that evolution in mankind had broadly passed from the genetic to the cultural sphere[180]. In combination with his last great work *The Expression of Emotion in Man and Animals* (1872) and his recently revealed passion against slavery, Darwin's inheritance moves rather closer to a similar view in contemporary neuroscience, that genetic evolution in man virtually ceased several thousand years ago[181], whereupon evolution took cultural forms, ever-increasing in speed and complexity.

I propose to explore here an alternative history of how the form of Classic Hollywood Cinema developed that sees it as an expression of cultural evolution in the Darwinian sense. The basic assumption on evolution is that it is an expression of nature, nature in action. The shift from genetic evolution to a conception of cultural evolution poses the question of whether culture is analogous to the processes of natural life. The notion of societies as living organisms goes back at least as far as Ibn Khalden in the 14th Century, and suggests why

---

180 See *L'anthropologie inattendue de Charles Darwin* by Patrick Tort, introduction to the French translation *Le filiation de l'homme*, Honore, Paris, 2013.
181 See V. Ramachandran op. cit. p. 134.

the principles of genetic evolution may apply to culture. A further assumption here is that evolution is not teleological and that would also go for the cultural variant[182]. It does include the notion that everything in it, literally everything, is derived in the final analysis from evolutionary forces[183]. Cinema is a cultural artefact and as such is a part of evolution – in the cultural sphere. I am less concerned, for this current purpose, with the issue of 'co-evolution', which suggests that genetics and culture interact. I assume here that they do, and the general principle of how culture emerges from genetic factors is allied to the term 'exaptation', the idea that something evolved for one purpose can be adapted for quite another purpose.

The key example in this case is what I see as the narrative impulse in the way the brain works, itself exaptated to become the stringent requirements of Classic narrative in the Hollywood film.

Affective Neurobiology yokes together three elements: emotion, the brain and evolutionary biology. I will look at them in regards to Hollywood firstly in relation to the brain – and the narrative form Hollywood film took, secondly in relation to evolution – seeing the particular formal paradigm as an example of evolution in the cultural sphere, and thirdly in relation to emotion: seeing the chosen period as realising a potential for 'making emotion visible'.

ii. Neurology and Narrative: Why Narrative?

From its inception, broadly dated to 1895, Cinema was a medium of expression in search of a form. By that I mean that it was the result of elements including certain technical inventions and the birth of photography around 1839, but as with any new medium it had its capacities and limitations and to explore its potential required considerable trial and error over a period of time.

The case I want to put forward here is that the Classic Hollywood Cinema realised that potential in certain ways and may be seen as a kind of apotheosis for the medium. That would seem to be counterintuitive in a cultural climate that has denigrated Hollywood as a crass commercial factory, a prison for creative minds

---

182 Culture is not seen here as necessarily progressing, nor as hierarchical.

183 Man is a product of Nature, and therefore everything that man produces also derives from nature. Evolution is the motor of nature. Culture is likewise a product of evolutionary forces, even through co-evolution, which nevertheless *always* bears the lineaments of the genetic evolutionary process from which it emerged. In the last instance nature is always the source and culture has only a limited and never total autonomy, dependent in every instance upon its genetic inheritance, however superficially remote and indirect that may be. Any other view tends to the anthropocentric.

where the best Directors struggled to maintain the integrity of their personal vision against the depredations of commercial interests, and in contrast to notions of a European Art Cinema that permitted vision and artistic integrity to survive and prosper.

Against these romantic images, I would like to suggest that the Classic Hollywood Cinema was an almost Leibnizian realisation of The Best of All Possible Worlds. That is to say that despite the constant pressure to profit, or rather because of them, a form emerged that was both biologically valuable and aesthetically coherent to a high degree, the Classic Hollywood Cinema as the Parthenon of the medium. The Hollywood Cinema was, as Andre Bazin insisted, a classical art.[184]

While the second element is concerned with the particular form of narrative expression that was developed in the Classic period through cultural evolution, this first element is about the adoption of the narrative mode itself, due to reasons based in genetic evolution.

I would like to propose a view firmly anchored in the natural processes of evolution.[185] I suggest that there is one major reason why Hollywood Cinema took the narrative form. Narrative is a fundamental mode in which the brain operates.[186] That mode is native to the functioning of the brain in a host of ways. For example, with both the Kuleshov experiments and those of Gazzaniga fifty years later, we see the impulse to connect stimuli together in such a way as to yield meaning, and that meaning has biological value – because of its unbroken connection to survival.

The relatively meagre information-processing resources of consciousness are deployed by the body/brain system to focus on the most relevant stimuli present in the external environment in which a subject is placed. The human subject will attempt to link the stimuli into a meaningful pattern and that pattern is what neuroscientists sometimes call 'confabulation', while I suggest we call it narrative. The brain tells a story because linking together stimuli was effectively seen by evolution as the most effective way of making sense of them. There is safety in numbers – a group of stimuli that can be linked into a pattern is more likely to

---

184 Andre Bazin, La Politique des Auteurs, 1957, has reservations about auteurism and includes the phrase 'the genius of the system' to refer to Hollywood.

185 Nature, seen from the point of view of evolution, it is worth reminding ourselves, is a disinterested force, whose logic is not that of man. It is not that biology escapes ideology, as it were, but that nature/evolution operates at a different level to human logic, it is illogical in human terms, its frame of reference is the planet and the universe not the local affairs of man.

186 For more on the narrative mode of the brain refer back to Commentaries section.

THE MATTER OF VISION

be understandable as a basis for action than looking at each one on an isolated individual basis. That choice was adopted by evolution as it was a better option than the alternatives in relation to the criterion of survival. In a broad sense I would also suggest that is the reason Hollywood adopted the narrative form for the new medium.

We interpret the world through narrative, and only through narrative. That is not an aesthetic choice but simply the least-bad method the brain has for making sense of the world via the feedback loop between vision and the body/brain system. Any other strategy is less likely to succeed as it goes against the grain of how the brain works.

Classic Hollywood produced the form of Cinema that it did because that was working with the grain to produce the biggest profits. It was not a question of abstract aesthetics or moral choice, but of evolution operating impersonally through the ants in the Hollywood ant-hill to develop a form of Cinema that stood the best chance of making the public return week after week to the movie-theatres.

That tendency towards narrative is also a reason that other forms struggle to make an impact with audiences. Such a view may be anathema to those with anti-narrative or avant-garde sympathies, a number among which I counted myself when I embarked upon film-making, but it is a view to which I have become increasingly drawn over the years and especially through the process of working on this project.

The brain, in this view, is driven by the biological basics of survival and reproduction. The struggle for survival is an effect of the drive to reproduction. The eye, for example, responds to movement, because movement may signal the approach of a predator. The reason for the pre-eminence of Vision is that evolution nominated it as the most effective survival-aid.

When the eye selects a number of stimuli in the external environment, what does it do with them? It passes the information back to the brain as part of a constant feedback process. How does the brain make sense of the diverse stimuli? Does it line them up and give them scores on the survival-threat front? Does it aesthetically appreciate their shape and colour and texture? The brain does these things and many more besides, but there is one overriding thing the brain does because it has proved to be the most effective action for survival. It makes sense of them as a whole, as a collectivity, by finding a critical path between them, by joining

168

them together in such a way as to make the most sense of them. It 'confabulates', it creates a story, a narrative.[187]

As indicated earlier this is no minor point about how the brain works, but appears to be central to the whole process in which the brain relates to the world. The underlying fact is that the world is composed of many stimuli – billions – but consciousness in particular is capable of dealing with only a few at a time. Therefore, if the brain (always in relation both to the body and consciousness) is to navigate us through the world, it has to have a method of making survival-sense of those few stimuli among the terrifying billions that it could be asked to respond to. Handling seven stimuli at any one time in working memory, said to be the maximum of which consciousness is capable among the potential field out there, is a frightening prospect as an abstract task. This is where the conceptual notion of narrative makes practical sense. If only seven from a range of billions is in view, what better way to manage them than to find some way of linking them in order to orient us to them – either as threat or opportunity, at base a matter of survival or reproduction.

Seven from a field of billions is a threadbare selection. If we assume the extraordinary efficiency of the body/brain system in selecting the seven most relevant to survival, there are still, to put it mildly, quite a few gaps. Therefore linking up stimuli is a least-bad rather than perfect solution, something typical of the logic of evolution rather than the logic of man. In this light the dynamic towards narrativity as a solution reminds us that natural law is a very different creature from the man-made. It is certainly not a question of reality in the traditional sense of a total view of out-there, but a remarkably discreet selection, the best that the body/brain system can do.

One might in that light see the aesthetics of Classic Hollywood as an exemplary adaptation of neurobiological realities in the sphere of culture (again in the evolutionary sense of that term). To turn the evolutionary selection of external stimuli into a disciplined aesthetic of classical rigour and proportion is an achievement in the realm of culture that should not be underestimated.

There can be numerous ways in which seven stimuli could be turned into a story and there is a sense that the brain's choice is not the only one – or even the best one – but one that is good enough to act as a basis for action. We are a long way here from a universal notion of reality or of logical perfection, but instead settle for a practical solution that offers itself as an option. This is the disinterested

---

187 This interpretation is my own, from a reading of the neuroscience literature in the light of thinking about Cinema.

world of nature, not the philosopher's dream of a rational universe. In that sense it may be the wrong solution, but in practice it is good enough. Nature is not philosophy nor engineering design.

There is a logical perfection operating in this process, but it is one composed of the peculiar logic of nature[188] rather than the logic of philosophers, especially those with a monocular attachment to language. In this way (and a range of others, such as the way the brain operates via metaphor) the brain turns the world into a story. Making up a story (which is not at all the same thing as identifying 'reality') is a natural mode for the brain.

And that, to put it simply, is why the Hollywood Cinema developed as a narrative medium. And it is also why, with a nod to Leibniz, it could – in a sense – have developed in no other way. It was not an arbitrary or bourgeois capitalist choice (even where it was), it was profoundly built into the way the brain has evolved to operate. It was a biological determination, not necessarily the only one available, but one that perhaps fitted the most relevant criteria.

iii. Anti-narrative?

That also gives a sense of the task any film-maker is up against in being against narrative. The efforts of an individual against the forces propelling narrative is a substantial challenge. A Godard or an Antonioni may heroically try to construct a workable alternative, but even they are working in relation to narrative, it is that they are reacting against. The result of loosening the ties of narrative drive, of ignoring or offending against the classical rules, is nearly always that the audience loses attention. In brief, it gets bored. That may be the elephant in the room in discussing these two film-makers, of whom I am inordinately fond, but it is the undeniable truth.

On the other hand, a Tarantino works more with the grain of narrative rather than against it, enlarging the options within the narrative tradition, retaining the key element of audience attention with variants on forward movement that do not sacrifice the attractions of the form. Despite the remarkable achievements of Godard and Antonioni in the early 60s I think reluctantly it would be fair to say that they did not create sustainable alternatives, and that is not due to any lack

---

188 To do justice to the logic of nature would require a treatise of its own, but the essence is that the superficially illogical choices that nature makes as strategy possess perfect sense when they are seen in the light of evolution, that is in terms of the requirements of survival. That logic shows up well in papers on neuroscientific experiments – see McGilchrist for numerous references to relevant accounts of experiments.

in their intelligence or creativity but to the deep roots of the key elements of the narrative form on the one hand, and the achievements of the classic Hollywood Cinema on the other. A Tarantino shows that narrative is a flexible medium, as long as the key rules of attraction are maintained, but even that is a tribute to the formal qualities of the classical aesthetic developed in the golden era.

With Godard the brechtian distancing from the characters, ironically our lack of emotional engagement with them, combined with picaresque narrative rather than the tightly disciplined classical narrative, eventually has an effect upon our engagement over time.

It is a mark of modernism to separate emotion from technique, but in so doing the bias towards the cerebral is at the expense of the emotional, and that does not sit easy with the native modes of the brain. In that sense Tarantino, with his relationship to Hollywood, financially and culturally, seems to have sought a middle-way that mixed distance with engagement. Doing that from inside American culture, as it were, might have contributed to the masterly management of tone he achieved in *Inglorious Basterds*, whereas the fun comic-book elements of mid-60s Godard in *Pierrot Le Fou* approaches American culture from the outside, with a French accent that can come across as occasionally arch rather than with the fluidity of an insider.

With Antonioni the lesson of Kuleshov is taken in almost the opposite direction to Hitchcock. The great achievement of the classical form means that in for example *Mildred Pierce* you feel that you always know where you are, the emotional narrative has a clear direction, even where it is ambiguous, a striking benefit of a classical aesthetic. With Antonioni, the opposite is the case. The neutral expressions on his actors' faces sustains the unknowability of their feelings, you never know where you are. That becomes tiring when the rewards of knowing fail to arrive. A Hitchcock film and a Curtiz film, for example, are rather different creatures, but they both operate under the discipline of the classical aesthetic. Hitchcock admired Antonioni's technique in *Blow-Up*,[189] but it would have been interesting to see how he dealt with the different direction Antonioni took the neutral expression of Mosjukine, almost the reverse problem of Godard's appropriation of Hollywood modes.

It also goes some way to indicating the difficulties facing non- or anti-narrative forms. The problem I was aware of in starting to make films was a strong sense

189 *Kaleidoscope/Frenzy* (1964-7) was inspired partly by *Blow-Up*. Hitchcock planned 450 shots and filmed and photographed test-material but the project was rejected by the studio as too violent, reducing Hitchcock to tears. http://the.hitchcock.zone/wiki/Kaleidoscope

that the rules only permitted certain kinds of things to be said and in kicking against those rules there was the ambition to say more and different things than it was felt narrative would permit. That came through particularly strongly in Godard's early films to the mid 60s, with him putting text on the screen, poetry, banner headlines, breaking the conventions of invisible technique, and how and where music was used. Exciting though those bravura innovations were in general they were one-off experiments – and the basic reason for that is the power that narrative has over us. It is not easy to hold an audience's attention in Cinema for upwards of ninety minutes and the same factors that have the brain operate in a narrative mode internally, as it were, make it an obvious solution for dealing with the lengths of time involved in feature films.

The highly disciplined narrative form of the Classic Hollywood Cinema was thus both a plus – its internal coherence created that classical aesthetic identified by Bazin, and a minus – there seemed to be so many things you can't say and so many ways you can't say them. In the end the discipline of the form almost comes down to one rule – show not tell. In a literary culture that alone is a hard task and the way Classic Hollywood achieved it by around 1939 was a triumph for the 'genius of the system'.

None of this is to say that narrative cannot develop or even that non-narrative forms will not come to dominate in some future time. Over the last twenty years one of the key developments in neuroscience has been the realisation that the brain is much more plastic than had hitherto been thought, constantly creating new connections, adapting to new circumstances, quite different from the older conception of a hard-wired system immune to change. This is not about an unchangeable natural dictatorship of the survival of the fittest, doomed to heredity and downgrading environmental influences (one nineteenth-century version of Darwinism). Along with that issue is a history of reluctance to accept evolution in the cultural sphere, seeing it as a reactionary force propping up the status quo. With the discovery of the plasticity of the brain, those fears would appear to no longer have the force they once had.

A Tarantino or a *House of Cards*[190] extends narrative possibilities, but within the overall framework of the form. However, the neurological factor does offer an account of one element in the domination of Hollywood Cinema. It is only a baseline, capable of almost infinite variation, but the tendency towards narra-

---

190 Both the British original (1990s) and the American version (2013) feature the main character talking to-camera, breaking the fourth-wall of the Classical form – although that was not completely unknown in Classical Hollywood in genres like the musical that had more narrative freedom than drama.

tivisation in the fundamental modes of the brain, like all evolutionary factors, remains an ineluctable foundation.

It would be interesting to apply the basic approach to a contrasting tradition to see how a different balance of forces created a rather different narrative Cinema, without many of the key features that defined Classic Hollywood. For example, from what I have seen of Ukrainian Cinema[191] it tends to be more poetic, lacking narrative drive and pace but with a more varied if less disciplined formal approach, a very different mix of elements to Hollywood Cinema. The slow pace may be a conscious reaction against Hollywood and a desire to create a distinctive national Cinematic tradition from resources within their own culture.

The relation to brain function was only opening the door to the narrative mode and, as the native mode of the brain, adapting the new medium of Cinema to narrative has obvious benefits. The medium is working with rather than against the way our brains work and thus has the best chance of surviving and prospering. The direction that developed – towards the classical form identified by Bazin – was the product of elements such as the intensively competitive commercial environment between the studios, the suitability of the feature-length film as a commercial product, and the ideological/commercial commitment to the invisibility of storytelling technique shared by studio heads, as well as producers, writers, directors and editors: the culture of Hollywood.

There is potentially a basis for the process of cultural evolution in the neurobiological facts about how the brain works in relation to narrative, movement, identification and emotion, but how that translates into the specifics of the Hollywood case would require a forensic examination of the connections between those general principles and the specific forms and variations Hollywood took, even in relation to the single sphere of the formal paradigm and its elaboration and development.

iv. Narrative, CHC and Cultural Evolution

The proposition is that the way the Classic Hollywood Cinema developed into the narrative form that it did is an example of a general phenomenon – cultural evolution. By that I mean cultural evolution, in the evolutionary sense, succeeded genetic evolution but follows essentially the same rules.

---

191 e.g. 'A spring for the thirsty' Yuri Ilyenko, 'Dancing Hawk' Grzegorz Krolikiewicz, 'Letters from a Dead Man' Konstantin Lopushansky, 'Narcissus and Psyche' Gabor Body, and the films of Paradjanov.

It is a familiar concept that genetic evolution is amoral in the human sense, a force of nature that operates according to the natural law rather than anything humans may wish it to do. Evolution has no design, and is unconcerned with man's deliberations. It proceeds relentlessly according to natural selection and adaptation. Evolution is non-teleological, it blunders relentlessly on, often selecting what a human designer or engineer would see as an inelegant or non-optimal path. Nature has its reasons but they are not the Enlightenment model of human Reason. Evolution is not something reducible to the anthropomorphic, which is a constant and unsurprising tendency in human thinking.[192] It is about the planet rather than just mankind, a force bigger than our deliberations, a massive, neutral and therefore somewhat frightening force that cannot be denied. The very impersonality of the forces of evolution is something that perhaps tends to inhibit us from this shift in thinking, and even when we make the shift, then to zoom in from the scale of genetic biology to a local scale of cultural biology takes another shift in thinking. The contention here is that the same impersonality applies to cultural evolution. It is not something in our control. We may make local impacts of relative significance for a given context (e.g. the rights of women, the right to vote) but the global movement of evolution goes beyond our species.

The difference between genetic and cultural evolution is that the latter is proceeding at a faster and ever-increasing rate. The notion that it is also more complex may be a human conceit, like the repeated desire to distinguish ourselves from the animals, as strong today as in Darwin's time. I have a sense that nature is more complex than culture, the ecology of nature exceeding the variables of the ecology of human culture, but that is only an instinctive feeling on my part. If one shifts perspective from the conventional way of thinking of human affairs and imagines that culture is, as it were, merely the successor of genetics in the larger field of evolution, then seeing cultural phenomena in the light of the principles of evolution begins to make sense.

The reason for focussing on the Classic Hollywood Cinema is to see it as the locus classicus of a certain kind of Cinema, what may be argued to be the dominant form of the medium – narrative Cinema.

While biological evolution may normally be seen in million of years rather than over the twenty-five years I am suggesting in relation to Classic Hollywood (1939–1964) that it is perhaps useful to consider that the pace of cultural change has speeded up massively compared to the timescales of genetic change. One only

---

192 'Man never knows how anthropomorphic he is' – Goethe.

has to think of the changes brought about by the invention of the web in the same time frame (1989–2014), to realise how cultural evolution appears to be constantly accelerating.

With the Classic Hollywood Cinema, the cultural institution of Cinema reached a peak of narrative discipline. By around 1939 this perfect engine of meaning[193] had all its essential rules in place, and the dominance of the American Cinema on a worldwide scale probably owes at least something of its position to that achievement.

By the mid-1960s the studio system that had bred that Cinema was in serious decline, which would only accelerate over the years to come. The appearance of *Star Wars* in 1978, called at the time by another movie-brat 'the worst film he had ever seen'[194] suggested that the dominance of drama centring on human emotions was losing ground in favour of a more spectacular and emotionally different Cinema, a trend set to accelerate over the next generation. This spectacular Cinema, aimed at teenage boys and arguably mirroring their emotional range, can be seen in one way to be a falling away from the highpoint of Classic Hollywood, where complex adult emotional conflict could be said to be at the heart of many of the films.

That fact alone belies the romantic notion of development towards perfection as the teleology of evolution. Evolution can quite as easily go what appears to be 'backwards' as it does not operate teleologically. It is not goal-oriented in the familiar human sense, it is nothing to do with 'Progress' as Rousseau and the Enlightenment conceived it. Change, yes, Progress, no. It's designs would not be approved of by engineers, as they are the result of the mechanisms of natural selection and adaptation and exaptation. It moves on, it changes, it adapts, but apart from survival of the species, it has no agenda. Even Survival is at the level of the species, not of a phenomenon like Cinema. And further than that, the planet has its own agenda, which wiping man off its face would be an unremarkable response should he get in the way. Evolution is not a moral force.

In that light it would be no surprise both that CHC happened, and then was replaced by what from certain perspectives is a backward move, the *Star Wars* generation of emotionally-simple spectaculars. But spectacle is a feature of Cinema, and so is action, so the *Star Wars* generation was suited to a new teenage audience and not to the audience for *Mildred Pierce*. That's evolution at work,

---

193 See the next section for a discussion of the formal qualities of Classical Hollywood.

194 Brian de Palma, a great fan of Hitchcock's kind of Cinema, reputedly said that to George Lucas.

rather than progress, a crucial difference. There are emotions in the *Star War* era, but they are of a different order to a *Mildred Pierce* or a *Casablanca*. And emotion is arguably not the centre of the story, or at least a different set of emotions, and at a different level.

Evolution and Classical Form

This element relates the development of the formal paradigm of Classic Hollywood to cultural evolution. I would like to set forward a view of the Classic Hollywood Cinema as an example of evolution in the cultural sphere, taking it as an apotheosis of the development of film form. In developing a certain notion of narrative cinema it created a perfect engine of meaning. This process I would suggest occurred largely informally, at both a conscious and unconscious level, among the few hundreds working in the studios who had a direct input to the process of making pictures – writers, directors, editors, and producers in particular.

Following the introduction of sound in 1926, it took around a decade for the technical limitations of the early sound-recording methods to be overcome creatively as well as technically, although some films managed a fluidity that belies their date of production – Raoul Walsh's *Bad Girl* of 1932, shot more on location than the average film, is one example. By the end of the 1930s the paradigm was pretty firmly in place, so that editors in particular were up-to-date with the techniques being widely used to interfere as little as possible with the process of telling the story. The ideal was invisible editing, and techniques had been developed bit by bit to further that goal. This was not primarily a creative impulse but the desire of Producers in particular, to hide the mechanics of storytelling as much as possible so that audiences would be seamlessly swept along with the story as they watched the fate of their favourite actors unfold on the screen.

The paradigm consisted of techniques that had been slowly developing since the birth of Cinema whose purpose was to achieve this invisibility of the mechanics. The paradigm consists of elements such as continuous screen direction, cutting-on-action and eyeline-matching. The essential purpose of these techniques is to make the process of telling the story as invisible as possible in order to minimise the disruption of the audience's concentration on the narrative. While the individual elements of the paradigm developed over the whole history of Cinema, with continuous screen direction coming relatively early on, for example, the development of the sound Cinema in the 1930s arguably saw a process of finessing the use of the paradigm elements so that by around 1939 a plateau had been reached. The early problems of the static camera required for the first sound-recording techniques had been overcome, and the fluidity of moving between close-shots and long-shots had been aided by cutting-on-action which was less visible under dialogue than it would have been with the silent cinema. Each element of the paradigm is an evolutionary story in its own right, but it is period when they had come together and the persistence of the plateau through a generation that is of interest here.

Hollywood 1939–1964

Setting the scene for Classic Hollywood between 1939 and 1964, from the era of *Stagecoach* to *Marnie*, the elements of film form relevant to classic narrative were in place a decade or so earlier.

In terms of how the key professionals worked with each other, a dip in audiences led to the introduction of production units in 1931[195], which would see key personnel – camera, editing, director, art department, writer and producer – work not just on one film together, but keep together as a team and have the chance to work on a succession of films. The impact of that is uncertain but it may well have been the case that it led to what I would see as the much smoother and more fluid application of the paradigm elements by the watershed year of 1939, which has been regarded as a peak of the Classic period, with a plethora of commercially successful films released, headed in the commercial sense by *Gone With the Wind*. Before 1931 production was centrally-organised rather than in units, and it was a matter for discussion that although it might have appealed to managers as a way of efficiently using technical crew on the payroll, it was thought to have led to undistinguished films that lacked character and distinctiveness. It would appear that perception was shared across the studio system as the change to unit production was implemented across the industry around the same year of 1931. With the same crew working together on film after film, it would be likely that it sharpened their ability to use the paradigm more effectively, not in terms of formal innovations as the elements were already established, but perhaps in the ways that they were used.

195 See *The Classic Hollywood Cinema*, Bordwell et al, Routledge, 1988, Ch. 25, p. 559 on.

My observations of films of the 1930s is that by 1939 there was a noticeable improvement in the fluidity of storytelling, so much so that it would be possible to distinguish between a film of the later date and one from the beginning of the decade. In terms of 'cutting on action', for example, films of the early 30s would often cut into close-ups without the disguise of movement, and would also employ 'three-shot continuity' rather than the 'master-shot' technique[196]. With the former method, shooting was planned so that there were links between the shot before and the shot after a given set-up, in order to assure they would cut together. That could see shots of similar scale cut together, whereas with a master shot, there would be a wide shot of the action then mid- and close-shots repeating the same action in order to give the editor (and often the Producer – who might have insisted upon being presented with choices for editing) a range of ways and timings to cut the scene together. Another aspect of this fluidity was perhaps also a more intent focus on emotion, discussed below.

I do not intend here to make a formalist argument about when and how the mode was established, but my feeling from seeing the films of the 30s somewhat a random is that the way the paradigm worked improved in efficiency during the 30s so that by 1939 most films obeyed its rules, in other words it was dominant by the outbreak of the Second World War.

Early 30s sound films often do not have the scene broken down into a master scene then into close-ups and reverse-angles, and close ups may not cut on action giving a jerkier feel than the later form imposed. Smoothness of the story-telling process had been finessed by 1939 to the point where it was more or less perfected as a set of principles.

The relevant issue was that studio bosses saw the role of form as helping to create an experience for the audience in which the story was the important thing and the telling, the techniques used, had the role of being as invisible as possible to offer as little distraction from getting wrapped up in the narrative as possible. Everything to do with the making of films – principally in the practical process of editing them – was aimed at reducing any disruptions to the audience experience. Invisible storytelling was the aim. While today we take for granted the techniques used in film-making the paradigm took from 1895 to around 1939 to develop and become established. Although many of the individual elements were devised many years prior to 1939 they were differentially established as

---

196 See *The 5 C's of Cinematography* on three-shot continuity v master-shot. Joseph C Mascelli, 1965.

ixed feature of the paradigm and the evolution process really only settled down ate on in the 1930s.

My sense is that by 1939 the finessing of the paradigm had plateaud. A film like *Mildred Pierce* (1945) has in place the key elements that persist to this day. Whereas many of the films of the early 30s have a stagey feel due to the technical imitations of sound-recording by the 1940s most studio films feel essentially modern. That difference would not appear to be in terms of formal innovations but more the finessing of techniques as film-makers found ways around the constraints imposed by sound.

Ideal Form

The ideal form of the Classic film emerged as a consequence of the highly competitive commercial environment between the studios in Hollywood. All the key players were committed to the belief that technique must be as invisible as possible to create the maximum focus of the audience on the emotional roller-coaster of the story. Technique must not get in the way and therefore the paradigm that developed reflected that guiding ideology. On the other hand it also reflected a certain respect for the effectiveness of the narrative form at its best.

The model that evolved as a result of these diverse, often unconscious, sometimes indifferent pressures on film form, constantly pushed towards removing any barriers between the audience and the emotional arc the films sought to create, was a highly-wrought, sophisticated and rigorous set of demands. In other words the Hollywood system created a classical aesthetic, internally coherent to a high degree, a narrative engine that is perfectly internally coherent as an ideal – in which nothing is wasted and everything has a contributory purpose. The irony is that all this essentially commercial pressure created an aesthetic that arguably bears comparison with any other in any art form, what may be thought of as the ideal Film. Capitalism creating classical aesthetics is perhaps a somewhat counter-intuitive concept, but had been identified as early as the 1950s by Andre Bazin, who christened it The Genius of the System.

Narrative was of course not a Hollywood invention, but the demands imposed by the medium of Cinema were particularly stringent and arguably it is those demands that led to the rigorous nature of the 'ideal form' for a film. The intractable character of the new medium means that the achievement of narrative fluidity was a considerable achievement in the face of the substantial difficulties posed by it. While a technique like Creative Geography, joining the eyeline of characters in successive shots, is in one sense an eminently practical solution to creating continuity of emotion, it is also a rather daring and imaginative spatial concept when thought of in the abstract – these eyes making contact across space and time in something like an abstract conception of space.

What these, often unsung, contributors were doing was creating a sort of apotheosis of the medium that began at the Station at La Ciotat in 1895. By the watershed year of 1939 the Classical form had established itself and developed to a point of high efficiency. The decline of the studio system saw that peak last only about a single generation, roughly the 25 years from 1939 to 1964. Cinema, in this view ends, as it were, with *Marnie*.

It would be another 15 years until the wave of documenting the form through the search for the perfect formula for screenwriting began, resulting in an increasing flood of books exploring the ideal form for the script. The classic rules inevitably still apply, but business conditions have changed unrecognisably since the rise of the internet, and audiences are now thought to be able to accept interruptions to the invisibility of technique – as shown in the constant asides direct to the audience in *House of Cards* (2013)[197].

Cultural Evolution

Evolution is a process of reproduction, adaptation and selection. Reproduction creates copies of what has come before, but it is not a perfect process and small variations can occur, and when those variations confer a survival advantage they can be selected and become part of the reproductive cycle. While that process was first outlined for genetic evolution, I would suggest it applies equally to evolution in the cultural sphere.

Everything in the human world, from unconscious processes to recorded history, has its origins in nature, that is to say in evolution – and thus in the basic processes of evolution – and that those basic processes – adaptation of random variations that provide some advantage in terms of survival and reproduction – are also found in the development of culture – in every moment of Cinema – formal and informal, conscious and unconscious.

---

197 As noted above that also occurs in the earlier British version, but American TV has perhaps tended to be more conservative with form, which is what makes this exception striking, and the series was launched on the net not on TV.

Cultural evolution may not be a familiar concept. In this context it does not mean culture in the sociological sense or in the sense of everyday language. In regard to narrative, if we think of the joining-up of stimuli that the brain performs as a survival strategy and then imagine that strategy adapted to the cultural sphere in the development of narrative in plays and novels and then in Cinema, that would be an example of cultural evolution. In it we see the passage from genetic evolution to cultural evolution, the 'exaptation' of something developed for one purpose adapted to another, and in this case also crossing the borders between genetics and culture.

This notion is broadly in line with 'DIT', Dual Inheritance Theory[198], the idea that genetics and culture form a 'dual inheritance'. There is much debate about how cultural evolution varies from the genetic form, but for the current purposes it is perhaps sufficient to embrace the notion that there are similarities that arise from the genetic inheritance, while culture would be expected to develop a certain degree of autonomy and therefore supplement genetic processes with those arising from the ever-increasing speed of cultural development, graphically shown in the rise of the internet.

From a biological perspective, culture is about the whole ecology of evolution in the social world of man, a rather broader concept than we are used to from disciplines such as sociology and anthropology. It could include the informal as well as the formal, tacit knowledge as well as academic knowledge, the unconscious as well as the conscious, always bearing in mind the watchword that everything comes from and is part of nature and always remains connected to it.

That last point is worth stressing simply because commentators of all kinds have constantly sought to effectively deny the part nature has to play in human society (even where that has not been either a part of their avowed purpose or even a conscious motivation), preferring a notion of autonomy that can arguably be traced back to Kant. The worthy motive in most cases was to combat conservative views such as inequality of the sexes, but the result has been to constrain scholarship in a range of areas. However, DIT has played a part in severing the connection of the idea of nature from the reactionary nineteenth-century elitist views of biology, allowing a new generation to approach important issues such as the differences between the brains of men and women in a spirit that embraces the plasticity and adaptability of the brain in cultural terms and allows us to admit of complementarity in difference, beyond the earlier fears of giving comfort to

198 See http://en.wikipedia.org/wiki/Dual_inheritance_theory.

181

ideological predelictions for seeing difference as a matter of inferiority an superiority, e.g. with men superior and women inferior.

On the other hand, it cannot be overlooked that evolution is literally a force c nature. Evolution is a disinterested force. It does not have the logic of mar although it has its own logic. What results from evolution is often far-remove from what a human design would produce, as it develops through nature rathe than through reason and the logic of philosophers. Evolution works through ma rather than with him. It has no interest in man per se. Man is merely anothe species on the earth, a small planet in one galaxy among billions, the lone surviv of the genus Homo.[199]

The plasticity of the brain supports the idea that culture can be formed an changed by man's agency. Nature as an implacable and disinterested forc suggests man's powerlessness in its face. The two are not irreconcilable and man' focus is naturally local. Battles for equality, for example, are themselves reflection of biological culture at work, reflecting changing realities differentiall in different societies. Votes for women were an outrage in Britain a hundred yeai ago and regarded as such in some arab countries today, but a century from nov may be commonplace there.

Hollywood and Nature

It is tempting to think of Hollywood as a phenomenon at the furthest remov from nature, but the fact is that as nothing in the brain has any source but th physical, despite what I would regard as mountains of mysticism to the contrar nothing in Hollywood is divorced in a qualitative sense from nature. Every singl thing, from the smallest to the biggest, can be traced back to evolution, and owe its real power to the pervasive presence of nature.

The conception therefore is that the evolution of CHC was analogous to th process of natural evolution[200], involving many of the same kind of processes an always linked to those processes, directly or indirectly, proximately or distantl but with the chain always intact. In this view culture is not autonomous, bu

199 This is not an original phrase, but I cannot place the source, elegant though it is.

200 Cultural evolution has not been much discussed in relation to Cinema or the arts, but has been the subject of muc debate since Darwin's *Descent of Man* (1870). The inegalitarian trend of the 19th century with Herbert Spence led to its disgrace in the 20th century, recouped in the 1970s, particularly with the Dual Inheritance Theory (DI1 approach of co-evolution between the genetic and cultural. The notion of a Universal Darwinism, proposed t Richard Dawkins and Daniel Dennett points towards evolutionary theory as a unifying force across disciplines, see in this instance as a potential to reunite the sciences and the arts.

grows out of genetic evolution and is always related to it. It has a relative autonomy but always bears the lineaments of its origins in genetic evolution.

The background concept of cultural evolution is that everything from unconscious processes to recorded history has its origins in nature, that is to say in the basic processes of evolution. Those basic processes, adaptation of random variations that provide some advantage in terms of survival and reproduction, are also found in the development of culture, in every moment of Cinema, formal and informal, conscious and unconscious.

Evolution in the sphere of culture is potentially the starting point for a Science of Culture, a holistic view of culture based in scientific method with the challenge of experimental testing of all ideas, so that the challenge for the development of ideas is to formulate them in such a manner as to be in principle submissable to laboratory testing.[201]

Cultural Evolution & Classic Hollywood

Biological culture involves psychology, sociology, politics, ideology, economics, etc, the informal as much as the formal, but also genetic elements as the foundations of biological cultural evolution. It covers everything in human affairs but goes beyond that to the workings of nature as seen in mankind as a species. In this view everything to do with man, the recorded and the unrecorded, are all part of biological culture. Nothing escapes it as everything springs from nature.

The evolutionary approach to the analysis of culture is grounded in history and highly flexible. The long-term we are used to in thinking about evolution have been cut down massively by the speeding up of cultural change. Again, one only has to think of the web to realise that.

Evolution is indifferent to human logic or morality. Nature has its reasons, but they are not the reasons of man. That fact is worth repeating as it has always to be kept in mind when thinking about the effects of evolution on human activity, particularly as it is a habit for man to anthropomorphise and forget our dependence upon nature, to dismiss it with the egotistical notion that we have somehow transcended it.

How might we imagine cultural evolution working in a context like the Holly-

---

201 A key feature distinguishing this approach from the variants of what is often called Continental Philosophy and that have played an important role in Film Theory.

wood studio system? The basic notion is that the particular narrative form of th Classic era was selected by cultural evolution, in a process that goes well beyon any individual, beyond conscious decisions, beyond business criteria and com mercial pressures in a process with millions, perhaps billions of tiny influenc coalescing in this remarkable ideal form of the Classic Hollywood film, or bearing all the hallmarks of a classical aesthetic, as identified by Bazin.

This is not a teleological process where there is some overarching guiding han that results in the form, and it is one in which no film actually realised th perfection implicit in the classical model, but every studio film shared to variou degrees in the common goal of the perfect narrative vehicle in which techniqu was wholly subjugated to the story, and interfered with the audience being swep up in the emotions of the story as little as possible. If anything fired the finessin of the paradigm of classical narrative cinema it was the constant fight in ever film to give prominence to the story by making the process of its telling a uninvasive to the viewing experience as possible. Invisible technique was the goa for fear the audience would lose the suspension of disbelief at some point or othe in the story. That was a conscious part of the process.

The image is one where perhaps a few hundred people at most in the Hollywoo studio system at any one time – editors, writers, directors and producers i particular – were consciously and/or unconsciously working towards perfectin a form for Cinema that became what we know as the Classic Hollywood Cinem. That process would involve substantial 'tacit' knowledge, that was not discusse or necessarily even verbalised, but was as it were in the ether of the times. Th everyday assumptions, such as invisibility of technique, would be assumed an largely unwritten.The notion of tacit knowledge is an interesting one, remarke upon in the context of film-making by Jonathan Miller[202] and in the book o Walter Murch by Michael Ondaatje[203]. Tacit knowledge is largely unwritten an often unspoken. It extends to every sphere of human activity but can be seen t operate in particular with craft-skills, whether carpentry or film-editing, whe people are doing something that involves highly-developed abilities, but it is ofte done silently and rarely becomes the subject of discourse.

While this seems rather abstract it reaches concrete form, for example, in the note sent by Hal Wallis to the editor of Casablanca, detailing cuts he required[204]. I one view this is the Hollywood Producer as tyrant, infringing the Director'

---

202 The idea was current in the 1950s in the work of the philosopher Michael Polanyi.

203 The Conversations – Walter Murch and the art of editing film, Michael Ondaatje, Knopf, New York, 2004.

204 See The Making of Casablanca, Aljean Harmtez, Hyperion, 2002.

184

authorial rights. That romanticism only serves to obscure the realities of the process. Hal Wallis was aiming for clarity and economy in storytelling, trimming or removing shots that did not, in his opinion, serve those goals. And it is the experience in reaching those goals that was shared by those few hundred people engaged in this common enterprise.

There is a further aspect to this example. While auteurism sought to elevate the Director to the status of creative artist, this biological view of cultural evolution sees the process as shared by anyone involved in finessing storytelling during the making of a picture. It is a quite different image from an individualistic romantic search for whose role was determinant in the finished picture. This vision is a grand view – of biology, in the form of evolution in its cultural guise, creating the Classic Hollywood Cinema, driving its way through history, via the individuals working in the system, through innumerable tiny changes wrought by those individuals, all sharing in the unwritten rules for making a film fulfil the narrative ideal.

The evolutionary process

This process I would suggest occurred largely informally, and at both a conscious and often unconsciously, among the relatively small number of people working in the studios who had a direct input to the process of making pictures – writers, directors, editors, and producers in particular. All these studio employees and employers, all in their offices, cutting-rooms, studios etc, coming together in the commissary at lunchtime, and in the screening room for viewings, and in the interstices, in the corridors, the breaks between reels, story conferences and editing lists, in all these cases flows the same tacit understanding – keep the story going, make sure the telling doesn't get in the way of the tale, cut out anything that gets in way or slows things down. A tacit ether laying over the whole of the studio world, with all the worker-ants slaving away under pressure to get the next picture out – but globally all sharing the same task – with the formal mode of that Cinema shaped by the commercial push to hide the mechanics, which in turn produces the paradigm elements that we think of today as narrative film form.

In that sense, even the idea of improvements in the application of narrative techniques in the 1930s is not perhaps conventionally rational in the sense of to do with aesthetic concerns. Their impetus would have primarily been commercial - from Producers and Studio heads concerned with return on investment rather than film-form. The Classic Hollywood Cinema did not develop its aesthetic achievement despite the money, but because of it. Aesthetic advance was to some extent an unintended, even unwelcome by-product of managers negotiating the vagaries of the market. An interest in art would have been considered a sign of unreliability in a Director, so that with a Hawks or a Ford, any aesthetic concerns are buried deeply behind an impenetrable facade of stoical professionalism: "My name is John Ford, I make westerns".

Hollywood is often pejoratively called a factory, because of the management's disinterest in art and the creative ambitions of those who worked there. Certainly the inhabitants work relentlessly towards something of which they themselves may have been either unaware or only partly aware, even for reasons of which they might have disapproved should they have been asked to make a judgement on it, but were all part of this 'blind' project that created Classical Hollywood. The studio system as a human beehive, with key workers, editors, writers, directors and producers making decisions about every element of a film, but all working towards a shared, if unspoken goal of the classical model that had been developed and inculcated since the earliest days of Cinema, advancing towards the perfection of the system that reached a kind of apotheosis around 1939.

This is not a story of documented history but of the unwritten, the unspoken, even the unthought, the interstices, of tacit knowledge, of an unconscious drive towards the perfection of a classical aesthetic that turned a stubborn and unwieldy medium into a perfect engine of meaning. Hidden in the highly competitive world of the Studio system was an implicit model of the motion picture, one without a textbook, an unwritten constitution, as it were, that nevertheless drove almost every key decision about each film from start to finish.

In the beehive all the workers carry out their individual tasks perhaps without any overall view of what the goal is, but each makes their contribution. The overall process whereby the classical form developed was something beyond the control of any one individual, beyond even Scott Fitzgerald's fabled six people able to hold the whole equation of pictures in their head. It was a product of the whole ecology of Hollywood, from the smallest item to the largest, including thoughts as well as actions, unconscious motives as well as conscious decisions. Despite the hostility of the environment to artistic ambition for individuals like directors and writers, it was ironically the commercial pressures as seen by the studio heads that pushed, even if blindly, in the particular direction that brought us the classic Hollywood Cinema. But that is precisely the disinterested character of evolution It is not at the behest of mere humans, who are at best its willing accomplices and

186

in some cases in Hollywood its unwilling instruments. It is a process that sweeps with it every element in nature and culture, and somehow in this case, through The Genius of The System, created an ideal immanent aesthetic form of perfect proportion (as seen in the ideal screenplay if not necessarily perfectly-formed in any individual film).

It is a remarkable in the tide of human affairs that such a commercially-driven enterprise as Hollywood should somehow come up with a perfect aesthetic, even if as an ideal. Every film failed to lesser or greater extent to realise that ideal, but the drive towards its values created a medium whose power we continue to underestimate today. It is as though the impersonal selective forces of cultural evolution had the ability to work through the studio system at that time and in that particular place to create something above and beyond the merely functional. Each film had the character of an artefact produced by evolution, imperfect, a copy with variations of the paradigmatic form, and if any one film came up with an element of any kind that was beneficial then it would find itself adopted and adapted in a continual process of evolutionary elaboration. The whole process combines the role of individuals – for example an editor discovering that cutting on action creates a smoother less visible transition from longer to closer shot – with the general ideology of the studio system that the role of technique was to maintain audience attention and suspension of disbelief.

However, the characteristic that evolution is non-teleological means it is not goal-oriented in the familiar human sense, nor about 'Progress' but only about change. Change, yes, progress, no. There is an argument that evolution has direction if not a goal, but it does not mean things progress, get better. Its designs would not be approved of by engineers, as they are the result of the mechanisms of natural selection and adaptation and exaptation. It moves on, it changes, it adapts, but apart from survival of the species, it has no agenda. Of course, survival (via reproduction) is the biggest agenda one could hope for in a sense. But again let us recall that survival is at the level of the species, not of Cinema.

Therefore it would be no surprise that CHC was replaced by what from certain perspectives is a backward move, the *Star Wars* generation of spectaculars. But spectacle is a feature of Cinema, and so is action, so the *Star Wars* generation was suited to a new audience demographic and perhaps not to the audience for *Mildred Pierce*. The emergence of a younger market, male and keen on the spectacular rather than dealing with the emotional suggests an economic and social understanding of those changes, which can be seen as differential development in evolutionary terms, technical advance and emotional regression. That's evolution at work in the realm of demographics, rather than progress. While it may be possible to argue that the CHC centred upon emotion, it might be harder to characterise other eras of Cinema in quite that way.

Biology, evolution, culture, cinema

'Nothing in biology makes sense except in the light of evolution'. Evolution brought to light the relationships – between what at first seemed to be disjointed facts in natural history – that constructed a coherent explanatory body of knowledge that describes and predicts observable facts about life on the planet. I would offer the suggestion that a similar case can be made for culture, with Cinema as a concrete instance, in extending genetic evolution to that of culture, a process which is not quite new, arguably dating back 10,000 years to the earliest settlements, and some would say to the 'Great Leap Forward' around 50,000 years ago, when man began to make clothes, dwellings, pottery, jewellery and art.

The mechanisms of genetic evolution transmuted into the realm of culture would suggest that nothing in *society* makes sense except in the light of evolution. Therefore in principle it would follow that we cannot explain the development of an instance like the Classic Hollywood Cinema without reference to those mechanisms. As it is the relatively recent past, and in many ways highly-documented, it would be an interesting and possible project to reconstruct the development of the formal element, for instance, from the particular point of view of seeing it as an evolutionary process. Valuable work has been done from a historical point-of-view (in the landmark studies by Bordwell, Staiger and Thompson), so there is quite some raw material from which to begin to elaborate a biological-cultural view. There is perhaps a sense in which the development from the early to the late 30s in finessing the paradigm is a particular area that would reward further study as it is arguably less about the establishment of elements of the formal paradigm, that were fairly-well established by then, as about other conditions, perhaps such as the shift to production units that saw the same teams work together more regularly.

Where else would you have so many people turning out so many works that were the result of so much pressure – financial, creative, psychological, organisational etc? Hollywood was a cauldron that produced burnished artefacts, honed to within an inch of their life. That is not to say any one of them was perfect, or was every likely to be so, but the model was a shared project among all the key players in this one place over a certain period of perhaps one generation.[205]

188

The commercial logic in general would be the same as in any business – the attempts of management to reduce risk and uncertainty of return for investment. Films were and remain a notoriously difficult product to guarantee as profitable. Views vary but it was common to regard one in ten as likely to yield substantial profits and the rest would be cross-financed, that is subsidised, by the one-in-ten. Of course no business sets out to make an unprofitable product and to that effect the aim of management was to reduce the number of financial flops.

In that context, film form is under pressure to give audiences what the heads of studios think they want – emotionally engaging stories told through techniques that minimise any disturbance to emotional involvement, so that the viewer sees only the story not the telling. While we may take for granted that goal today, it was not by any means guaranteed as an outcome in the 1930s, and the battle to create that perfect machine for profitable emotion was a constant one between producers, writers, directors and editors, to make each film as effective as possible in mesmerising audiences and thus increasing the potential of each project for turning a profit.

Behind the pressure to invisible technique lies the collective instinct that narrative was the path to follow, a clear trajectory from the birth of the medium. The difference that a neurobiological view proposes is to see that impulse towards narrative as both genetic and cultural, a co-evolution between the way the brain has evolved to work – joining up stimuli to make sense of them – and the exaptation of that basic mechanism to produce the play and the novel and a certain culmination in the Classic Hollywood Cinema.

This collective effort, among a few hundred studio employees at any one time was largely unwritten and unrecorded. It was not in the interest of those involved, certainly not the studio bosses, to release that kind of 'Intellectual Property' beyond their gates, as this elite knowledge was part of the mystique of Hollywood. Making storytelling invisible was accompanied by keeping trade secrets secret. Film-makers in general could pick up tips from seeing other studios' films, but not from buying a book on screen-writing, something that would emerge only in the 1980s in a very different context.

The paradigm was both ever-present and invisible, in the sense that it was not the kind of thing that was written down, even as a guide from studio bosses to

205 The context changed with the rise of Television and the power of the studios made a return in the 21st Century in a different nexus of circumstances, with the model retaining its power as seen in the myriad books advising on screenplay writing.

underlings. It was something in the air, a condition for being on the plot was to have it in your veins. This was tacit knowledge at perhaps its most developed.

There is a certain irony that the creation of the perfect engine of meaning, the ideal method for handling time in the motion-picture, was an evolutionary outcome in the sense that it was not just unintentional but if anything unwelcome, as that was not what it was all about to the studio heads and producers. Even writers and directors would be wary of owning up to aesthetic interests in such a climate. The silent stoicism of a Howard Hawks or John Ford was a defence-mechanism against any suspicion of artistic intentions as unmanly, where professionalism was valued above everything else. Hawks' first rule of directing was "Don't annoy the audience".

Professionalism, doing a good job was the esprit de corps of Hollywood. The idea that they were creating something over and above their intentions – a classical aesthetic that can stand alone as an object of analysis – might have amused them, and at some level I suspect Ford's gruffness and Hawks's toughness were conscious strategies to disguise aesthetic interests. In comparison Hitchcock was almost effete, but even under questioning at length by Truffaut,[206] he tends to describe the different challenges he set himself in each film as 'technical'. Directors like these, as well as writers and some Producers would have been well aware of what they were doing, of this collective project, even where they would not think of it in terms anything like a Classical aesthetic.

The pressure-cooker environment of Hollywood that created this form for film cannot be explained adequately in sociological, ideological, psychological or economic terms. Anthropology might get closer, but only an anthropology that took into account the neurobiological origins of the pressure towards narrative, in other words an evolutionary anthropology incorporating neuroscience.

Evolution of film form

It is worth going back to the earliest days of Cinema, when we might imagine that any number of directions for the development of the medium are possible, many of which appeared in those early days, from What The Butler Saw to abstract Cinema. In a global evolutionary sense, why then would a direction emerge that embraced narrative?

206 *Hitchcock – Truffaut*, Revised Edition, Simon & Schuster, New York, 1986.

The positive reasons are not hard to fathom – novels and plays were the obvious precursors, and it was partly the prestige of those middle-class media that prompted DW Griffiths to seek respectability for a medium that had both begun in fairgrounds and was considered unsuitable for respectable people to attend. The early Cinemas were a popular venue looked down upon with a certain disgust by the middling classes as literally odorous places smelling either of body-odour or disinfectant or both. In that sense *Birth of a Nation* was a breakthrough in terms of respectability, despite its overtly racist theme, perhaps rather more than its formal triumph in creating a three-and-a-half-hour presentation that also made more profit than any film before or for a generation afterwards (i.e. *Gone With The Wind* in 1939).

The negative reasons rarely get an airing. The new medium is, in certain ways, highly intractable. The tableau shots of early Cinema, where the whole scene is covered in a wide-shot, makes understanding stories almost impossible – at least when seen from today's perspective. The elements of the paradigm, such as eyeline-matching, otherwise known as 'creative geography' are rather extraordinary inventions when thought of naively. Someone imagined an invisible line that connects two pairs of eyes in abstract space. Imagine that line existing without the eyes on either end of it, and then imagine the two sets of eyes also in abstract space, and then imagine connecting each pair of eyes to opposite ends of this invisible line. A little mad, no? And that is only the start.

Of course, the process would probably have been nothing like that. Evolution is adaptation. Film-makers, that is principally cameramen, editors, directors and producers, would have been intensely familiar with screen direction principles – the Cavalry going left to right therefore the Indians going right to left. That was already well in place before 1910. Imagine a baby watching a character go off screen, to one side of the frame, say the right. Where have they gone? If the next shot has them coming into frame from the right – well, why not? Have they not just come back, having left? Even if the background space is different that might well be a reasonable mental assumption as we are probably more interested in the character than the background, especially if the character is moving, as movement attracts the eye. On the other hand, if the character appears in the next shot from the left, again moving towards the right of the frame, then we seem to think that person is in continuous movement, moving from one place to some other. We might not notice the background too much, but it can help if it is different as that emphasises the focus of our attention is moving through different spaces. If that person stops, still looking in the same direction, then we might wonder what s/he is looking at? Now if the next shot has someone else looking in the opposite direction, that is from right to left, and both are static, then might we not think that they are looking at each other? What a discovery!

What seems perhaps 'natural' to us, as a fine example of cultural learning, would have been potentially neither natural nor even perhaps understandable to an imaginary first person making such a 'mistake' in putting two shots next to each other in succession. A sharp eye somewhere might have thought – that seems to work, what is going on here? A less sharp eye would have simply got on with taking the shots apart and correcting the mistake. Imagine an editor running that cut back and forth, back and forth, seeing whether her eyes were deceiving her (women cutters seem to have been more common than camerapersons), until she was no longer sure whether she was imagining something useful or just getting tired.

Historically it might have been twenty years of more before that mistake became a firm fixture in the paradigm of narrative film-making. Imagine the millions of times that cut passed back and forth across a light source on thousands of film before it evolves from an error to a fixture. That is my image of evolution.

In fact, there is more to it than that. The eyes looking left to right must appear to be looking at the eyes looking right to left. If either are looking too high or too low, or to one side or the other, the wonderful fiction of 'creative geography' or in eyeline-matching falls apart to a greater or lesser extent. It is no surprise how important eye-contact is when we gain so much information from looking at the faces of other humans. That physiological fact lies behind the importance of the eyeline match, a further example (along with the narrative tendencies of the brain) of how evolution plays a part as a foundation of culture.

How abstract is that conception can be seen in the fact that gives its name to 'creative geography' is that the person looking left-to-right can be in Moscow and the person looking right-to-left in New York, yet we still take it as they are looking at each other. That indicates the power of eye-contact in how our brains apprehend the world. Our focus is on the person not the background, on the face, on the eyes, on the direction of look of the eyes, and then we 'confabulate' the notion that these two people, ideally in one sense a man and a woman, are looking at each other. Biology again, reproduction calling the tune.

This fine example of cultural learning is a nice mixture of the physiological and the 'cultural', in the sense that it is something new that had not existed before, at least in its precise sense of a technique in Cinema. Of course, it is a translation, or adaptation if you like, of us observing two people talking to each other in front of us. But it is not one that is unmissable as a conclusion. It takes a certain set of circumstances for something we do naturally and take for granted to be seen in an abstract way as the solution to a problem in the new medium of Cinema. Now we take it for granted there too, as we have been trained by repeated exposure to the technique, echoing a perfectly normal natural one in social relations, through our time spent watching films and television. It is ironic that our learning has been so good that we take it, and much of the rest of Cinema, for granted.

Imagine an exercise where all the familiar devices of narrative are taken apart, reverse-engineered as it were, to create a kind of anthropology or evolutionary process in reverse, where we are de-familiarised with what we now take so much for granted. Before our eyes Cinema falls apart, goes back to its earliest days, and the intractability of the medium, the source of headaches every day for film-makers across the world, appears before our eyes once again and becomes evident, and we are returned to those early days and the apparent near-impossibility of doing something with this combination of mechanical and chemical devices that will make any sense to anyone. Think of that Policeman in Leeds, called in to view the first moving-images projected on a wall in 1888 by Louis LePrince.

The use of the medium to show people doing things is an obvious one. Monsieur LePrince filmed traffic crossing a bridge but also family in the garden. From there to a tableau of the proscenium arch of theatre, as in *Les Films D'Art* of 1908, is no great advance, in fact arguably a retreat, a literal stepping back. The problem of breaking up the proscenium space in order to achieve a greater legibility of the individual pieces of the action is however, an issue worth devoting some thought to. In simple terms, that leads us to the paradigm of Classical Hollywood Cinema.

I am fond of that definition, apocryphally given by Sam Goldwyn, of documentary, "Films without women". If the commercial future of the new medium makes sense as portraying people, then the next step is to replay the positive force of evolution, reproduction. Desire, love, reproduction. If the negative is survival, the positive is reproduction. Hollywood as films with women.

Evolution example: Cutting on Action

'Cutting on action' is one of the paradigmatic techniques developed in order to facilitate smoother storytelling by hiding a cut from a long shot to a close shot. An editor of the Classic era might have seen it in Cinema, and might even have

193

returned to watch it more than once if it caught her or his eye. But, in a time before studying films closely was possible, that would be as near an editor might get to seeing a 'new' technique, and they would then have to try it out themselves in the cutting-room to work out precisely how to do it. Editors used to cut before or after the action, and cutting on the action involves choosing the frame where the most movement or most suitable movement occurs in the shot, and then cutting in the close shot, a matter of trying things out.

From the first editor who came up with the idea, perhaps by accident or through constant reflection upon the problem, or both, to the second editor who happened to see it in Cinema, to the third who took it up etc, it would be some time before the technique was universally adopted.

The process of thinking about the technique may well have been partly conscious and partly unconscious. There is physiology involved to realise that the audience won't notice the cut during movement and then the testing to see where in the wide shot is best to make the cut to the close shot. As film-makers were rather busy in the studio system, it may have been some time before a technique used by one editor was spotted by another and the passing on down the line to the point where a technique was universally adopted could have been a matter of years.

In what sense, you may ask, is this culture? In the combination of physiology, conscious and unconscious thinking and gradual adoption it is not a bad example of evolution in the cultural sphere in the Darwinian sense.

One may imagine the process being observed by a director during editing, and him asking how it was done and what was the principle. That would be a necessary step in the adoption of the technique on a regular basis, because both the wide shot and the close up have to have the movement required. A close-up without the preceding movement will result in a jump in the cutting, which indeed is noticeable in both silent and early sound cinema. Therefore the original insight would have then to transfer to the planning of shooting by a director. Without the movement on both shots the cut cannot be disguised and to have it requires deliberate planning of how to shoot both wide and close shots. So the process of adoption of this variation of film form requires a number of steps to happen before it can begin to be more widely adopted. Perhaps in this simple example we have an illustration of how film form might have evolved to the classic period.

There is another important factor about this particular technique, mentioned earlier. The fact that it contributes to smoother storytelling, eliminating the jump

194

between wide and close shot would have potentially recommended itself beyond the editors and directors to the producers and studio heads. The reason for that is a broader commitment within the Hollywood industry to minimising the visibility of film-making technique in a film. The business end was concerned with giving spectators the best experience that would have them returning to Cinema week, in week out. Anything that got in the way of their being swept up in the story and in the fate of the stars was counter-productive. Therefore the lowly role of film form was to get in the way as little as possible. Each element of the paradigm (eyeline matching, continuity of screen direction, cutting on action etc) was there not to develop the medium in any abstract sense, but in order to make the illusion as strong as possible and to create as little distraction from the narrative as possible. In that sense, film form in Classic Hollywood had an economic function above all.

With cutting-on-action, the technique plays to the brain's inability to notice certain changes that occur during movement, and there is a substantial empirical body of work that explores that issue.[207] A historical approach can identify when it happened,[208] a biological-cultural approach can explain its significance – not just in terms of the physical reasons, but also potentially taking that further into the epistemological questions about what we know, how we know it, and the significance of physical phenomena such as not noticing particular kinds of changes. For editors it was a practical discovery that helped to smooth the storytelling process, and in so doing met the parti pris of producers and studio heads.

Imagine editors cutting before or after the action on hundreds of Hollywood films before one happened to try what must have seemed like a counterintuitive development, perhaps something discovered by accident, or by someone with an instinct about the brain and movement, perhaps a skill encouraged by the multiple-camera interlude (1929–31) into becoming more general and then as single camera came back into use, working through the master-shot method transcribed to single-camera. This may be a good example of how evolution works in culture, combining perhaps an individual's instinctive knowledge about how

---

207 Viewers famously missed a man in a gorilla suit entering the frame as they were distracted by the action. Also quoted in Dehaene op. cit p. 35 etc.

208 In *The Classical Hollywood Cinema* book the term 'matching on action' is used and mentioned in relation to the classical paradigm, but the illustrated example is from a 1944 film *Mr Skeffington*, and another quoted is from the 1941 *Play Girl*. The suggestion is made that multiple-camera shooting, which dominated from 1929–31, facilitated cutting-on action as multiple choices were available to cut from master-shot to closer shots. It may well have been in that period that the cut-on-action became a standardised skill for editors (p. 305). Bordwell earlier describes it as an expensive and time-consuming technique and discusses it in relation to temporal rather than visual continuity (p. 46).

the brain works (e.g. movement blindness) with institutionalised requirements (invisible storytelling) and technical/commercial developments (the multi-camera phase intended to restore some fluidity to the sound-film compared to that of late silent-Cinema to offset what was seen as the static and boring effects of the limitations of early sound-recording), coming together over time so that what was perhaps an isolated discovery in editing becomes more widely taken up for diverse reasons and then becomes established as part of the paradigm. Reproduction with variation leading to adaptation, the genetic evolutionary process transferred into the cultural realm.

Why it exists is partly down to a mixture of the biological base and the social conditions that made invisible storytelling a key aim. However, it also poses questions on the big issues of consciousness and truth – if we only see certain things and effectively do not see others what does that tell us about what consciousness is and the age-old question of the nature of the truth consciousness perceives?

There is the implicit suggestion that 'biological' truth is a rather different creature from 'philosophical' truth, precisely because experiments can demonstrate how the brain works is quite different from how philosophers have assumed it to work[209]. It is possible that what we notice and what we don't notice is decided by what has biological value, in other words what is regarded by the body/brain system as relevant to survival. Perhaps what we don't notice we don't 'need' to notice from that perspective or, on the other hand, the fact that we don't notice certain things is an evolutionary fault in our systems that constrains and influences not just the literality of how we see the world, but also the philosophical implications as well. Or perhaps both.

Creative Geography

The notion of 'Creative Geography' is a delightfully abstract element of the formal paradigm of Classic Hollywood. The development of each element of the classic paradigm is an evolutionary tale in itself, but it is important to realise the scale of the task facing film-bosses in the early days of Cinema. The way I realised that myself was in the process of learning about film-making, when one is

---

209 The origins of a distinct philosophical truth, as discussed in the second section of the book, arise with Kant, the notion that philosophy can lay claim to a truth the equal of that claimed by experimental science. The problem is that such a claim can be the 'tumbling ground for whimsies' that William James saw in the notion of the unconscious later adopted by Freud, and amply demonstrated in the various idealisms since Kant.

suddenly faced with the practical problem of how to manage this rather abstract relationship between the space in which the action takes place and the process of story-telling that becomes focussed in the cutting-room. For example, eyeline matching (creative geography) is a very artificial process that occurs in separate shots that may have been filmed hours or days apart, but when cut together appear to be happening in real time. What is being produced is the simulation of two people talking to each other simultaneously in one space, but the technique of achieving that outcome is highly regulated in order to create the dramatic presentation without being distracted by the techniques involved, sometimes called 'artificial geography'. If however the rules are not properly observed, then it is disruptive to the viewing experience – if the eyelines don't match then we are immediately aware something is wrong and our attention will be taken by that fact rather than what the drama is about at that moment. We will be thinking 'he is not really looking at her', for example, and that could either be experienced as undermining our suspension of disbelief or even worse we might try to explain it in terms of the characters' psychology – he looks shifty, or he doesn't really mean what he is saying to her. If we reverse-engineer the process by which that technique came to be discovered, there might well have been a moment in an editing room when an editor realised by chance or through making an error, that what is key in people talking to each other is eye-contact, and then working out how to achieve that in a practical way in staging the filming in order to preserve that eye-contact when creating the scene in editing. A way of seeing the difference is to look at films made before eyeline matching was the rule and then it becomes clear what an improvement it made to the fluidity of the story-telling. For example, if you have to film two people together in the same shot in order to show eye-contact there is no flexibility in being able to focus on the reaction of the person listening. If, then the form reaches the stage where an 'insert' shot cuts into close-up of the listening person, the cut will be noticeable in moving from a wide shot to the close shot of one of the participants, partly because the shots are of a different scale. So the rule becomes established that the shots of each person involved in the eyeline match technique should be of a similar scale in order to cut down the jarring effect of the cut. Even better if the person to whom you are cutting moves their head in reaction – and then you can also cut on that action to the close-up, so that the cut becomes virtually invisible, as our eye is taken by the movement of the head, instead of the cut from a wider shot to a closer shot. In that last case the process becomes invisible and makes the least distraction to the storytelling, the aim of studio bosses and therefore of the cameramen, editors, directors and producers involved in the practical production process.

'Creative geography' and cultural evolution

In one way 'Creative (or artificial) geography' is quite a magical idea, but the reality is that it obeys a biological law – although law is a little formal as a term – but the idea is that we humans look at each other as a priority, hence the 90% of our information about the world from faces. We are attracted to faces 'naturally', that is for biological reasons to do with survival and reproduction, and so it is unsurprising that is where our focus lies. Film-makers in some way recognised that fact and came up with 'creative geography' as a way of tuning in to this biological fact. That was of course not their purpose, they were simply trying to find ways to tell stories better. The practice would have taken time to be adopted and a further period before it became virtually universal in Hollywood practice. One may imagine it being seen in one film and an editor, director or producer noticing the technique and proposing it on their next production.

In this sense evolution in the sphere of culture is about the same processes of adaption that are familiar from genetic evolution, that of exaptation. Cinema is an example of that in broad terms, as many of the elements that are features of Cinema work with the grain of how the brain itself works (narrative, mirror-neurons and copying, identification with characters and shared circuits). Geography works with how and why we use our eyes in relating to others and allows the audience to keep returning to the relationship between two people, developing the thread of that relationship over time, serving a narrative purpose. What was at first a technique to link characters in space had turned, by around 1939, into a tool for creating emotional relationships of depth and complexity. The technique itself had evolved, not fundamentally in its mechanics, but in the uses it was put to. By the time of *Casablanca* two people in space became an aid to expressing unspoken emotions with a history as Bogart and Bergman summon up the anguish of their past in Paris amid the tensions of wartime Casablanca.

We make stories as a fundamental survival technique, and that way of the brain operating goes some way to suggest why the Classic Hollywood Cinema became hegemonic. CHC, of which Creative Geography forms a key part of the paradigm, works with the grain of the brain, as it were. (Of course the matter is more complex than that, US economic power and a host of lesser factors must be included in the overall picture).

This is evolution working itself out in the realm of culture. The timetable of evolution, of millions of years is here shortened to a few decades for the whole paradigm of Classic Hollywood, a tiny indication of how cultural evolution has perhaps accelerated and continues to do so.

The Screenplay and the Ideal Film

A second significant element is the paradigm of the screenplay. It is one of the ironies of the Hollywood story that it was really only long after the demise of the Classic era that the screenplay paradigm emerged, through textbook guides, investigations into how good screenplays worked, and gurus selling their advice on how to write the perfect script. This development only began around 1980 and has seen countless books published on the screenplay, whereas in the Classical period there was only the odd one and writers learned on the job rather than taking a course.

The Ideal Film is implicit in the rules of the classical screenplay. Those rules are highly internally-coherent and although they were formalised to a greater extent many years after the classical period, they were evolved by the 1940s, adapted first from the theatre and then developed specifically for Cinema. There were very few textbooks of screenwriting before the 1980s, but what is clear from the analyses dating from this later period, is that the rules were and are very strict and precise. As with any temporal work of art, the opening has to lay out the principal themes that the later stages will thoroughly explore before finally resolving them – in a way that is both 'unexpected and inevitable'. In other words the climax of the story has to have resolved all the themes in a coherent way stretching back to the opening, but with a skill that retains an element of surprise. There are a host of other rules,[210] such as – at random – 'show not tell', 'character is action', always come into the scene at the last possible moment, that together constitute a formidable classical system, ironically only really made explicit since the 1980s with the growth of screenwriting courses in higher-education. The craft skills that evolved to create the ideal screenplay were largely in place by 1939 and are evident in for example *Casablanca*, *Notorious* and *Stagecoach*, but my feeling is that one could not say quite the same of early 30s Hollywood films.[211]

---

210 See John Truby: *The Anatomy of Story: 22 Steps to Becoming a Master Storyteller*, Faber & Faber, London, 2008. Truby's book but also his software for helping screenwriters is a revelation of the complexities of what I term the Ideal Script, showing how many balls need to be kept in the air at the same time by the aspirant screenwriter. His software forms a kind of working diagram of the key narrative elements, and in its own way is part of the tacit knowledge of the film industry, explicit in the software but a 'technical' tool only of interest to the writer struggling with all those balls.

211 Chapter & verse would be useful to back these feelings, and I intend to return to the topic. The skills were in existence, so there must have been other factors such as the staginess imposed by sound-recording limitations – which is what makes *Wild Girl* (1932) exceptional as a location film shot in a forest. Production factors, such as those that led to the formation of teams suggest executives realised the early sound films lacked appeal so perhaps there was more emphasis laid on script – but that is only speculation at this point.

Blue Jasmine & *the Ideal Script*

One concrete way of showing what the Ideal Script is about is to look at a contrasting example. The studio system was effective in developing the classic narrative model and although that tradition carries on today with film-makers oriented towards the visual qualities of that narrative model, the decline of the studio system saw the rise of independent film-makers, both those who had been trained in Hollywood but set up outside the studio system, and others who had never worked in that system. Of the latter kind, they often favoured the greater freedom of subject-matter and treatment that working outside the Hollywood system, for example in New York, afforded. One example is Woody Allen, working in New York, starting as a comedian before turning to Cinema, and creating his own brand of films based upon his reputation for comedy. *Blue Jasmine*, 2013, was said by some critics to be his best film for 20 years, and received generally strongly-favourable reviews in the press, and was nominated for an Oscar for screenplay in 2014. I have only seen the film once but it struck me for its departures from the model:

1. Show not Tell: Towards the end of *Blue Jasmine* the heroine's sister tells us that her sister was always one to turn the other way when there was something she did not want to face. That line was a summation of the film in a way, but in another way it came as a revelation, a surprise, an "Oh, I see" moment – and for that to come near the end of the film – and in dialogue, is a mark that the film had not established – by filmic means – what it had to deliver in dialogue. It had not shown us successfully, what it told us in dialogue. For that to be a surprise, it meant that it was not a confirmation of what the film had told us by other means, that we would then use that dialogue-information to confirm what we already knew. On the contrary, it meant that I was running the earlier parts of the film over in my head to check that statement against what I had been shown. The problem is that the dialogue was effectively providing me with new information late on in the film. It is another rule of the ideal script that it should not, if possible, provide important new information about the main character late on as it will disturb the rhythm of the narrative for us. That particular line did just that in this case. I did only see the film once, but my recall of it would suggest that this was far from an isolated incident. In fact, my general impression of Woody Allen films is that they do a lot of telling instead of showing as they are heavy on dialogue and light on visual dramatisation. His films have a strong following and have been commercially successful as a 'brand', which goes to show the CHC model is not the only route to connecting with audiences, and that as culture changes so do the forms of Cinema that work for audiences. It is an irony that the studio system produced a pure form of Cinema that later freedoms have seen a falling-away from, as its disciplines and control over form declined.

2. Character arc: The main character in the CHC goes through a process of change, grows, develops, faces challenges and evolves through them. In *Blue Jasmine* the impression is that the character is the same at the end as she was at the beginning. She has gone through external changes, but that is not reflected in her personal development as the classic model requires. The tear-stained woman rambling to herself on the park bench in the last scene felt similar to the widow near the start of the film. That would suggest no character arc. In terms of the CHC, that would be seen as a basic failure that would be very unlikely to be allowed to pass in the studio system. It felt like a crowd-pleasing negative ending – the character has learned nothing and therefore deserves her misery and decline. One of the US reviews made a point about the unrealism of the ending, that those who got rich in the way her husband did rarely ended penniless. The review regarded that as regrettable, but there is an irony in the film rewarding a liberal audience with wishful-thinking that turns its face away from something it would have been a tougher challenge to face, just like the accusation of her sister against the main character.

3. Deus ex machina: When a plot does not have designed into it the resolution of certain issues, dropping in a matter of chance to solve them is called a 'deus ex machina'. In *Blue Jasmine* the heroine is about to escape poverty with a wealthy new beau. They look in the window of a fancy jewellers to choose an engagement ring and are about to enter the shop when – lo and behold – at that precise moment a character turns up who can upset the apple cart and destroy her plans. He is the ex-husband of her sister, who lost his money under the main character's husbands business scheme that collapsed when his fraudulent dealings caught up with him. His revelations, including her having a son she had not revealed, shock her prospective husband so much he pulls out of the romantic bliss they were seconds away from confirming. Quite why the ex-husband of her sister, who was supposedly working in Alaska, turns up on Fifth Avenue at the moment the heroine is about to achieve salvation from poverty and a return to the life of a rich woman is not explained. Deus Ex Machina, God pops out of the machine to solve the plot problem. In the CHC chance never can be dropped in to correct faulty plotting. Chance as a solution would be seen as a beginner's mistake, something that might come up as an idea but would be quickly dismissed as the weakest of weak solutions, and one that raises more questions in the audience than it solves, thereby going against the cardinal rule of making the story process as smoothly invisible as possible.

4. Pure Cinema: Hitchcock opposed his idea of Pure Cinema to 'Pictures of People Talking'. What he meant by Pure Cinema was the age-old quest in every medium to identify the unique features of that medium in order to develop those features, thus making the most of the particular qualities of the given medium.

It is sometimes the case that people that transfer from one medium to another, in contrast to that idea, carry over their attitudes from their original medium rather than adopt the specifics of a new medium, and hence it can be that writers – novelists, dramatists and the like, are less interested in the pure aspects of Cinema when they make films.

Blue Jasmine is almost a locus classicus of the tendency, as it features a lot of dialogue, and a lot of telling with the dialogue rather than showing with the images. Hitchcock contrasted dialogue-driven films with those where the story was told through visual dramatisation, showing not telling.

5. Audience orientation: There is a sense in watching a Classic Hollywood film that you always know where you are – that is to say the emotional status of the hero/ine is made abundantly clear in visual ways, rather than through dialogue alone. Dialogue plays a crucial part, but it does not carry too much of the burden of the the plot or character. The achievement of that 'geographical' security is no mean achievement, nor was it ever easy to create – hence the codes of Classical Cinema. With a Hitchcock film he will establish that clarity in order to undercut it by casting doubt over the status of the hero/ines' emotional situation. But in order to do that, the film has to create a clear sense of one direction before holding out an ambiguity in an other direction. Without clarity in the first sense, ambiguity would not work as the audience would not have the strong sense of who the character is before the ambiguity is worked in to undermine that sense.

The problem with *Blue Jasmine* is that the film does not manage to achieve position one before moving to position two. It is unclear 'who' the main character is – is she strong or weak, innocent or manipulative? She has elements of each and shifts from weak to strong, from innocent to scheming without the key anchor of giving us a centre to her character. The problem again is the reliance on dialogue instead of showing us action that lets us draw conclusions about her strength or weakness. We don't know exactly 'who' she is, and therefore when variations happen – when she is strong after being weak, it is easy to be confused about what she is supposed to be.

These issues with the script of *Blue Jasmine* are rather basic failures, seen in the light of the classical model of the Ideal Script. Woody Allen is perhaps not subject to having a Hal Wallis point out in no uncertain terms errors of structure and characterisation, and instead enjoys the freedom to pursue his own vision, one in which he has had commercial success. There is a double irony in the strictures of the Hollywood factory often producing highly-disciplined script structure, and the later freedom of a 'name' writer/director having such substantial errors in a finished film.

Woody Allen has enjoyed commercial success and critical acclaim despite those problems of course, not because of them. That goes to show that the Classical Hollywood route is not the only one to provide audience satisfaction, and the remarkable resilience of the narrative film is capable of infringements of the Ideal Script to quite a substantial degree when they are offset by other factors of audience appeal. As with the 'fourth-wall' element of *House of Cards* (2013), the audience's ability to deal with what would have been regarded as intrusions into the ideal of the seamless spectacle shows their greater sophistication, by which perhaps means familiarity with the forms as might have been assumed with the drama in ancient Greece, than would have been assumed in the Classic period.

Kate Blanchett won an Oscar for her performance in *Blue Jasmine*, and it remains the case that women leading-characters are few and far between[212], Joan Crawford won her only Oscar for *Mildred Pierce*. The contrast between the Classic qualities of the script for *Mildred Pierce*, based on a James M Cain novel, and the basic failings of *Blue Jasmine* is a striking lesson that evolution is not at all the same thing as progress.

Classical aesthetics and the Ideal Script

One interesting feature of the recent fascination with script is the emergence of a theme stated by Andre Bazin in 1957 – that the Hollywood Cinema is a classical art. With script-tutors such as Robert McKee *Story: Style, Structure, Substance, and the Principles of Screenwriting* (1999) [213] and in particular John Truby, in *The Anatomy of Story* (2008), there is a strong sense that the narrative script is a remarkably coherent and integrated aesthetic system, rigorous and unforgiving, highly-developed and highly-demanding. It is a system where the classic aesthetic principles appear – that nothing is wasted, everything has its role and ideal position, in other words a perfect engine of meaning. These guides are not

212 *Gravity*, which won best-director at the same Oscars, had a female scientist main character in Sandra Bullock.
213 McKee, Faber, London. Truby, Faber, New York.

academic exercises, but practical manuals intended to aid the writer in constructing a *screenplay*. They are sometimes based on empirical research into the most successful scripts in order to extract from them general principles that can be applied by those setting out to write a script (e.g. Syd Field, *Screenplay*). The object they have produced might be thought of as the Ideal Script, and it has all the marks of a classical aesthetic in narrative guise.

It is an irony that such guides were not available to a Ben Hecht or a Jay Presson Allen, and while the odd book had been written in the 20s and 30s, for the most part writers learned their skills on plays or novels and would learn on the job in Hollywood. The knowledge of screenwriting was esoteric as the number of screenwriters would have been comparatively small, and may have been of the tacit kind rather than explicit and conscious. Is was only really from the 1980s that such knowledge has been extracted and formulated into the numerous guides available today. Reverse-engineering from the model today to the screenplays of the classic period suggests that there was at the very least an implicit ideal form in the Classic Hollywood Cinema that fully lives up to Bazin's claim.

The one area where the development of the paradigm of the ideal film may be traced is in screen-writing, or rather in screen-writing books written ironically long after the classic period, but all trying to fathom the basis of a successful screenplay and in so doing tracing the lineaments of the Ideal Screenplay. Hollywood in the early days didn't bother with scripts – Chaplin would try things out directly on film and it was apparently only in the 20s that written scripts became de rigeur under the influence of the likes of Cecil B De Mille – another attempt to bring the medium under more manageable control. A less well-documented evolution of script-writing rules accompanied the visual rules of form that occupied editors[214] – and a hands-on Producer like Hal Wallis.

The rules of screenwriting make the strict nature of the ideal Hollywood model clear. There is no leeway in the rules, a form so tightly integrated that it could work like a Swiss watch – every piece had its place, nothing was out of place, nothing was wasted, and the form had reached a level of perfection that at least in part may be held to account for the dominance worldwide that Hollywood reached in the heyday of the studio system in the sound era.

---

214 A rare example gone into print is Edward Dymytrk 'On Editing', which includes for example the rule about 'cutting on action', one of his seven rules. Focal Press, London, 1968.

Aesthetic cohererence & integration: Marnie

Many of the narrative rules were of course known from literature long before Hollywood, at least among writers interested in reflecting upon their craft. Failure to obey any of the rules was potentially to court disaster. That is not to say that films were not made that failed the rules in one or more points. The rules were so strict that it would have been almost impossible for a writer to follow them with complete success, but the rules portray a perfect case, an ideal, an ambition, and there is at least one striking case where a film-maker tried to follow one of the most demanding rules – that of scene structure. In *Marnie*, the last of the sequence of great films from Hitchcock that began a decade earlier with *Rear Window*, Hitchcock, perhaps as another example of his approach of taking on a technical challenge in every film, seems to have taken on that particular challenge in 1964.

I noted earlier that the rules for the ideal screenplay is the notion that the writer should come in at the last possible moment in the scene – just before a change takes place in the fortunes of the hero/ine, show the change taking place, and then end the scene. Go into the next scene again at the last possible moment before a change, show the change and finish the scene – and repeat until the story ends – in a way that is both unexpected and inevitable. Hitchcock seems to have tried to follow this particular rule as closely as possible with *Marnie*. Every scene comes in at the last moment, the change happens and then bang into the next scene with the same pattern. The result is a train crash as the pattern is repeated scene after scene. How far had Cinema comes since La Ciotat? These 'rules' are more folklore than formally codified, but will be familiar to screenwriters among a host of other rules, all of whose purpose are to create a narrative with an unrelenting forward-movement.

The Ideal Screenplay – a Perfect Engine of Meaning

The narrative form of the ideal screenplay is a perfect engine of meaning, an exemplification of Bazin's contention that Hollywood Cinema was a classical art. Although very difficult to achieve in practice, because of the superficially con-flicting requirements built into the rules[215], in an ideal case there would be – as for any creative work – nothing lacking and nothing in excess, everything would

---

215 An example is that the ending should be inevitable & unexpected, which on the surface seems contradictory, but means that the ending should resolve all the issues set up by the narrative but holding a surprise in the way it happens.

contribute to telling the story in the most effective way, any subplots would feed into the main plot at just the right time and in the right way, and the audience would be led into a labyrinth whose way out surprises them while fulfilling the expectations it had created along the way, finishing with the correct combination of satisfaction and unexpectedness.

Quite a tall order for the poor writer, but as the craft developed, the ability to hone the form of the screenplay increased, and writers and editors, readers and directors as well as the more hands-on Producers all knew the rules inside-out, so that as often as not they would remain unspoken but ever-present in the ether around the making of a studio film. That is not to say for one moment that scripts became necessarily better, as each story and each situation of its production involved different challenges every time, but only the idea that by around 1939 everyone knew what the game was and what the rules of the game were, and that by time the notion of Hollywood as a classical art had become concrete in the form of the ideal screenplay.

The Genius of the System

Bazin proclaimed the Genius of the System of the Classical Hollywood Cinema, and in contrast to the 'politique des auteurs' in which he had been instrumental. Instead of this or that director taking credit for the classical qualities of the Hollywood Cinema of his time (the 1940s and 50s) he ascribed it to the Hollywood culture, a most unlikely insight. There was a sense that auteur theory had a romantic element in promoting individual directors struggling against the disinterest in or opposition to their artistic integrity, and that would not disturb any lingering anti-american and anti-capitalist sentiments that would not be unusual in French culture. However, Bazin's formulation set a cat among those pigeons in the sense of giving credit to high-capitalism and to a system otherwise known for crass vulgarity, excess, greed and venality on a large scale. Clemenceau said of American culture that it was distinctive in having passed from barbarism to decadence without pausing at the intermediate stage of civilisation. To attribute the qualities of classical aesthetics to such vulgarity could seem perverse and contrary, an intellectual pose of wilful flippancy. Bazin was not of that character and his attribution was both serious and profound. What did he see in the Hollywood system that could give rise to such an anachronistic claim? I suggest that it was just those qualities that he saw in a film like *The Searchers* or *Vertigo* but perhaps also in a 'C' picture like *Detour*, and in the less respectable genres of film noir and comedy. What they all did have in common was the immanence of the Ideal Film based on the Ideal Script. The classicism was not individual films or directors but in the narrative model of the Classic Hollywood era. Every film to a greater or lesser extent had this ghostly presence of the immanent model hovering over it, the sense of a common project that was shared by people who may individually have been sworn enemies, but who shared a cultural presumption about popular narrative and its mechanics. There were always variations in the skill and happenstance of how well the Ideal Film would fare in individual circumstances, but in every case directors and editors, producers and camera crew, studio bosses and scriptwriters all shared in the clear sense of how a film should work. It may have been, as Fitzgerald famously said, that only half a dozen men 'held the whole equation' of motion-pictures in their head, individuals like Hal Wallis, but a wider circle of what would have been perhaps a few hundred personnel shared the key elements of the common project. The Genius of the System was a result of commercial pressure more than aesthetic ambition, an apparent contradiction that it took an Andre Bazin to see through to the truth – that from so sordid a beginning endless forms most beautiful and most wonderful have been, and are being evolved.

3. The Affective: Making Emotion Visible

One of the great achievements of the Classic Hollywood Cinema was to make emotion visible. The heart of that achievement was ironically to make emotion invisible. The silent cinema had a tendency to wear its heart on its sleeve, actors would show their feelings in facial expressions. The defining moment of Cinema is what might be called The Face of Robert Mitchum. He perfected a kind of minimal acting perfectly-suited to Cinema, a neutral expression that goes back to Mosjoukine and Kuleshov.

When a woman asks Robert Mitchum if he loves her, his face is a mask. Because of the way the brain works we go into overtime to flesh out that mask, to bring meaning to it, to narrativise it. Because we see no expression we fill it in, we compensate for the neutrality by running over in our minds the options of what he could be thinking. We need to make sense of that absence. We cannot help but join things up, to create a narrative that satisfies the stimuli with which Cinema has presented us. A woman asks a man she loves if he loves her. There can hardly be a bigger question. The moment of *Mildred Pierce* when Mildred's selfish daughter tells her she loves her, cupboard love to get what she wants,

Mildred's face gives us no clue on what she is thinking. We may be wondering if she believes what she hears, or recognises Veda's cupboard love for what it is, and if so ignores that from guilt or stores it away to return to in the future, or even thinks Veda is right to behave like that to get what she wants, and what Mildred never had but is working to get now?

The drama has been carefully structured for these moments, moments of discretion, of withholding the obvious expression of emotion on the face in favour of a neutrality that shifts the work from the actor's face to the audience's brain.

Hitchcock added to Kuleshov's neutral expression followed by the bowl of soup a third term, the closure of the syllogism, the reaction shot. The profound nature of the reaction shot, the moment it becomes the apotheosis of Cinema, is when there is no reaction. It was implicit in Kuleshov, actor-soup-actor-baby, but throw the baby out and there is the syllogism, the actor looks, we see what he is looking at, we see his reaction to what he has been looking at. A world created in abstract space. The bowl of soup could be in Honolulu and the actor in Vladivostock, but Cinema can join them up.

It is the witholding of emotion, the neutral face of Robert Mitchum that for me is the heart of Cinema. That discretion marks an advance over most silent cinema and claims a moment for sound cinema that its predecessor could not have. As we look at Robert Mitchum simultaneously we hear the actress ask him if he loves her. Over that neutral expression – Mitchum's biography was called 'Baby I don't care' – we speculate on his feelings. It is the witholding of expression that sets our minds whirring. Arguably it is even more effective with Mildred as she is perhaps a more complex character in emotional terms, but the principle still obtains.

The great discretion of the CHC was putting emotion on the screen, making it visible, precisely by rendering it invisible. Emotion is not literally visible in this notion of Cinema, it is immanent in the moment, the moment of our looking at The Face of Robert Mitchum.

* * *

ANB & Cinema: The Campaign for Real Science

The question of what kind of theory is proposed here is important, not least in the light of the notion that Film Theory was not a real theory as it had no xplanatory powers. The start of this enquiry was to gain a proper understanding f 'the power of cinema', and that is what the ANB approach to Cinema would laim to do.

'he claim is that ANB offers the potential for a superior depth of analysis to revious frameworks, tied as they have been to the sleight of hand that reduced linema to Language. Instead of linguistics, semiotics, and psycho-analysis, ANB atures the real Sciences of Biology and Neurology, evolutionary biology and euroscience together as neurobiology, and ANB could be part of a 'Campaign or Real Science' in the study of Cinema.

s an example of an experiment-based approach that is about the relationship etween brain function and evolution, a paper by Indersmitten & Gur tackles ie question of the differences between the left and right hemispheres' expression f emotion through respective sides of the face (note that a hemiface is one half f the face, the left relating to the right-side of the brain and vv):

Ve replicated the finding that emotions are expressed more intensely in the left emiface for all emotions and conditions, with the exception of evoked anger, 'hich was expressed more intensely in the right hemiface. In contrast, the results ıdicated that emotional expressions are recognized more efficiently in the right emiface, indicating that the right hemiface expresses emotions more accurately. 'he double dissociation between the laterality of expression intensity and that of :cognition efficiency supports the notion that the two kinds of processes may ave distinct neural substrates. Evoked anger is uniquely expressed more intensely ıd accurately on the side of the face that projects to the viewer's left hemisphere, ominant in emotion recognition'.

xpression intensity on the right and recognition efficiency on the left, suggesting listinct neural substrates' conforms with general expectations, but nuance of the xpression of anger by the left brings in a further factor that accuracy of expression ıay be more important for survival than intensity:

\s pointed out by Sackeim et al. (1978), evoked anger is unique in that its urpose is to prepare the organism for conflict. The greater RHF intensity of ʌoked anger would project to the perceiver's right hemisphere, potentiating the npact on the hemisphere more dominant in emotion processing and thereby ıcreasing the likelihood that the intensity of the emotion will be appreciated by ıe perceiver. Thus, anger could be an evolutionarily important sign for action, hich is elaborated more thoroughly by the left hemisphere (Buck, 1986)'.

This example, which used photographs of actors as the stimulus for interviewees suggests the interrelationship of brain function and survival, that is to say evolution. Anger intensity in the right brain requires action – which is the left-brain's job to elaborate. The complementarity of the hemispheres is high lighted by the emotional expression perhaps most clearly relevant for survival.[216]

While this example deals with differential responses between the two hemisphere to photographs of facial expressions of emotion, it is suggested that a focus for ANB & Cinema would be to begin to untangle the relation between consciou and Automatic emotional information input from films.[217]

The ultimate purpose and function of ANB is to on the one hand understand Cinema at a greater depth than has hitherto been possible, but also on the othe hand to have film-study make a contribution to understanding more about how the brain works, through participation in the design and practice of laboratory based experiment, a practical raison d'etre for film study that would be something of an innovation for the humanities.

Every film is a moment of evolution. In that moment a film is a vessel that capture a wide range of phenomena, facts and techniques, thoughts and unconsciou impulses, histories personal and institutional, formal and informal, a microcosm of the evolutionary tale of the wider world. That story is seen as covering a broade field than traditional forms of enquiry in film. It would incorporate the informa tacit areas of knowledge as well as traditional formal kinds, ranging beyond the areas of disciplines such as sociology and anthropology in order to begin to construct an archive of Cinema, based on scientific-method, that would also b a contribution towards the development of a science of culture grounded i neurobiology with an affective slant.

Affective Neurobiology & Cinema: Summary

1. Cinema is **Moving-Picture**s. Moving-Pictures move. Painting and photogra phy cannot. Theatre has people moving, but not in an interesting way. Interestin means jeopardy, or at least change. There is that in theatre, but not in th concentrated, relentless way it is there in Cinema, especially in Classic Cinema. The essential focus of Cinema is that Vision comes before the word, symbolise

216 Indersmitten, T. & Gur, R.C., 'Emotion processing in chimeric faces:hemispheric asymmetries in expression an recognition of emotions', *Journal of Neuroscience*, 2003, 23(9), pp. 3820–3825. Quoted in McGilchrist, op. cit.

217 A task that has occupied Dehaene for fifteen years in relation to Consciousness. Dehaene op. cit.

n Cinema abandoning the proscenium arch early on and moving the camera loser to the characters and the action. "Action" means what it says, even when t is only people talking, at least in Classic forms.

Movement is important because the eye is attracted to movement. It can't ignore t, it just has to look. The reason it has to look is biology, evolution, survival. We ave to look in case it might be the movement of a predator. We can't help it. nd that is why moving pictures move. The first case is movement in the frame. That is the classic situation in which we are looking at the frame, even out of the orner of our eyes, and when something moves something in our heads clicks nto action. The camera moving is the second case, and briefly that may be hought of as following the story, a more sophisticated idea, that brings up the econd kind of movement.

. The task of the story is to follow change. **Change** is the movement in the motional status of the hero/ine. The story creates a critical path of those changes, hat is its modus operandi (in the Classical model).

As we follow physical movement for biological reasons, we follow **emotional movement** for other biological reasons. **Emotional change** attracts the brain as hysical movement attracts the eye. The essence of the early breaking up of the roscenium space was to clearly follow the hero/ine. Watching early films with he proscenium space intact it is difficult to know who is who.

Breaking up that space with closer shots of the hero/ine focusses our attention on he main character. Our interest in the main character is partly created by his/her ccupying more of the frame and more of the time of the story, but that is emented by their trailing the string of emotional change that attracts us like a nagnet.

motion is created by survival. What we are interested in when having our ttention drawn to the hero/ine is their survival, and connected to that basic ife/death concern, is love/hate, rich/poor, happy/sad. In other words we are nterested in their fortunes as an adaptation of the basic life/death interest, an xtension of it, or 'exaptation' as the technical term goes.

. An extension of following the fortunes of the hero/ine is that another brain unction is the **narrativising** one. Again, as a survival strategy, we make the best ve can of the limited information-processing capacity of Consciousness by oining the small number of stimuli that we can perceive consciously at any one ime. My interpretation of that is it reflects a general brain-method of rationalis-

211

ing for survival. In this case it means joining up the stimuli we can see to best serve survival. That means making a story from them, the most viable one (biologically) possible. If we see yellow stripes moving through a bush opposite to us in a clearing we might jump to the conclusion that could be a tiger and it might want to eat me. If we are in a supermarket aisle choosing between an eco-cereal and a choco-cereal, the process may well involve various self-images of who I am to choose one or another. I would argue that the link is intact with the life/death scenario, but adapted to what we might call culture rather than nature.

Narrativising is thus viewed as a fundamental survival strategy – it makes the best use of the limited resources of Consciousness to devise a scenario as a basis for action where there may be danger. I would also argue that it is not too much of a leap to suggest that is a reason why the **narrative mode** became dominant in Cinema, exemplified by the rigour of Classical Hollywood.

4. A related issue is the operation of Emotion in the sense of **empathy**. Neuro-science has another potentially interesting perspective on the traditional question of how the audience identifies with the hero/ine in Cinema. *Mirror Neurons* show that we copy physical movements of others as a basic mode of operation of the brain.

5. The more recent discovery of what has been called *Shared Circuits* extends that operation from the physical to the emotional. When we follow the emotional status of a hero/ine in Cinema we **Automatically/unconsciously empathise** with their experience. That is part of a much wider mechanism that makes us social beings, able to relate to other humans through visible information, what we know as body-language, facial expression, sound information like sighs, anything and everything that – for the most part outside conscious awareness – helps us to **share the emotional experience of others**.

6. Finally, the burden of what we see when we watch a film enters the brain outside our conscious minds. We are aware of only a fraction of the mass of information that enters the **Automatic**. While that may be quotidien information in everyday life, in the intense and dramatic context of Cinema, that material has a high proportion of Emotion involved. Cinema is **a theatre of Emotional exercise** one which can leave us exhausted at the end of a film. The combination of the Emotional intensity and the volume of information goes a long way toward explaining the power of Cinema.

These elements together provide an account of the attractions of Cinema which combines genetic inheritance with cultural evolution in the biological sense.

* * *

A Theory of Cinema: 10 points:

ANB is a Theory of Cinema that sets out to explain the 'Power of Cinema' – tracing the relationship between how the brain works and how Cinema works with audiences:

1. Cinema combines the power of Vision with the drama of Emotion.

2. 99.9999% of the information we absorb from a film enters the Automatic.

3. Cinema is structured like the brain (not like language) & likewise centred on Emotion.

4. The eye is attracted by movement (a question of survival) – physical movement.

5. The brain is attracted by movement – emotional movement (a question of reproduction).

6. Narrative is a mode native to the brain – hence the dominance of narrative Cinema.

7. Kuleshov (2 shots) to Hitchcock (3 shots) to Gazzaniga (confabulation) – narrativisation.

8. We unconsciously identify with the screen hero/ine via Shared Circuits and Mirror Neurons.

9. The Classic Hollywood Cinema shows culture adapting to biology – making emotion visible.

10. Every film is a moment of evolution – a beginning for a Science of Culture.

5

On Method

Epistemology

I f you are interested in a book of contradictions, this one may recommend itself to you. It is about Cinema with no images, against the word but in words, for Vision but with nothing of Vision. It proposes a scientific analysis by a non-scientist, and a philosophical position by a non-philosopher. It is against philosophy yet in its own odd way is a sort of philosophy book, a book by someone who would not think of himself as a philosopher, and would prefer not to be, and knows nothing of Philosophy. It rejects all current Theory, the work of the last fifty years, all French thought of the 20th Century, and the whole of German Idealism going back to and including parts of arguably the greatest philosopher of the modern period, Kant. In other words it consigns the whole of what is often insularly described as 'Continental Philosophy' to the scrapheap. It proposes a return to a Scottish philosopher of the earlier part of the Eighteenth Century, whose tradition is all but forgotten. It is about Cinema but with no analysis of films, and proposes the chaining of Language, Consciousness and Reason, three glorious pillars of being human, in favour of three virtual unknowns – Vision, the Automatic and Emotion. It takes against formal analysis and knowledge, regarding them as often as not on the autistic side, while proposing only informal, and usually both invisible and unarticulated, analysis and knowledge, the very instincts Kant regarded as absurd and no grounds for judgement, as superior. Not merely superior but infinitely so. It adopts neuroscience with no details or troublesome knowledge of how the brain works, adopts evolutionary biology with an unreconstructed fundamentalist notion of evolution, agreeing wholeheartedly that it is 'the best idea anyone ever had'.[218] It proposes that thought takes place in Vision based on a hunch, and against almost 100% of general opinion (with a handful of notable exceptions). It caps it all with a demand that all ideas are

---

218 A comment of Daniel Dennett.

formulated to be testable under laboratory conditions, yet proposes no experi
ments of its own. If you should wish to dine on contradictions, then you have
found yourself a feast.

In those lights the 'essays' that form this book may be most favouritively described
as 'thought experiments', a term scientists give to speculations based on research
experience. Unfortunately, I have none of that, except through some years of
film-making, my touchstone.

There is, however, an unlikely happy ending to this picaresque tale. The more
thought about the hegemony of the word the more impossible it seemed to devise
strategies to overcome it, so deep and pervasive is the embedded culture of the
ideology. What I failed to realise, stupidly, was that right under my feet and in
plain view changes are occurring that would do the job for me, fortunately
without the least effort on my part. "Events, dear boy, events" had come to the
rescue. The migration of websites to video, the success of Instagram for a
generation for whom Twitter was of no interest, and the $4bn purchase of an app
to send photos that disappear in 10 seconds after they are received, all signalled
that a tectonic shift was underway, one that would sweep away the old regime of
the word like a tsunami, obliterating it and leaving it a vague memory – and in
the space of rather less than a generation. The time of Vision is returning, prepare
the celebrations, line the streets, practice your hurrahs. Long live the Once and
Future King, warmly applaud as the noblest of the senses ascends to the throne.
And don't forget to prepare the lowest, most remote dungeons to shortly receive
their new prisoner, the once haughty word.

A lesson from film-making

When I began making films there was a feeling of suffocation about conventional
narrative, that one was prevented by the formal rules from saying what one wished
to say. There was a mismatch between the energies of wanting to say certain
things, with the optimism that they were new and worth saying, and what one
was learning about the strictures of the form. That experience of railing against
convention was accompanied by the frustrations of trying to find ways of battling
against the overwhelming walls of the narrative city. Which ever way one turned
it seemed impossible to overcome the impressive structure that was so coherent
and comprehensive while strictly shutting out so much that one wished to say.
That led to the pleasure in seeing other film-makers who were fighting the same

216

ight – the bravura and imaginative intelligence of *Pierrot Le Fou* and the more
.ober and rigorous contravention of the rules in the opening hospital scene in *La
Votte*.

.earning about a medium is to learn its rules, to learn precisely what is permitted
>y those rules and what is forbidden. That part is rather easier than learning why.
There seems to be no obvious answer to why you can't say *that*, or at least not in
hat way. Narrative is a mighty engine, perfect in its own way, not easily slighted,
ind never without cost. One learns eventually that the slightest slip will be
>unished by the audience's attention wavering or simply being lost. Narrative is
i demanding master, resourceful and implacable. You are only one person and
10 matter how much you twist and turn, and even if you were to have the
>rilliance of a Godard, it is relentless and will eventually wear you down and make
/ou see why it insists upon its own way. When you are brought to heel, you are
eft with the fact that you are only limited in what you can say by forming it in
uch a way that it can be squeezed within the rules. You have to find a way to say
vhat you want to say but in the ways that narrative allows. You have to be
esourceful in recasting what you wish to express within the rails upon which
1arrative drives relentlessly forwards. There is always a cost. You lose something
>f the freshness of how you wanted to say it, you lose something of the freedom
>y complying with the limits of the form. There is no doubt that you lose
;omething, but also in learning through that painful process you learn that there
ire different ways to say what you want to say, as long as you have the flexibility
·o shift your way of thinking, your mode of expression, so that the essence of the
:hought is somehow retained, perhaps transformed, perhaps almost unrecognis-
ible, but in that transformation faithful to the core, the real essence of the idea.
[n undergoing that exhausting remaking the best thing that happens is that the
:ore finally shows itself to you. What you began thinking was the core is still
:ontained within the new formulation, but is clearer, burnished in the fire that
destroyed the early freshness, to reveal the same essence in some ways purified in
:he process. It took that wearisome process to get things clear, a necessary process
:o say what you want to say, but to say it better.

That is my background, buried in the past of this project. It is not a background
:hat equipped me as a scientist or a philosopher when I began to look to science
ind philosophy for guidance.

A sense of the rules of academic writing increasingly became a similar kind of
>bstruction to saying what was necessary to the rules of narrative in my film-mak-
ing experience. The challenge was to find a way around those particular restric-

tions without compromising what was important. There is a kind of discourse to the academic mode in the Arts and Humanities that pretends to objectivity by the use of a quasi-scientific language that is often specialised as part of seeking a rigour of expression which in reality has no real connection with the essential disciplines of science. It is a comforting shield to hide behind, a satisfactory ruse often to disguise a profound lack of clarity and poverty of ideas, and therefore difficult to come out from behind. To instead plump for ordinary language and the plain exposure of what ideas one has is a tricky choice. I have been very fortunate, I realise, in actually having that choice. For many the choice is effectively ruled out as falling outside the accepted norms within which their peers operate.

One stands the risk of the ideas becoming invisible when they are not expressed through the given formulae, but one is also freed to do what proved so difficult in my early film-making *education sentimentale*, that is to try to say what cannot be easily said within the rules. As one obsessed, as anyone who reflects upon their creative challenges is, with matters of form, I was both concerned and exhilirated by the task of saying what could not be accommodated within the normal academic styles. Concerned in that I would have to stray beyond the acceptable boundaries, but exhilirated by the opportunities that opened up.

I began to realise that not only was such a move necessary for me personally lacking the scientific background and therefore unable to adopt a scientist's way of writing with any degree of honesty, but there was a unity between the more informal approach that permitted saying what might otherwise be unsayable, and the essence of this project. After all, the big breakthrough that I feel is so crucial in neurobiology is the inclusion of Emotion within the golden circle of scientific method. That inclusion of the 'subjective' in the world of the 'objective', of Reason, pointed to parallels with writing about ideas in a more subjective manner. Not only was it the only real way that I could proceed, but it simultaneously reflected in the form, as it were, the heart of the content.

Much of the scientific writing I have read was written in ordinary language, and it was ironically only my background in the arts and humanities that carried with it an insistence on putting the appearance of rigour into the language rather than genuinely into the content. In contrast, I wanted to leave the science to scientists, omit the pseudo-scientific language of Film Theory, and the result is – a book of essays.

ssays

have always rather liked the term 'essay'. To essay is to explore, try something ut, a tentative attempt, an expedition with a suggestion of risk. In that sense, his book is a series of essays rather than anything definitive. It is exploratory, ith propositions, suggestions rather than authoritative definitions. It has to be hat way as my tiny knowledge of science and philosophy prevents any greater mbition. But there is something about the essay idea that I find much preferable) the academic form. There is something dishonest about the kind of academic node, of argument that is essentially derived from quotes of the work of others. If the ideas are good can't they stand on their own feet?) There is a 'left-brain', teral, accountancy sort of lack of imagination about the tendency. In the cholarship I admire that does not obtain, but it is rare. I think of Anthony Blunt n the Quattrocento, a sense of thinking things out for himself rather than relying n other authorities for the ideas to respond to.[219] For the rest the mode tends to he predictable and formulaic, the more so the fewer the ideas. On the other hand, should be honest and say that I concluded I could do the book in no other way. didn't want to hide behind formalities and what is more there is an element in hem, as noted above, that disallows a more informal element, which ends up neaning that a lot of what you really want to say cannot be said without ransgressing the canons of that style.

here is, however, a sort of greater ambition, in the sense of an attempt, an 'essay', t finding a way of saying what I most want to say, alongside the bows to quotation nat show others have thought in similar ways. I realise there is a kind of rhetoric) doing that, an admission that I found myself forced into it in order to say the nost important things, which wouldn't fit in in any other way. Behind that is an ːssay' at an ambition to give rein to a 'right-brain' way of writing, one that is roader and freer. I would like to propose the suggestion of a 'right-brain' hilosophy. It would seek its knowledge in the unarticulated, tacit, instinctive vorld that is so much more the reality of life than the narrow pecksniffian mode f much of the Academy, if not the best of it. Those two things together, a need nd a principle, make fortunate bedfellows and again I am very conscious of the rivilege of being able to give them room.

f the ideas are good enough (as Howard Hawks might have put it), they can ːand on their own feet – and don't need to quote others as support. That is partly

---

l9 Anthony Blunt, *Artistic Theory in Italy 1450–1600*, Oxford, 1963.

the risk here, but one I prefer to take instead of seeking security behind the dominant rhetorical conventions – my small *essay*.

Formal v Informal knowledge

There are epistemological questions of interest in the differences between the formal knowledge of the Academy and the kind of informal knowledge that exist as, for example, craft skills. The philosopher Michael Polanyi brought these questions up in the 1950s with his notion of 'tacit knowledge'. The original insight is that there are all kinds of knowledge that are not captured within the formal boundaries. The role of Emotion, so important to this study, would be one such, but there are a range of others such as the nature of the 'cognitive unconscious'. One of the hunches that set this enquiry off was that we take in most of the information we absorb from a film unconsciously. The nature of that 'unconscious' is largely unknown at present, but if it is substantial a feature as my instinct suggests, then it plays an important role not just in watching films but in all our mental life. Craft skills, as found in the film industry, for example in film-editing, tend to be largely unwritten as knowledge as they are eminently practical skills but also ones that point to a different mode of knowing. Polyany felt that tacit knowledge was the largest source of knowledge, much greater than the formal kind. Knowledge written down and codified is a poor creature in comparison, one limited by the kind of narrow focus that has been associated with a 'left-brain' orientation to problems. The other kinds of knowledge, the 'right-brain' sort, are more numerous but far less easy to articulate in language. The parallels with the debates over Emotion are close. As science has begun to apply objective study to the formerly 'subjective' area of Emotion, it would be an interesting expansion of that theme to look at tacit and other informal types of knowledge as their impact on our daily lives is indubitably far greater than the academic sort. Capturing the modes of those kinds of knowledge leads to complex epistemological questions, which currently neurobiology seems best-placed to tackle at the experimental level. Incorporating such kinds of knowledge into the formal schema is like dealing with Emotion in a rational framework, and neurobiology has made advances in that over the last generation, while it has to be admitted it remains an area of controversy even within neuroscience. For Spinoza intuition was superior to Reason, its inferences direct, with no need of reference to general rules, its mode of thought distinct from Reason, and best of all its followers less subject to evil passions.[220]

---

220 Quoted in Spinoza's Theory of Knowledge, Ch. 6, p. 76, *Bacon to Kant*, Garrett Thompson, Waveland Press, Illinois 2002.

A Return to Nature

Such a debate, it seems to me, is part of the questioning of the adequacy of rationalism seen as autonomous, which goes back to Kant, what might be called a critique of Impure Reason. As neuroscience shows that Reason is in fact contingent upon Emotion that notion seems less and less defensible. The other side of that coin is a sense that the Academic approach in general has moved further and further away from a connexion with nature and that man has to some extent lost sight of our foundations in the processes of evolution. The fashionable notion that man has transcended nature is of a piece with the nineteenth-century desire to distinguish man from the animals. The ridicule heaped on Darwin's head for suggesting man's descent from apes has certain parallels with the notion that man's cultural development has broken his ties with nature. That tendency is partly driven by resistance to the idea that we are prisoners of nature, especially a nature red in tooth and claw and the conservative social implications that man cannot change inequality between the classes and the genders.

As neurobiology discovers more about the plasticity of the brain, its constant making of new connections, the notion of a rigid social order as a reflection of nature becomes less and less tenable. In this sense cultural evolution does not transcend biology but is profoundly based upon and facilitated by it. It is in that context that a return to nature seems possible. The denial of nature and the denial of science have often gone hand-in-hand as philosophers of all kinds have felt able to see the world exclusively in terms of an autonomous social culture that has left biology far behind. That 'Idealism', arguably with its roots in German Idealism, has led to theories about everything divorced from Biology, resulting in the 'Castles in the Air' of which Schopenhauer accused Hegel.

The foundations of German Idealism were laid by Kant and, interestingly, one of his two main targets was David Hume. Hume was of the tradition that linked experience and experiment, derived from Newton, and while one might have expected him to be a fanatical adherent to Reason, in fact his most famous statement is that 'Reason is, and must always be, the servant of the Passions', a particularly modern and percipient claim. While Kant was highly critical of 'Pure Reason' he nevertheless arguably was effectively on its side with his desire to establish a certain autonomy for Reason in his Categorical Imperative. Such an autonomy is implicitly rejected by Hume, and finds an echo in the recent discovery in neurobiology (e.g. Damasio and LeDoux) that you can have Emotion without Reason, but not Reason without Emotion. In other words, Reason is not autonomous but contingent upon Emotion. That arguably decisively overturns Kant's ambitions for Reason. It is also an argument for the superiority of the materialism of science over the idealisms of a philosophy effectively divorced from Nature.[221]

The influence of German Idealism extends from Kant through Hegel to Marx and, more relevantly in regards to Cinema, to French thought in the twentieth-century. Quite why the tradition of Port-Royal, with its pride in the clarity of French, should end up with the opacity of the writers behind Film Theory is another story, but the result of connections to that tradition permeated French thought's desertion of clarity, joining Hegel in the Castles in the Air.

I have noted earlier that another striking element of French thought in the twentieth-century was its striking and perhaps unexpected orientation against Vision, an idea found in Martin Jay's ground-breaking book *Downcast Eyes: The Denigration of Vision in Twentieth Century Thought*. Those two elements created a perfect storm that saw French theorists of film intellectually formed by ideas that were both idealist and logocentric. It is one of those little ironies that they were almost universal in their protestations of devotion to materialism, but in effect a materialism of the upside-down Hegel type, as it were Castles in the sand. Those versions of 'materialism' were in fact, dare I suggest, wholly in thrall to an idealist inheritance, and the result was a Film Theory irredeemably idealist and logocentric, and one into the bargain that rejected any connection with the proper materialism of science.

That tradition proudly asserted another of Kant's claims resulting from his desire for an autonomy for Reason, the independent 'truth' of philosophy. In that convenient fiction (which I believe to some extent) philosophy had its own autonomous truth quite separate from but of course equal to that of science, the truth derived from experiment. The autonomy of philosophical truth sounds like William James's description of Freud's unconscious: 'a tumbling ground for whimsies', and the stream of ideas built on nothing firmer than the rhetorical philosophies of the idealist tradition were likewise placed uneasily one on top of another, all the while getting further and further from even the idea of solid foundations in material reality.

French thought of the twentieth-century that went on to inspire what was to become Film Theory matches the description given by the Nobel physicist Steven Weinberg: 'the unreasonable ineffectiveness of philosophy'. It was inherently

---

221 see A Lesson for Kant below.

doomed to that role by its idealist inheritance and rejection of a connection with science, and through that with nature. Instead of an appropriate humility before nature, French intellectuals (and not only French) – for the most part – displayed a disregard for and complete ignorance of science. The gap between their version of materialism and the kind of materialism found in laboratory experiment and in particular in the rootedness of evolutionary biology in time and the process of history just seemed to increase year by year. If a philosopher was criticised the reaction was often to claim that he was not understood. In a climate of rhetorical idealism (tracing its legitimacy back to Kant) that constitutes an adequate defence, and allows the spiral of rhetoric to continue its ascent.

The logocentric inheritance of French culture expressed itself in two founding statements, one about Cinema and the other about the unconscious. In the first it was claimed that Cinema 'is structured like a language'. In the second it was claimed that the unconscious was 'structured like a language'. It would be hard to demonstrate the idealism and ahistoricism of that philosophical tradition better. Cinema derives its power from Vision. The eye has a history going back over 500 million years. Language is perhaps 40,000 years old. Only a pervasive Logocentrism could fuel such a declaration (scientists might agree but would be more circumspect). The unconscious is not structured like a Language. The unconscious is structured like the brain, by adaptation via evolution. In that process Vision is pre-eminent and Language is a relatively recent arrival. Language is not a cause but an effect of evolution. Again, only a thoroughly ahistorical idealism divorced from the materiality of biological evolution and its historical process in time, combined with a disregard for the relevant science, could occasion such a claim for Language.

In the place of that 'ineffectiveness' this project suggests a return to nature, by which I mean a return to evolution, to evolutionary biology combined with neuroscience as a proper scientific basis for analysis. In principle all ideas should be eligible for testing under laboratory conditions, that is able to be used as raw material for the formulation of experimental designs that can be submitted to the rigours of scientific method.

While the ideas put forward here may be speculative 'Thought Experiments' at this point, even as a principle the very notion of putting forward ideas in a scientific spirit would be new to the arts and humanities, while it is standard in science. I would see that as a useful caution to speculative philosophising which, in itself, is a natural part of the development of ideas. But, without the kinds of rigours that testing implies it has no boundaries, no expectation that it will take

223

responsibility outside itself, the 'autonomy' of philosophy that has always evaded
such a duty.

The purpose of such a discipline is to encourage the aim of formulating ideas, in
this case about Cinema, that can contribute through their testing to our further
understanding of how the brain works. The archive of Cinema is also a concrete
resource that has the potential to making a substantial contribution in addition
to our understanding of how culture evolves. It is suggested here that 'reverse-engineering' from Cinema as a concrete instance of culture – that is again to
emphasise the notion of cultural evolution as a biological phenomenon successor
to genetic evolution, rather than in the sense the term is used in other disciplines
– to Nature, as it were, a preferable and more effective direction than the opposite
direction of enquiry that would proceed from nature to Cinema. It would be a
massively complex undertaking to conceive of the path from nature to Cinema
in its every moment. On the other hand it is considerably more possible to retrace
the steps of this recent medium to the forces that have given rise to it – as with
the case of the evolution of the eye and its relevance for the development of
Cinema.

A Lesson for Kant

A central tenet of Kant's theory is the 'transcendental unity of apperception'. It
is a bold and difficult notion by which Kant means the unity of consciousness.
As we have discussed, consciousness is fleet of foot and can move at lightning
speed from one stimulus to another, from one mode to another, with ease. From
staring at the stars in the heavens of a rural night sky my foot slips on the damp
grass as I turn my head from the Milky Way directly above me to a shooting star
that grabs my attention from my peripheral vision. From the Milky Way to my
slipping foot is a journey of a fraction of a second in my head. My attention shifts
at speed, and back at speed to the further wonders of the night sky.

Kant believed that such unity requires one to be able to think of my experience
as mine, to have the thought that 'This is my experience'.

There is a key term to be added to Kant's formulation, a 'formal' unity of
consciousness. From the subjective insight Kant derived a principle. He moved
from the well-observed unity of consciousness to a formal proposition – that the
ability to think of the experience as mine requires judgement and hence categories. The categories organise intuitions into experience by a process of synthesis

akin to judgement. For Kant, experience becomes experience when it is organised by logic.

That development is a crucial one as he moves with it from an observation to a formal principle. The question here is whether there is a necessary connection between the observation and the principle and implications of such an assumption. It may not be a necessary connection but it is the device by which Kant brilliantly overcomes certain philosophical problems in the territory between the empiricists (e.g. Hume) and the rationalists (e.g. Leibniz). With the erection of the principle Kant moves from subjective insight to philosophical conceptualisation. And that is where the problem lies. Arguably there is no necessary connection between the insight and the principle.

A lesson from recent neuroscience is that the study of consciousness cannot erect principles from subjective introspection. The leap forward that has liberated the study of consciousness, emotion and dreams is to regard subjective experience as raw data not evidence.

In taking introspection as the basis for his philosophical principle, Kant effectively took it as evidence and then superimposed upon it the notion that experience is governed by logic. Hume's famous statement on emotion, had he fully taken it on board, should have warned him against such a move.

A supplementary lesson from neurobiology is that the logic of philosophy and the logic of nature are incompatible creatures. In conflating the two Kant slides from the nature of experience to a conception based on the logic of man, eliding the logic of nature and thus casting that long shadow which encouraged the increasing divergence from the materialism of science to the idealism that permeates Continental Philosophy.

In paving the way for the autonomy of philosophical reason, Kant makes a fundamental error that condemns philosophy to the condition of 'unreasonable ineffectiveness' that so disappointed Weinberg. Intuition and Logic are oil and water rather than the companions Kant wished them to be.

Introspection is admirable material as raw data but may be unreliable as evidence. The logic of nature is not logical. Hume saw that, Kant did not.[222]

---

222 After writing this note I discovered that it chimed with a criticism by Schopenhauer, see 'Fundamental error' in http://en.wikipedia.org/wiki/Critique_of_the_Kantian_philosophy.

Expansive Materialism

One of the criticisms often levelled at science, when it tries to offer an analysis of art, is that it is a hammer to crack a nut, offering only crude generalisations where subtle, sensitive and complex appreciation of particular works are quite beyond it. I believe that situation has changed with the advent of Emotion as part of the field of scientific method (as discussed in Commentaries) and that, on the contrary, science is within sight not just of being able to equal the richness of analysis offered by traditional methods of all sorts, but to infinitely surpass them in depth and breadth.

For example, where scientific explanations have often had an arid formality, a stiff rationalism to them, the one thing they have been missing above all is the sense of feeling, of expressiveness that is at the heart of art. With the inclusion of Emotion in the paradigm of scientific investigation that all changes. I don't mean to suggest that it is an open-and-shut case, that the change in the formal system achieves that depth at a stroke. The proof will come from the quality of analysis that begins to be encouraged by this opening to what have been described as 'right-brain' attitudes – the holistic, the creative, the visual, the emotional. It is what might be called a right-brain rationalism that has the potential to provide the kind of depth that has been missing hitherto.

The usual criticism of science in relation to the arts is that it can only offer 'reductive' formulas that create a simplification of the object of study, and are inadequate to its complexities. Again, I would contend that with the introduction of Emotion into the equation, that is outdated as a criticism. With the vastly-increased reach that Emotion brings, it is now possible to practice an 'expansive' materialism, that goes substantially beyond anything that is even capable of being offered by traditional approaches.

Neuroscience is beginning to be able to offer descriptions of how the brain works that identify fundamental modes of operation – and ones which I would contend offer striking parallels with what have to now been thought of as literary strategies rather than the product of the evolution of the brain reflected in cultural exaptations – in the field of literature and cinema. That sense of the priority of the mode of operation of the brain over what have been thought of as the products of the practice of Language provides a shock-effect in shifting our perspective on the origin of such things. We can begin to see that much of what we thought were the products of culture operating through Language have much deeper roots in the evolution of the brain, and that their appearance as techniques in literature and Cinema is a consequence of that process rather than originated by and through Language. In effect, Language has been riding as a passenger upon vastly older and deeper products of evolution, and has been almost universally lauded as the author of things of which it is merely a reseller.

The traditional modes of analysis have also followed our culture in general in prioritising conscious processes. Where the unconscious was invoked it has been generally in the context of Freud, whose methods had very little support or credibility in the scientific community due to their failure to observe the most basic procedures of science. The most basic procedure of science is observation. Psycho-analysis very deliberately eschews observation, literally turning its back upon the patient. What Freud offered instead of observation was to listen to talking. The 'talking cure' could hardly be a concept more in the pocket of Language. More recently, the analysis offered by Dream Science, a branch of neuroscience, has comprehensively undermined every major theoretical pillar of Freud's practice: 'the Freudian emphasis on wishes, censorship, and the dream work is secondary at best, which means that Freud was wrong on all of his main hypotheses'.[223] '... all of the features of dreaming that Freud wanted to explain with his wish-fulfilment, disguise-censorship theory, are explained in just the way he hoped might ultimately be possible – by the physiology and chemistry of the brain.'[224]. However, the study of the unconscious has assumed a new priority through the arrival of Emotion on the scene, as it is generally argued by theorists and researchers of Emotion that it largely is about unconscious processes.[225]

Cinema is, in that famous word, Emotion. Therefore Emotion, the identification and following the path of Emotion in a film, would be central to a kind of understanding that has not been rigorously followed in the past. It is now possible to conceptualise that what the audience follows over the time of a film is the graph, as it were, of Emotion affecting the hero/ine. Making the focus of film-study the analysis of Emotion would place it on a properly scientific basis with its foundations deep down in the way the brain operates. As the eye is eons older than Language, and developed as a survival aid, Emotion is the output of the body/brain system, the telltale of survival issues registered by that system. There could hardly be a more profound basis upon which to build an analysis of Cinema.

---

223 Domhoff, describing Hobson's position in: Domhoff, G. W. (2005). Refocusing the neurocognitive approach to dreams: A critique of the Hobson versus Solms debate. *Dreaming*, 15, 3–20. While Hobson's own theoretical position has been seriously questioned, his view of Freud seems impeccable and one generally shared by a wide range of scientists.

224 Hobson op. cit., p. 102.

225 e.g. Ledoux, op. cit.

In that evolutionary perspective that includes both the genetic and the cultural, every level of Cinema, from the history of an industry to the characteristics of a single shot, part of a shot, the smallest detail imaginable, there is nothing that is not deeply rooted in those elements. Everything in Cinema originates in nature, seen from the perspective of Evolution. There is nothing in Cinema that does not have its own evolutionary history, in the biological sense – both genetic and bio-cultural. However distant, however superficially tenuous, there is an unbroken link between the principles of natural selection and that most artificial of things, a film. Man has not, cannot and never will transcend biology. Adaptation, exaptation is the mode of connection that culture has to genetic origins, but the chain remains unbroken and man ignores it at a price. The 'unreasonable ineffectiveness' of philosophy is just one such price, and the only resolution of that problem, should you consider it a problem, is a return to nature, a certain humility before nature, a recognition of the unbroken chain of life, of which we are merely a part.

Perhaps the most important implication of the neurobiological context for Cinema goes back to the basic insight about the power of the eye, the enormous amounts of information it sends to the brain every second, and much more importantly still, what I would argue is the extraordinary quality of the information it absorbs.

For me the real essential quality of Cinema is this hitherto underrated, ignored and/or denied range, depth and extent of information that Cinema is capable of presenting to the viewer. While the same applies in broad terms for Vision in general, Cinema deliberately set out to amplify and intensify that impact with the darkness and the light, and the intensity of emotion portrayed on that 'window', the screen. The result was reality but more, emotion but more, more than in real life. Cinema became virtually a laboratory for emotional exercise. The irony of all this is that we hardly realise it. We take that immense information-processing ability for granted, more than that we absorb it without being aware of the fact, unconsciously, Automatically. We see more than we know.

It would seem to me that Neurobiology is the only analytical framework capable of penetrating that depth. I do not say that it has yet done so in the way I suggest, but that it has the potential and that far beyond what any other framework could offer, even in principle. Through its burgeoning understanding of the eye, of Emotion, of empathy, through Mirror Neurons and Shared Circuits, it offers a framework far superior in all dimensions to those that have come before. It can go further, deeper and broader – and through the discipline of science and a scientific method immeasurably enhanced, as I would see it, by the inclusion of Emotion within the paradigm.

The case of metaphor offers a glimpse into how neurobiology can overturn our preconceptions and the limited understanding offered by analysis not based in science. A similar process applies to every single function of the brain and by extension every aspect of Cinema. In this view, to reiterate, there is nothing in Cinema that does not come from Nature, from either genetic or cultural evolution in the tradition established by Darwin. That grounding in the deeply historical aspect of Evolution, with its unrelenting focus on survival, provides the most solid basis for an 'Expansive Materialism' that alone has the capacity to reunite the Two Cultures under the banner of science.

The limits of materialism & metaphysics

I would like to add a necessarily brief note about the boundaries of materialism and where it crosses over from, as it were, physics to metaphysics. It must be brief as my knowledge is limited, but what has interested me is thinking about how far a materialist explanation can go, and where it runs out of steam. Evolution feels like solid ground due to its historical depths, but seeking an explanation for Consciousness, for example, stirs a whole retinue of demons.

There are two seemingly conflicting views of Consciousness that could be characterised as seeing it in the first instance as solely an outcome of material forces – the view I would take – one that has no truck with the fear that the sum cannot be greater than the (material) parts. A second instance would be that Consciousness is everywhere and in everything – sometimes called Pantheism. Often that view is thought of as being anti-materialist, but there is in Leibniz, who espoused the latter view, a possible resolution of the apparent conflict. Jonathan Edwards[226], who has written on Leibniz's concept of monads has put it that: 'The whole point of monads is to explain how there can appear to be causal chains ... Leibniz was about ... dynamics, action, force, connection – ... that was everywhere. There is also the standard mistake of thinking that the monads are something other than 'physical'. Monads are what makes the physical physical – through their ways of aggregation. They are metaphysical in the sense of being the root of the physical.'[227]

226 Review editor of the *Journal of Consciousness Studies*, and Professor of Immunology at University College London.

227 Email communication shared with an informal discussion group on Theories of Consciousness, February 2014.

Beyond that sense of the metaphysical I am unable to travel, but with Monads a a conception of the smallest possible units of existence, there is some comfort in seeing them as the root of the physical.

A Practice of Film Theory

The task I would identify for film-study is to find ways of working with neuroscientists in order to excavate and recover the huge amounts of information from a film that I suggest enters the realm of the Automatic. It is not an easy task to disentangle conscious from unconscious input,[228] but I believe that not only would it begin to reveal the still largely-unsuspected depths of Cinema, but would at the same time potentially make useful contributions to our understanding of how the brain works. The realm of the Automatic is still largely a terra incognita

That is where I would see the potential of the *affective neurobiology* approach for exploring an 'expansive materialism' of greater depth and breadth than anything that could even be dreamt of being offered by any previous theoretical framework.

As part of the attempt to pursue the information absorbed into the Automatic there are some basic approaches that can be taken. Film Study since the 60s practiced close analysis of individual films. With the availability of VHS to study films in detail in a way that was very rarely possible before, the kind of work I did with students on *The Searchers* began to show the amount of information that was present within Hollywood films in particular that had previously been thought of as merely vulgar entertainment not worthy of serious study. While such close study tends to be unfashionable these days it feeds into a notion I would put forward here, that sees every film as an instance of evolution in the cultural realm, each with its own particular history that bears upon and bears the marks of cultural evolution in every detail, formal and informal. In theory each film could have its own archive that builds up the information about it, beginning perhaps with close study of it in the traditional way in order to reveal the wealth of information that escapes an ordinary viewing – or should I say the conscious mind during a normal viewing. Added to that would be information relevant to that audit about its construction process from the Director, writers, editors, Producer, Production Designer, Composer, anyone involved in its production.

---

228 A point made to me informally by Christian Keysers, but Dehaene has made a valuable start with his threshold approach.

From that material a researcher could begin to try to uncover what might be thought of as immanent material within the film itself. For example, with the first scene of *Psycho*, there is so much suggested about the circumstances and backgrounds of the lovers in the hotel room, that there is the start of a trail that not only leads through the time of the film itself, but potentially outwards to the process of the construction of the story, the work on back-story – what were the lives of the characters off-screen? In *Psycho* there is a lot unspoken but suggested in the interstices – which is what makes a Hitchcock film such a rich source of analysis. Following those strands in terms of the lives, conflicts and social mores of the characters would add considerably to the 'external' information, what has been called 'exformation'[229]. In this conception the film is the tip of the iceberg and the hidden part remains to be discovered by such procedures.

Charles Bennett's notion of Logical Depth[230] suggests that 'the value of a message is the amount of ... work plausibly done by its originator, which its receiver is saved from having to repeat'[231]. Logical Depth is a measure of complexity, and 'perpendicular to information content', a way of determining how much meaning a message contains. The more work the sender has done the greater the value of the message. The meaning arises not from the information in the message but the information discarded in formulating the message. A message can be edited to the shortest form possible to enable a Turing machine to formulate it – for example when the laws governing planetary motion are turned into a table of solar eclipses. The compressed information has to be unfolded, which takes time, and this time is measured as logical depth. It is a measure of the process that leads to the message, rather than the information transmitted. Complexity is a measure of the production process rather than the product. The work behind the message may be invisible. The facility of the message is in proportion to the amount discarded to make it easy for the receiver to absorb. Clarity requires depth.

I would like to suggest that there is a link between Logical Depth and Hitchcock spending $225,000 on the script of *Marnie*. The process I propose for uncovering the hidden history of *Vertigo*, for example, is in the spirit of establishing the Logical Depth of the film. With *Marnie*, if we allow that perhaps Hitchcock was trying to achieve what I suggest – the Ideal Script with change relentlessly at the

---

229 See Norretranders, op. cit., pp. 92–96. The concept is that a mass of information present in the process of the formulation of a message is discarded, leaving only the message. The approach I am suggesting would aim to recover that and other information relevant to e.g. the opening scene of *Psycho*. See below for the notion of Logical Depth which expands on the theme.

230 Referred to in Norretranders, op. cit., pp. 79–82. I have taken much from his definition.

231 Charles Bennett, 'Logical Depth and Physical Complexity', in *The Universal Turing Machine: a half-century survey*, Rolf Herken, OUP, 1988 pp. 227–257, quote from p. 230.

heart of every scene – the difficulties of balancing that abstract theoretical desire (his 'technical' problem for that film) with the demands of narrative, plot, characterisation, climax etc, would be substantial, even with his great experience. He is prepared to spend money on a succession of writers to get what he wanted, shaping their input rather than replacing it himself. There would be a great deal of material discarded in the process, both formally and informally (in discussion and in the unspoken communications of 'tacit' knowledge), and the notion here is that the more that is discarded, the more discreet the process of rejection and alignment with the principles of suspense and showing not telling, the greater the logical depth of what results as the film. It's what you leave out more than what you leave in. I believe that it is that process that creates the rock-solid feeling I had in that warehouse-gallery watching Judy emerge from the bathroom in *Vertigo*.

Even with one of his TV half-hour episodes, when Hitchcock directed the results could bear out the depth of his control – in an experiment with audiences using fMRI scanning. Discussing results from *Bang, you're Dead* (1961), Hasson et al put it that 'The fact that Hitchcock was able to orchestrate the responses of so many different brain regions, turning them on and off at the same time across all viewers, may provide neuroscientific evidence for his ... famous ability to master and manipulate viewers' minds. Hitchcock often liked to tell interviewers that for him "creation is based on an exact science of audience reactions" (Douchet 1985).[232]

Detailed study of a film would take as its task to assemble as much of that 'discarded' material from the making of the film, the archive of its 'Logical Depth'.[233] With that archive assembled, it would be possible to construct an experiment that asks subjects to record their conscious recall of a viewing of the film. Then they could be prompted about other information from the archive, perhaps including false information as a control element. Accessing the conscious material could also involve fMRI procedures to compare activation in different parts of the brain (as Hasson carried out) with the conscious recall patterns. There

232 Hasson et al., 'Neurocinematics: The Neuroscience of Film', *Projections*, Vol 2, Issue 1, Summer 2008, pp.1–6, op. cit.

233 The Elephant in the Room here is once one leaves Hitchcock behind, how many films would have that depth, a question that would take us back to the auteurist debates of the 60s. As all films are underestimated in their visual information, the provisional answer would be that an audit of any film would throw up unsuspected depth and riches of information, but for Cineastes some films are more interesting than others. A *Detour* may be cheap and shot in five days, but its director's skill and intelligence made it stand out among 'C' pictures. A British 'quota-quickie' may tell us about social mores and show streets since irreparably changed – it depends what we are looking for. Every film has greater depth than we imagine, a storehouse largely untouched for future generations to mine - in a 'History' of Cinema with criteria drawn in a variety of ways, yet to be explored, from ANB rather than the traditional ones.

are a variety of ways in which it would be possible to try to access conscious recall or awareness, including a running-commentary by the viewer as s/he watches the film.

A later stage of research could be hypothesis testing, for example focussed on Emotion. As Emotion is the heart of the conception of Cinema I put forward here, it would be interesting to test the notion that the audience follows the graph of emotions, particularly those affecting the hero/ine. It is possible we could learn more about the operations of both Mirror Neurons and Shared Circuits by using films as a virtual laboratory, with measurement of audience responses via fMRI combined with reporting by viewers.[234] The nature of empathy, its dimensions and variations could potentially tell us a lot more about human motivations, especially as responses to more complex emotions portrayed in certain films.

The great advantage Cinema offers is that this material is already laid down on the film and therefore the 'input' remains consistent. What varies is what we are trying to access and how, plus elements of how different people react differently. Experiments to date have rather confirmed that audiences tend to react quite similarly, but for example with autism and other variations in brain-status, films may be a useful 'control' against which to assess the differential effects of brain status, particularly in regard to how viewers relate to emotion as portrayed on the screen.

The principle remains throughout this conception of a Film Theory that ideas are required to be formulated in such a way as to amenable to testing. Hypotheses about how we react to others, how emotions work, and how strategies are laid down in memory for use in unfamiliar situations (how to behave like the hero, for example), could all be made the subject of experimental design and then tested under laboratory conditions.

This sort of approach would be my answer to Christian Metz's question of fifty years ago – how scientific can analysis of Cinema be? If we approach Cinema with contemporary scientific method, instead of the red-herring of various frameworks beholden to the word, then it can be properly scientific. All the usual pitfalls of experimental design and the interpretation of results remain, but we would be in a new era where the questions are no longer solely academic but could potentially also have an impact in the real world – in increasing our knowledge about how the brain works. We would of course also learn a lot more about how Cinema works, and I have a sense that ironically it is only be concentrating on the

---

234 This crucial combination of objective and subjective is discussed by Dehaene, op. cit.

functional issues about the brain that we will really increase our knowledge about Cinema. It is not exactly a mere by-product, but more that in focussing on what it is tempting to call Real knowledge, through Real Film Theory, it is possible to produce knowledge with real purchase, that both contributes to our understanding of the brain but by doing so opens up new depths of understanding about Cinema.

Confessions of a Convert

There are few more rabid in conviction than a convert. I was as excited as anyone by the exotic glamour of the 'semiotic moment' in the 1970s when French Film Theory arrived in England. Against the dowdy worthiness of the empiricism of the time it seemed both shocking and rigorous. Only when I tried to square the circle with my experience in film-making and failed did the worm of doubt begin to grow. As Colin McCabe once asked: "A theory of what?". Implicit is that question is the epistemological doubt that for me eventually cracked wide open the whole project. 'Theory' in the humanities is a latter-day inheritance of Kant's 'Copernican Revolution' in philosophy, the part that asserted an autonomy to the kind of 'truth' that philosophy pursued, a revolutionary claim for independence that has had doleful results, a 'tumbling ground for whimsies', certainly in relation to Cinema. Enough of Castles in the Air. It is time for a return to a certain humble empiricism, but a New Empiricism that has its own, Newtonian-scale Revolution, in the inclusion of Emotion in a revised and revived paradigm of scientific method.

Testing is not a panacea, it is not a guarantee in itself that ideas will be more productive. However, it has behind it vast experience of refining techniques and patient persistence with observation, just the thing that Freud curiously deserted in literally turning away from the patient. The truth from experiment is always conditional, always subject to overturning, always subject to criticism on methods and interpretation. That is the way of scientific knowledge – and it strikes me that with any amount of reservations it is infinitely superior to the discourse of Theory that possesses none of that apparatus. Testing is no panacea but it is a damn sight better than not testing.

From the point-of-view of science, the word and its derivatives, including the Talking Cure, are simply not science. No end of disguise in the garments of language aspiring to the appearance of science changes that fact. In science all ideas must be tested. In Cinema that simple principle would revolutionise its study. Such a revolution is proposed here.

Left/Right brain – Science & Philosophy

The left/right brain debate has a certain echo in this book. In standing up for instinct and emotion one is being very foolish in a scientific context. Not only not a scientist nor philosopher but standing up for not exactly anti-rationalism, which would not be the case, but for ways of thinking that go beyond the narrower conceptions of reason. My feeling is that we only have our instincts. Second-guessing what others might think in a given situation is the royal road to mediocrity. Whether our instincts are good or bad they are all we have, and I have come to the view that in the main one's instincts are solid. That is entirely subjective and introspective and refers only to me, whilst allowing that sometimes I get it wrong, probably like most people. Where the Left hemisphere is said to locally-focussed, in such tasks as choosing the right word, the Right has a wider search, looking at several words, for example. As this is a book of words, but words about Vision, it might be thought of as (a) mad (b) an interesting experiment in using the word to discuss Vision. It is worth reiterating that the populist left/right debate should not take credit from the many experiments that both investigate the different approaches the hemispheres take to problem-solving and link how these elements have, like everything in the brain, evolved in the context of survival. The two hemispheres do not restrict themselves to certain tasks, but both deal with words, for example, just in different ways. This complementarity is part of a wider pattern researchers have observed in the brain where evolution creates a number of systems with overlapping functions. Because they overlap does not mean there is redundancy in the system, but that each system brings, as it were, a different perspective as it is approaching a given problem from a different conjuncture of elements. Evolution works by providing a number of different angles on a given problem, each contribute their distinctive approach founded in the fact that they evolved to solve a different problem or range of problems. What evolved to solve say visual problems (thinking of the Right hemisphere) might bring a 'visual' orientation to words, a bit like the Visual Thesaurus[235] that shows a word with lines around it linking to related worlds. The lines are dynamic, so if you choose another option the words and their connections shift around to reflect that new emphasis. That seems quite like what I imagine a right-hemi-

235 See http://www.visualthesaurus.com/

sphere approach to words might be, compared to the left focussing narrowly on one word and excluding other possibilities. In this simple example one can see the outlines of the way the hemispheres and the brain in general works – with both the narrow goal-oriented focus and the broader, more holistic overview contributing usefully each in their own way.

One thought behind this book is that both science and philosophy have on occasion tended towards a narrow rationalism – the distrust of emotion in the ranks of many scientists might be one such case. A broader rationalism, analogous to the right-hemisphere approach, could benefit both science and philosophy – and the study of emotion is one step in that direction. The style of this book tries to cast aside a certain defensive formalism of language, although that was less a principle than force majeure, as the material I wanted to include felt as though it was at different levels and the only way to unite them was to try to write as simply as possible – fearful though one might have been about the degree of exposure such simplicity involves. Hiding behind formality is certainly more comfortable although something of a restrictive corset in matters of expression. A concern with 'matters of expression' would seem to go along with matters of Vision.

As neither one nor the other it would not be quite right for me to suggest to scientists and philosophers that they expand their purview to a more holistic attitude. However, there is a sense that philosophy has lost the plot with its 'unreasonable ineffectiveness', and there is in the distrust of many scientists of emotion, room to do so, as Lady Bracknell might have put it. There is a revolution that one could glimpse in such a development – if I may put it simply – a right-brain philosophy would be so much more relevant than the rather stick-like creature we know today. This book is not an exemplar, but it is an attempt to say things that certain formal restrictions make it difficult if not impossible to say, and that notion of widening of what it is possible to say could be beneficial across a range of disciplines.

Endnote

A central plank of the sentiment put forward in this book is that speculative philosophy in the tradition I would trace back to Kant has been in fundamental error from the beginning in working from the assumption that it is possible and indeed desirable for philosophy to lay claim to an independent but equal truth to science. The argument goes that reason is contingent upon emotion and that has been demonstrated by neuroscience and that in that single moment the notion of a certain autonomy for reason is, I would argue, decisively demolished and simultaneously and neatly the superiority of scientific method exemplified.

On the other hand the contradictions in this project that I have already noted are that it is a book against the word in words, on neurobiology by a non-scientist, on philosophy by a non-philosopher, for testability of ideas but without detailed experimental designs, a Theory of Cinema without much in the way of films, and finally a variant of speculative philosophy that is against speculative philosophy.

Scientists call their speculative ideas 'thought experiments' and one common factor with the speculations I put forward here is that behind them lies the intention to devise experiments in which those thoughts become hypotheses testable under laboratory conditions. I fall short of that goal but I share that intention. The ideas put forward here differ from those normally found in the arts and humanities in that they are genuinely sympathetic to science. They are in favour of a proper scientific analysis of Cinema (and by extension of the arts and humanities) and aim towards hypotheses as a basis for experimental design.

They also challenge head-on the fear that applying science to art is inevitably reductionist, forcing wealth of expression into categories that impoverish it. That fear is an almost automatic defence-mechanism in the arts & humanities, an instant dismissal that prevents one from having to face up to the North face of the Eiger of science. The claim here is the obverse – that in reality it is Language and its associates that have a very limited ability to express the dimensions of human experience. In contrast, the claim is that Vision sees everything, understands *everything*, touches everything (and what Vision does not see science reveals). What Vision sees Language struggles to put words to. That is its job, but it is a fundamental error to mistake the medium for the source. I see therefore I am.

The faith expressed here is that science is up to the job, and then some. We will never understand Vision by taking the road of Language. We can only comprehend Vision by understanding the brain, and that through neurobiology centred upon Emotion. With the proven tools of science we can begin to unlock the unspoken riches of Vision, the moment Judy emerges from the bathroom, suffused with a blue light, drenching Scottie in emotions he has been fighting, a scene that felt to be carved from rock yet is only there in light. Language will never penetrate the depths of the iceberg, only science in the service of Vision can accomplish that. Objective correlates of subjective experience are now available through neuroscience. They may be limited by what is reportable but I am certain that my feelings about the scene in *Vertigo*, as Judy emerges from the hotel bathroom, will one day be able to be articulated through that process, revealing the depth of Hitchcock's construction and the glory of Cinema – and that day approaches.

Brecht said of contradictions that he could abide nothing else. I am with him on that. More I am with Joyce; the ineluctable modality of the visible ... though through my eyes. Thought occurs only in Vision. In my experience the most unlikely ideas, dug up somehow by the Automatic, are *without exception* the most fruitful. It is a service the Automatic provides to the conscious mind, so what is mere contingent reason to contradict it?

There is one concluding comment, a realisation to which I stupidly came only at the very end of work on this book.

The history of all hitherto existing analysis in philosophy and discussions of science quite as much as about Cinema has been in thrall to language. In philosophy, the continuities from Kant to Wittgenstein, for example, lie for a large part in the issue of language. Likewise we are still battling with discussions about the philosophy of science centred on language, while Film Theory is wholly its prisoner.

This project proposes the shift from language to Vision, based not only on the depth and breadth of the power of Vision but also on a firm grounding in evolution after Darwin. We can only break out of the often circular quandaries of philosophy and discussions of consciousness and the 'hard' problem, for example, by jettisoning abiding idealist conceptions and replacing them with a materialism rooted in the simple fact that the brain, as a part of nature, has evolved. All brain functions, without exception, have their own evolutionary histories. Metaphor and narrative are modes of the operation of the brain first and creative techniques second.

From language-based idealism to vision-based materialism is a long journey, but one which nature, in the form of cultural evolution, may well be in the course of making for us.

Bibliography & Filmography

The ideas put forward in this book go back to doubts about Film Theory that arose in the 1970s. They began to take shape over ten years ago and the following represents only the main books that, at one time or another, were particularly stimulating in that process and in the order I discovered them.

Books:

Tor Norretranders, *The User Illusion*, Penguin, New York, 1999

Daniel Dennett, *Darwin's Dangerous Idea*, Penguin, New York, 1996. (Thanks to David for that suggestion)

Martin Jay, *Downcast Eyes: The Denigration of Vision in Twentieth Century French Thought*, University of California Press, Berkeley, 1994

Antonio Damasio, *Descartes' Error: Emotion, Reason and the Human Brain*, Putnam, New York, 1994

Joseph LeDoux, *The Emotional Brain*, Weidenfeld & Nicolson, London, 1998

Iain McGilchrist, *The Master & His Emissary, the Divided Brain and the Making of the Western World*, Yale University Press, London, 2009

Vilayanur Ramachandran, *The Tell-Tale Brain*, William Heineman, London, 2011

Christian Keysers, *The Empathic Brain*, Social Brain Press, 2011 (first issued as a Kindle book)

Charles Darwin, *The Descent of Man*, 1871 (2013 French translation, introduction by Patrick Tort)

Stanislas Dehaene, *Consciousness and the Brain*, Viking, New York, 2014

Films and Directors mentioned in the text:

Leeds Bridge & Roundhay Gardenshots scene, Dir. Louis Le Prince, 1888

The Train Entering the Station at La Ciotat. Dir. Louis Lumière, 1895

Les Films D'Art, 1908

The Kuleshov Experiments, Dir. Lev Kuleshov, 1917

Wild Girl, Dir. Raoul Walsh, 1932

Shadow of a Doubt, Dir. Alfred Hitchcock, 1943

Detour, Dir. Edgar G Ulmer, 1945

The Big Sleep, Dir. Howard Hawks, 1946.

Mildred Pierce, Dir. Michael Curtiz, 1946

The Searchers, Dir. John Ford, 1956

Vertigo, Dir. Alfred Hitchcock, 1957

Psycho, Dir. Alfred Hitchcock, 1959

Bang You're Dead, Dir. Alfred Hitchcock, 1961

La Notte, Dir. Michelangelo Antonioni, 1961

Marnie, Dir. Alfred Hitchcock, 1964

Kaleidoscope, Dir. Alfred Hitchcock, 1964–7

Pierrot Le Fou, Dir. Jean-Luc Godard, 1965

The Good, the Bad and the Ugly, Dir. Sergio Leone 1966

Star Wars, Dir. George Lucas, 1977

Inglorious Basterds, Dir. Quentin Tarantino, 2009

House of Cards, Episode 2, Dir. David Fincher, 2013 (released on Netflix)

Blue Jasmine, Dir. Woody Allen, 2013

Gravity, Dir. Alfonso Cuarön, 2103

Ukrainian Cinema:

A spring for the thirsty, Yuri Ilyenko

Dancing Hawk, Grzegorz Krolikiewicz

Letters from a Dead Man, Konstantin Lopushansky

Narcissus and Psyche, Gabor Body

Paradjanov

Ingmar Bergman

Bernardo Bertolucci

Robert Bresson

Brian De Palma

Nagisa Oshima

Martin Scorsese

Acknowledgements

have had noble help from friends, who rallied to the last-minute cause of my trying to eliminate at least some of the innumerable repetitions, and the worst errors of ignorance with donations of time and consideration for which I am most grateful. Particular thanks to David Bowen for taking the trouble to give very useful detailed comments but also for his forbearance over many years with non-scientist blundering around in the dark. Thanks to Simon Raggett for his detailed work and suggestions, & not for the first time. Thanks to Jonathan Edwards for being the most positive first reader one could dream of and the sole cause of my floating down Malet Street several inches above the ground. Thanks to Alastair McDonald for notes both typically thorough and amusing, and to my younger son William for very practical suggestions and the idea of a blog to carry on the project after publication. All kindly read and commented with hours to go to my deadline, which was a lot to ask. Thanks also to Ted Dixon, who I'm afraid got bored very quickly, to Paul Kerr, a film person amongst mainly science people, for keeping on trying to make things clearer, but most of all thanks to Kate, who didn't complain and without whom this opportunity and such happiness would not have arisen. I would also like to thank my publisher, John Libbey, for giving me the chance to discharge my duty to these ideas, one that has been incumbent upon me for many years now. A final debt, to Mr Thomas, Dirk Strauss and the team at The Royal Marsden. My father, a good teacher, wrote a book called *Self-Expression Through Composition*. It was never published, but at the last moments of completing this book for some reason it came to mind that although he might wince at the composition part, he might see a faint echo in the chance I have had here to express ideas that have been bothering me, as he used to put it, 'for the better part of some time'?

Index

247